5

£25

WAGNER AND LITERATURE

For Janice

WAGNER *and* LITERATURE

'Wagner I approached along the paths of literature'
Lord Berners

RAYMOND FURNESS

 Manchester University Press

St Martin's Press, New York

Published by Manchester University Press,
Oxford Road, Manchester M13 9PL

British Library cataloguing in publication data
Furness, Raymond
Wagner and literature.
1. Wagner, Richard – Influence
2. Literature, Modern – History and criticism
I. Title
809'.03   PN701

ISBN 0–7190–0844–1

First published in the United States of America in 1982 by
St. Martin's Press, Inc.
175 Fifth Avenue, New York, NY 10010
Printed in Great Britain

Library of Congress cataloguing in publication data
Furness, Raymond.
Wagner and literature.
Bibliography: p. 149
Includes index.
1. Wagner, Richard, 1813–1883.   2. Music and literature.   I. Title.
ML410.W13F95   782.1'092'4   81–14391
ISBN 0–312–85347–5   AACR2

Photoset in Garamond
Northern Phototypesetting Co., Bolton

Printed in Great Britain
The Alden Press, Oxford

contents

illustrations

Richard Guhr's 'Regeneratio' from the collection *Aus der Dresdener Richard-Wagner-Ehrung im Scholß Albrechtsberg*. It is reproduced by kind permission of the Richard Wagner Museum, Bayreuth — *page ii*

Pauline Eigner's 'Tristan. Akt II' first printed in *Die Jugend*, Munich, 1900 — *viii/ix*

A diagram by Charles Morice in his *La littérature de tout à l'heure*, Paris, 1889. It is reprinted in Lilian Furst, *Counterparts*, London, 1977 — *1*

Siegfried by Aubrey Beardsley, an imaginative representation drawn after a visit to the music-drama in 1892 and given to Burne-Jones — *31*

Arthur Rackham: 'Siegfried! Siegfried! Our warning is true . . .' from *The Ring of the Niblung*, 1939, translated by Margaret Armour. By kind permission of William Heinemann Ltd. — *69*

'Wagner Comics'. These are reprinted in Hartmut Zelinsky's *Richard Wagner 1876–1976. Ein deutsches Thema*, Frankfurt am Main, 1976 — *108/109*

'Richard Wagner. Höher geht's nimmer' by O. Gulbransson, commemorating the centenary of Wagner's birth, 22 May 1913. Reprinted in *Der Deutsche in seiner Karikatur: Hundert Jahre Selbstkritik*, Stuttgart, n.d. — *141*

acknowledgements

For this book I owe a heavy debt to many persons, above all to my colleagues in the Faculty of Arts at Manchester University, whose patience I sorely tried with my constant pleas for information; without their valuable hints and clues this book could never have been written. I am indebted likewise to my students for their stimulating remarks and their fortitude during our long Thursday afternoons: rarely can Wagner have had such a band of alert and vivacious followers. For financial assistance I must thank the Deutscher Akademischer Austauschdienst, whose generosity enabled me to spend an indispensable month in the Richard Wagner Gedenkstätte, Bayreuth, and I express my special gratitude to Dr Manfred Eger, director, and Herr Günter Fickenscher, librarian, for their unstinting support. Above all my good friend Peter Skrine must be thanked for his interest and encouragement: his great breadth of reading afforded many a useful insight.

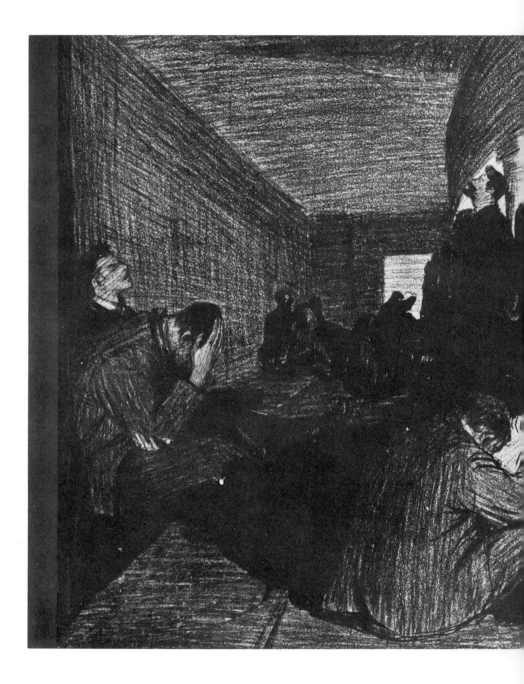

introduction

In his brief but perspicacious study on *Aspects of Wagner* Bryan Magee comes to the conclusion that 'Wagner has had a greater influence than any other single artist on the culture of our age',[1] a statement which gave rise to much speculation on the part of the present author and ultimately to the idea for this book. With perception and sympathy Magee points to the presence of the Master in many aspects of European culture, and it is here but one of those aspects, namely literature, which has been selected for amplification and development. Corroboration concerning the wisdom of dealing with Wagner and literature was further derived from reading the excellent articles of William Blissett which, arguing lucidly that 'the impingement of Wagner on literature is profound and persuasive, and increasingly as the years pass it becomes necessary to examine the mediated as well as the direct influence',[2] held out a daunting prospect. For references to Wagner which are simply incidental or topical would be of peripheral interest only; the explicit treatment of Wagnerian themes and persons might prove a worthwhile study, but the far more elusive construction of fiction with a totality derived from the use of Wagnerian techniques also demands an imaginative analysis. For the major European novelists stand beneath his sway, as well as an abundant florilegium of minor figures, not only in their reference to the man and his art but in their imitation of his method; the composer who provided a common source of inspiration for the subtleties of Virginia Woolf, the vagaries of the decadents and the religious yearnings of the myth-makers must have been of uncommon stature. That a a *musician* should have had such an overwhelming effect on *literature* is even more remarkable, but the age was ready for a shift towards music in the arts, and it was Wagner who provided a unique and almost mystical stimulus. It was he more than any other artist who was able to fructify and enrich imaginative writing: it may safely be claimed that without Wagner the literature of at least a century would be immeasurably impoverished, as regards topics as well as structures. His Protean abundance means that even the literature of decadence could be fired by his work, which can provide the tortured *frisson* as well as radiant myth and luminous symbol. The use of the interior monologue in many a modern novel is the narrative equivalent of Wagner's constantly modulating river of sound and the literary leitmotif, developing, intensifying and establishing complex inter-relationships, stems directly from his

technique of polyphonic expression of complex states of awareness.
' "Music" was one thing, "Wagnerian music" quite another, and there was no common measure between them; it was not a new pleasure but a new kind of pleasure, if indeed "pleasure" is the right word, rather than trouble, ecstasy, astonishment, "a conflict of sensations without name".'³ C. S. Lewis describes in his autobiography how, even before he had heard a note of Wagner's music, he had experienced the very shape of his name as a magical symbol. Such was the force of Wagner's mythical vision that Lord Berners, entranced by the legendary landscapes, the green and glittering waters, rainbow bridge and magic fire concluded — likewise before he had heard a note played or sung — that the music must indeed be marvellous if it at all corresponded to this enchanted world: the mere sight of the score of *Das Rheingold*, glimpsed in a shop window in Windsor, caused an agitation which made him claim: 'So must Dante have felt when he saw Beatrice on the bridge in Florence ...'⁴ And when this music *was* heard, and heard after a gap of thirty years, then the impact was indeed overpowering. Willa Cather's *A Wagner Matinée* is a most poignant statement of the transcendent joy which Wagner's music brought into the drab life of the central character, as well as of the sickening sense of loss that Georgiana Carpenter experiences as the musicians leave and bleak reality returns. The radiant glory of the Prize Song from *Die Meistersinger*, exemplifying the triumph of beauty and art, is but a brief incandescence, and the middle-aged woman must face the journey back to privation and hardship, to the inconceivable silence of the plains.⁵ In a gesture very similar to that which Thomas Mann would describe some forty years later in *Dr Faustus*, where Leverkühn's mother attempts to shield her son from the uncompromising intensity of music, Georgiana Carpenter had sought to save her nephew from too close an attachment to this art, lest its loss prove intolerable; Thea Kronborg, in Willa Cather's later book *The Song of the Lark*, is more ruthless in her triumph in the great Wagnerian roles. In the same novel a Frau Ottenburg takes to her bed on the news of Wagner's death — an ironic touch? Possibly, but the blasé intellectuals and aesthetes of d'Annunzio's world felt genuinely impoverished at the passing of the Master: 'Richard Wagner is dead! The world seemed diminished in value ...'⁶

But what of the great satirists and denigrators? Lest the tone of this book prove too portentous they will have their say, for a rich source of humour may be found in those writers who delight in debunking excessive Wagnerolatry. Unable to detect in Wagner transcendent purity, or nostalgia for other, more noble worlds, or mystic spiritual harmonies, some writers preferred to see Wagner as a pompous disseminator of clamorous confusion, his work full of visceral eroticism, elephantine coupling, hoydenish glee and insufferable attitudinising; devotees were castigated as being blatantly unmusical, neurotic, coarse-fibred or morally suspect. But the detractors also pay a back-handed compliment to Wagner's stature:[7] the greatest victim of them all knew full well that his exaggerated praise of Bizet's *Carmen* was a self-conscious attempt to find *some* antidote to the irresistible sorcery radiating from Bayreuth. Political objections to Wagner's *oeuvre* are, however, only of secondary importance in this book, which is concerned with the richness and diversity of the literary response to Wagner rather than with the repetition of moral strictures; the abuse of Wagnerian archetypes by confused mystagogues is relevant only in so far as literary models are concerned. (Deryck Cooke's skilful repudiation of political criticisms levelled against Wagner, whom he calls 'one of the greatest minds the world has ever seen'[8] is exemplary, although the present author is aware of the dangers which an unqualified adulation of Wagner can bring.) Reduction to absurdity, deflation of nimiety and a salutary reminder of the ludicrous aspects of hyperbolic praise provide a welcome relief, and Chapter Four contains examples of those writers who prefer satire to fulsome panegyric and the febrifuge to the intoxicant when confronted by the Wagner phenomenon.

At the end of his useful book on Wagner and certain aspects of the English novel John DiGaetani concludes: 'Those most antagonistic of the arts, music and literature, were harmoniously joined in some great modern literature through the rainbow bridge of Wagnerian patterns'.[9] I prefer not to speak of antagonism, but would rather begin this book with Wagner's own striking simile of poet and musician who set off to journey across the world in opposite directions, the poet across the land and the musician across the sea; many hazards are experienced, but ultimately it is the poet who enters the musician's boat, rejoicing in the 'giant bolted' framework of the ship which travels across the vastness of the ocean. 'The musician had taught him how to handle the helm, to trim the sails and how to use the cunningly devised expedients for breasting storms and tempests. Sailing the wide seas at the helm of this glorious ship the poet, who before had toiled to measure hill and dale step by step, now rejoices . . .; let the billows rear themselves never so proudly – from *its* high deck they seem to him the willing, faithful bearers of his high fortune, that fortune of the poetic aim.'[10] The ship, Wagner tells us, is the orchestra, and the poet who embarks upon it learns to marvel at the mysteries of the deep which it enables him to experience.

I have attempted to cast my net wide on this journey through European (and American) literature, but crave indulgence for those figures who have eluded me. The translations, sometimes inadequate paraphrases, are my own unless otherwise stated, and have been incorporated into the text, rather than relegated to the back, to facilitate argument and illustration. The original languages are to be found with the notes.

Notes

1 Bryan Magee, *Aspects of Wagner*, London, 1968, p. 86.

2 William Blisset, 'D. H. Lawrence, D'Annunzio, Wagner' in *Wisconsin Studies in Contemporary Literature*, VII, 1966, p. 34.

3 C. S. Lewis, *Surprised by Joy: the Shape of My Early Life*, London, 1955, p. 76. The collection *They Stand Together* (ed. Hooper), London, 1979, testifies to the enduring importance of Wagner for C. S. Lewis; there are many references to the composer and his work and one particular letter, dated 1 February 1931, shows how the presence of Wagner never left him: 'In that fir wood I suddenly got a terrific return the other day of my earliest Wagner mood, the purely Nibelung, Mime, mood before the Valkyries rose on my horizon. You know — very earthy, and smith-y, and Teutonic. How *inexhaustible* these things are . . .'

4 Lord Berners, *A Distant Prospect*, London, 1945, p. 73.

5 Willa Cather, *A Wagner Matinée*, in *Youth and the Bright Medusa*, New York, 1956, pp. 225–6.

6 Gabriele d'Annunzio, *Il fuoco* (Mondadori ed.), Milan, 1977, p. 333: 'Riccardo Wagner è morto! Il mondo parve diminuito di valore . . .'

7 Vilification can, of course, also be a prerequisite or forerunner of appreciation; W. H. Auden claimed that *The Wagner Case* first taught him to listen to Wagner, about whom he had previously held silly preconceived notions. See his Oxford inaugural lecture of June 1956, entitled 'Making, knowing and judging', printed in *The Dyer's Hand and Other Essays*, London and New York, 1962.

8 Deryck Cooke, *I Saw the World End*, Oxford, 1979, p. 264.

9 J. L. DiGaetani, *Richard Wagner and the Modern British Novel*, Cranbury, N.J., 1978, p. 163.

10 Richard Wagner, *Gesammelte Schriften und Dichtungen*, Leipzig, 1897, IV, p. 160: 'Der Musiker hatte ihn den Griff und die Handhabung des Steuers gelehrt, die Eigenschaft der Segel und all' das seltsam und sinning erfundene Nöthige zur sicheren Fahrt bei Sturm und Wetter. Am Steuer dieses herrlich die Fluthen durchsegelnden Schiffes wird der Dichter, der zuvor mühsam Schritt für Schritt Berg und Thal gemessen, sich mit Wonne der allvermögenden Macht des Menschen bewußt; von seinem hohen Borde aus dünken ihn die noch so mächtig rüttelnden Wogen willige und treue Träger seines edlen Schicksales, dieses Schicksales der dichterischen Absicht.'

1

SYMBOLISM *and* MODERNISM

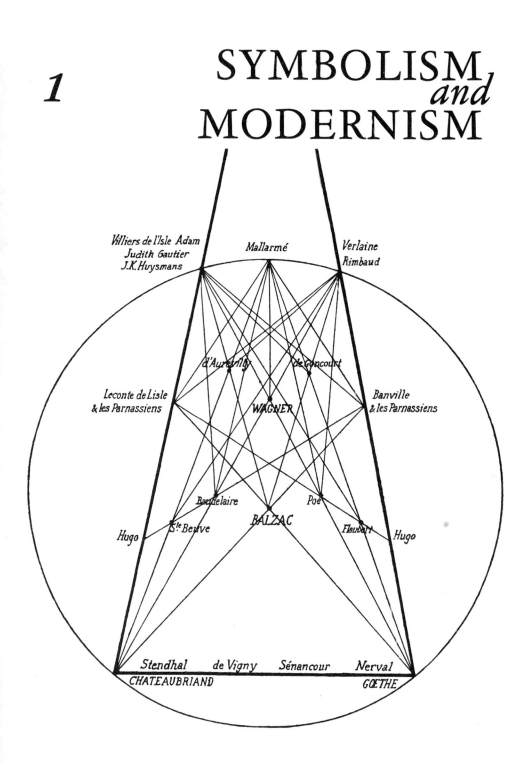

Villiers de l'Isle Adam
Judith Gautier
J.K. Huysmans

Mallarmé

Verlaine
Rimbaud

d'Aurevilly

de Goncourt

Leconte de Lisle
& les Parnassiens

WAGNER

Banville
& les Parnassiens

Baudelaire

Poe

BALZAC

Hugo

S.te Beuve

Flaubert

Hugo

Stendhal   de Vigny   Sénancour   Nerval

CHATEAUBRIAND

GOETHE

'Puzzled we may be, but it is primarily because the music has reached a place not yet visited by sound.'
  Virginia Woolf, Bayreuth, 1909

Writing from Paris on 20 April, 1841, in a series of letters for the *Augsburger Allgemeine Zeitung* which were later to be published under the title *Lutetia: Articles on Politics, Art and Social Life*, Heinrich Heine, whose company in Paris Wagner found most stimulating and whose journalistic skills he strove to emulate, describes the paramount importance of music in Europe at that time. Of all the art forms, Heine wrote, music enjoyed undisputed hegemony, so much so that the age should be termed the age of music, and in speculative mood he continued to sketch a historic order of the arts in which the spirit, finding stone too intractable a material, strove for realisation in painting, but which then, becoming more and more subtle and abstract, could only find in music its appropriate medium. The Romantic world, Heine implied, moved towards an ever-increasing remoteness and spirituality: intensified spirituality ('gesteigerte Spiritualität') and abstract thought ('das abstrakte Gedankentum'), strove for sounds and tones to express a stammering transcendence ('eine lallende Überschwenglichkeit'); the dissolution of the entire material world into surging sound was the goal. And music, Heine claimed, is perhaps the last word in art as death is in life; to him it was of great significance that Beethoven became deaf at the end of his days so that even the invisible world of tones ceased to have any resonant reality for him: 'His last creations were simply memories of tones, ghosts of expired sounds ...'[1] It is the movement towards inwardness which Heine describes here, that specifically German Romantic tendency to bypass the domain of things and to seek pure patterns in the mind. To music is assigned the highest rank within the arts because it is the most *meta*physical of them all, that art form to the condition of which, Walter Pater believed, all the other arts aspired and which Rilke, in his *Sonette an Orpheus*, proclaimed as being existence itself.

  Heine's witty and frequently satirical tone precludes heavyhanded interpretation, but in this article he has touched upon a profound truth concerning the triumph of music, its elevation to an almost divine status in European – and particularly German – Romanticism. The musician, above all the lonely impoverished and misunderstood musician, becomes visionary and seer: despised by the world he achieves ultimate bliss by communing with a world of pure harmony, unsullied by material dross. In the same year as Heine's important article, in fact three months before, there appeared in the *Gazette musicale* Wagner's revelatory and semi-autobiographical story *Death in Paris* which was praised by Berlioz in the *Journal des Débats* and, in fact, shown by him to Heine, who is reported to have said that E. T. A. Hoffman could not have done better. The emaciated German musician R., after struggling in vain for recognition, expires, uttering his famous creed:

> I believe in God, Mozart and Beethoven, likewise in their disciples and apostles; I believe in the Holy Ghost and in the truth of the one and indivisible Art; I believe this Art to be a divine emanation that dwells in the hearts of all enlightened men; I believe that whoever has steeped himself in its sublime delights must dedicate himself to it forever and can never deny it; I believe that all men are blessed through Art and that it is therefore permissible to die of hunger for its sake; I believe that in death I shall attain the highest bliss – that in my life on earth I was a dissonant chord, which death will resolve in glorious purity . . .[2]

The art of Mozart and Beethoven guarantees salvation for R., Beethoven particularly, as Wagner's story *A Pilgrimage to Beethoven* portrays. Those statements allegedly made to Bettina Brentano by Beethoven, namely that music was a higher revelation than all wisdom and philosophy, that it was the sole gateway to a higher world of truth, and that art alone was divine.[3] may be unreliable (the authoress did, however, visit Beethoven in 1810), but demonstrate again that the Romantic imagination felt the need to extol music as a second – or indeed as the only – religion. The supreme portrayal of the Romantic musician, that lonely figure who believed that music was the key to an invisible world, is Wilhelm Wackenroder's Berglinger, who knew that the non-representational world of music reflected an ultimate reality, but also exacted a fearful penalty: loneliness and alienation from normal life. The early deaths of Wackenroder's Berglinger and Wagner's R., and the madness of Hoffmann's Kapellmeister Kreisler represent the dangers of self-abandonment to this undifferentiated vision: that which is called the 'musical' tradition in German thought and writing will, indeed, claim many an illustrious victim.

Whether or not Wagner had read Wackenroder is unknown (he had, of course, read and greatly admired Ludwig Tieck, collaborator with Wackenroder on the *Effusions of an Art-loving Friar*, and met Tieck in 1847, discussing *inter alia* the Lohengrin legend), but Schopenhauer did read Wackenroder's *Reveries concerning Art* in 1806 and was greatly moved by Josef Berglinger's distress. The plight of the idealist and the triumph of the banausic which Wackenroder described could not but strengthen Schopenhauer's pessimism, and Wackenroder's praise of music as an ultimate revelatory experience certainly foreshadows Schopenhauer's claim that music, being non-representational, comes closest of all the arts to expressing the ultimate essence of existence itself. (Hoffmann's Serapionsbruder Cyprian had similarly asserted that no art stemmed more from the inner spirituality of man than music, no art needed more than music that which was purely spiritual and etherial).[4] That which links Romantic aesthetic theorising with Schopenhauer's noble system is indeed the privileged position allotted to music; a brief diversion might be permitted here, for it is Schopenhauer and Wagner who exerted a profound influence on the symbolist mode and through this on what may be called European modernism.

For Schopenhauer ultimate reality, the Kantian *Ding an sich* (thing in itself), is the will, a blind, furious and purposeless striving which may be transcended either by utter abnegation (the way of the saint) or by the transformation of the will into an idea, an object of aesthetic contemplation. To stand *outside* the meaningless thrust of existence, to recreate it objectively, is the privilege of the artist in his inspired moments, and it is the musician above all who claims our attention here. For whereas the representational arts simply imitate the manifestation of the will in phenomena, music, which does not rely on images and concepts, represents more directly the will itself, not its external manifestations. All the other arts, according to Schopenhauer, reflect the illusory world of nature, they are, in a sense, mere reflections of reflections; music, representing nothing specific, reveals absolute reality, the ceaseless energy behind all phenomena, the will itself:

> As our world is nothing but the appearance of representations in their multiplicity . . . so music, which transcends these appearances, is also quite independent of the world of appearances, ignores it completely and could, in a sense, still exist even if the world did not, which could not be said of the other arts . . . Music is not, like the other arts, the reflection of appearances but is a *reflection of the will itself*, which is objectified in these appearances; that is why the effect of music is so much more powerful and penetrating than that of the other arts, for these tell us about shadows, while music portrays the essence.[5]

A remarkable statement indeed – that music could, to a certain extent, exist even if the world did not, for it is the immediate projection of the will, not of its multiple manifestations. What if the will, however, is blind and hectic, an amoral activity? By a sleight of hand which was to have profound consequences for nineteenth-century aesthetic theory Schopenhauer proclaimed that music is the art form closest to salvation because it is a projection of the will and at the same time its miraculous transfiguration into form and harmony; a reflection of senselessness, it mysteriously *transforms* senselessness. Music is not a means to redemption, it becomes redemption: free of empirical sense it reveals a universal longing without purpose or object, an emotional absolute, reality in a true and original sense. And Heine's statement concerning the increasing 'inwardness' of the arts is here most profoundly corroborated: music has indeed replaced sculpture as the primary art of the West, and the free composition of private, self-sufficient universes will increasingly replace the imitation of natural forms. In painting a movement towards abstraction, in literature the increasing use of private images and autonomous metaphors, abstracted from their context, demonstrate the way in which empirical experience becomes of lesser importance: it is true to say that the adoption of the principles of musical composition by the other arts is the most dominant characteristic of modernism.[6]

The effect that such a philosophy had upon Richard Wagner was immense: his attention was drawn to Schopenhauer's *The World as Will and Idea* by the poet Herwegh in the autumn of 1854 and came as a revelation, for it powerfully reinforced Wagner's own emotional intuitions and the growing awareness that Feuerbach's optimism was not conducive to his temperament. Between October 1854 and the summer of 1855 Wagner read the work frequently, understanding for the first time the meaning of Wotan's destiny and submitting to the doctrine of renunciation which Schopenhauer preached as the only course for men trapped within the flux and turmoil of existence. How much this suited Wagner's mood during the composition of *Tristan und Isolde* and how — amazingly — he speculated upon modifications of Schopenhauer's doctrine of denial will be discussed in the next chapter; here let it be noted that Schopenhauer's comments on Wagner's text of the *Ring* (Wagner sent him a copy, printed on impressively thick paper and neatly bound) were hardly complimentary, and the philosopher suggested that Wagner should cultivate his poetic, rather than his musical, talents. Preferring Rossini, Schopenhauer had little time for *Zukunftsmusik* and indulged in his ambition to play through all of Rossini's work on the flute. 'It is one of the most adroitly ironical scenes of intellectual history', writes Erich Heller, 'to imagine the grim pessimist and metaphysician of "Music as Will" fluting *La Cenerentola* in his austere bachelor's quarters while Wagner, all silk and velvet, composed music metaphysically inspired by Schopenhauer.'[7] The philosopher may have had little time for his most ardent musical disciple (he did not know that Wagner and certain other political exiles in Zurich had attempted to find him a teaching post in that city), but Wagner owed him an enormous intellectual debt, as did Nietzsche. It was not simply the doctrine of renunciation (one which Wagner did not naturally adhere to) which impressed him, but the elevation of music to a means of salvation; sixteen years after reading *The World as Will and Idea*, in 1870, Wagner could write in his essay *Beethoven* of the state of ecstasy called forth in a musician when he saw through reality to the ultimate itself, when inspiration overwhelmed him and he knew that he had seen through the turmoil of life and gained that wisdom which only the saint achieved in his imperturbability. Such visionary states of rapure, Wagner writes, alternate with moans of anguish when the world of futility and meaninglessness asserts itself, and yet even the suffering is blessed. 'And this suffering again, allotted to him as penalty for the state of inspiration in which he so unutterably entrances us, might make us hold the musician in higher reverence than other artists, yes, almost gives him claim to rank as holy. For his art, in truth, compares with the communion of all the other arts as *religion* with the *church*.'[8]

Art as the key to the world of absolutes, music above all as a redemptive revelation – the way is prepared for the luminous mysteries of symbolism. Schopenhauer's *The World as Will and Idea* became, in the words of Lilian Furst, 'so current in France in the 1870s and 1880s as a result of Théodule Ribot's book *La Philosophie de Schopenhauer* (1874) and a veritable avalanche of articles that Cantacuzène's translation seemed almost superfluous when it finally appeared in 1886';[9] similarly Schelling's mystical nature philosophy and Hartmann's *Philosophy of the Unconscious* became well known in France at this time. Indeed, French symbolism is arguably the 'second flood of the same tide as Romanticism'[10] and of German Romanticism (especially *Frühromantik*) in particular, with Wagner as the priestly intermediary: the sympathy with death and the cult of the past, the themes of dream and trance, isolation and longing link the German Romantic tradition with Wagner, who ravished the symbolists with his treatment of the remote and the legendary, the mystically erotic and the esoteric; likewise his insistence on the artist as priest, his emphasis on the need to mythologise the historical, his concept of the fusion of the arts and the use of the leitmotif. It was the *Revue Wagnérienne* which experienced Wagner as the supreme catalyst to the symbolist movement, not simply as musician but as guarantor of ultimate artistic triumph. What Baudelaire had sensed some twenty years before (to be described in the next chapter) now became common knowledge: that Wagner was magus, and that his art was a religious celebration, elevating the celebrant to highest spiritual beatitude. It was through the manipulation of redolent symbols – or, rather, the symbolic extension of the leitmotif – that Wagner created a world enriched beyond measure, and determined the *musical* pattern not only for the world of harmony, but for literature and the theatre, which is our concern here.

The symbolists were preoccupied by the nature of music and its relation to poetry: art was to be symbolical rather than representational and an attempt was to be made in writing to 'musicalise' the inner universe. A music of words was to be elaborated, 'a tight, organic form based on associative structures, logical ellipsis and image-transformation' was sought.[11] A poet of the stature of Mallarmé feared that the literary mode would become jejune and limited if it could not emulate musical patterns, and by 'musical' he meant Wagnerian. A clarification of the term 'leitmotif' is necessary here, for this concept is central to Wagner's compositional method, and reached out into literature where its powers to enrich and enhance were found to be of unprecedented intensity. Debussy's jibe at the 'cartes de visite' technique should be seen as resulting from a grudging awareness of the awesome presence of Wagner at practically every stage of the composition of *Pelléas et Mélisande*; Wagner himself never attached labels to his musical ideas.[12] These musical ideas, or 'carriers of feeling' were completely uncircumscribed: no intellectual description could do justice to their high emotional pressure. The unique nature of Wagner's music, its phenomenal power of compressing into a few bars the most profound emotional and psychological experience, and the endless harmonic and orchestral transformations of these 'carriers of feelings', or leading motifs, exerted such an overwhelming influence on literature because psychological cross-reference and associations, and inter-relationships between clusters of images and symbols, could be established, the impact being enormously increased thereby. It is here that Wagner's influence is most profound: to say that a poem, or even a novel, is musical in the Wagnerian sense does not simply mean that there is an allusion to a musical work, or that the use of the tonal and rhythmical resonances of words reinforces their conceptual meaning, but rather that its use of the literary leitmotif intensifies the quality of the feeling by repetition, unifying the various parts of the composition and relating the various parts to the whole.[12] Verlaine's demand that all art be subordinate to music, and Mallarmé's suspicion that poetry may have become the lesser achievement both derive from Wagner's colossal example: the leitmotif, that characteristic theme which is always the same yet never the same supports the whole vast fabric of Proust's *oeuvre* as well as much of the work of Virginia Woolf and Thomas Mann and many a minor modern writer. And further, a drama of suggestion rather than statement, of inner rather than external movement is adumbrated here, where suggestiveness, musicality, mystery and reverie oust the traditional development of character and exploration of human relationships: the symbolist theatre of Mallarmé and the experiments of Meyerhold demonstrate once more that insistence upon the superiority of the inner vision over mere external actuality. And further still: when the leitmotif-symbol assumes the shape of an independent character, or, rather, when a symbolic character ceases to be a

Thomas Mann – Death in Venice?

true person but a functional idea of the work, an aesthetic attribute, then the theatre of expressionism is not far away. When the leitmotif-symbol points not outside the work, but inward, back to the work, then the character becomes something like a musical note, not representing anything objective or external, but becoming a function of a self-contained, artificial world.

'Symbolism? . . . Don't understand . . . I suppose it's a German word, is it? What's it supposed to mean? Me, I'm not interested. When I suffer, or feel glad, or cry I know perfectly well that's not a symbol. Look, all these distinctions – they're a lot of German stuff – why should a poet bother about what Kant, Schopenhauer, Hegel and other Boches think about human feelings!'[14] Verlaine's tetchy reluctance to admit that the word 'symbolism' meant anything, his rejection of the term as being meaningless and Teutonic, an abstraction remote from actual reality, may be seen as an unconsenting recognition of the hegemony of things Germanic at this time: the victory of 1871 was not simply a military one. Wagner's name, capitalised in René Ghil's *Traité du verbe* (1886), conspicious by its focal position in Charles Morice's mystic diagram in *La littérature de tout à l'heure* (1889) and held as a glittering monstrance above the centres of European civilisation, became an unimpeachable guarantor of excellence; the *Revue Wagnérienne* exemplified that proneness to use his name to reinforce those tendencies which the symbolists held most dear. 'The *Revue Wagnérienne*', wrote Block, 'was important for its illumination of the aims and values of the French writers themselves, who used Wagner as a mirror and image of their own theories and aspirations.'[15] Camille Mauclair, writing in 1922, sums up the position succinctly: 'Wagner was more than a passion for us – he was a religion. Through him we really possessed a spirit of collective mysticism.'[16] Of that sodality which formed the nucleus of the *Revue Wagnérienne* two names will be selected for discussion here, Stéphane Mallarmé and Edouard Dujardin, for from these two radiated, under Wagner's influence, varied and fruitful speculations concerning a new theatre and a new form of novel. By dint of constant appeal to the spirit of the Master, the highest authority, both Mallarmé and Dujardin explored new and recondite worlds, whose treasures were to enrich immeasurably the paucity of the domains thirsting for new sustenance. It is to Mallarmé, without doubt the greater figure of the two, that we shall turn first: although Dujardin had considered the idea of an 'armchair theatre', a 'spectacle dans un fauteuil',[17] and Téodor de Wyzewa, in the same journal, had written that 'a drama which is read will appear, to sensitive souls, more real, more living than the same drama acted in a theatre by living actors',[18] it is Mallarmé who pushed to extreme limits the possibility of a drama of suggestion rather than statement, an inner rather than an external drama, an 'interiorisation' or 'musicalisation' of dramatic action.

Mallarmé had long speculated on the possibilities of new forms of drama: the nebulous concept of '*l'Oeuvre*', the vast dramatic projects of the 1860s and 1870s exemplify this. It was doubtless Baudelaire who opened Mallarmé's eyes to Wagner's greatness: Baudelaire's critical writings, published in 1869 as *L'Art Romantique*, were profoundly influential, as was Edouard Schuré's *Le Drame musical et l'oeuvre de Richard Wagner*, which appeared in the *Revue des Deux Mondes* in the same year. A most important intermediary was Villiers de l'Isle-Adam who, obsessed by the German composer, visited him in 1869 and again in 1870, shortly before journeying to Mallarmé in Avignon. (Villiers's poem in prose 'Azrael' is dedicated to 'Richard Wagner, au prince de la profonde musique'.) From these diverse sources Mallarmé received confirmation of Wagner's cardinal importance: the concept of a synthesis of the arts and of the theatre as a holy shrine, the emphasis on ritual and mysticism greatly appealed to Mallarmé and Baudelaire's insistence on seeing Wagner as pointing towards an internalisation of drama, towards a portrayal of complex inner states, quickened the sensitive interest of the French poet. The testimonies to Wagner's unique genius, the eulogies following his death in 1883 and the founding of the *Revue Wagnérienne* some two years later all led to new levels of Wagner fever: Mallarmé's remarkable contribution to that journal, half article, half prose-poem, the *Richard Wagner: Rêverie d'un poëte français*, is an act of homage which helped Mallarmé to clarify his own ideas regarding a new theatre. In Block's words: 'The description of Wagner's ideal art work is set forth in religious and ritualistic terms: the theatre is to become a temple and the spectacle a ceremony in which the masses participate in a sacred rite ... throughout the *Rêverie* Mallarmé is passionately concerned with the impact of the new art form on the audience, and the re-ordering of the relationship between the stage and the mass public.'[19] The 'sortilège' which Wagnerian theatre had created, its suggestiveness, spirituality and essential intensity were unique, and reservations concerning Wagner's usurpation of the poet's role (it was the poet, for Mallarmé, who must control the interplay of the arts in the theatre, not the musician) are hushed before the testimony to Wagner's gigantic achievement. The great *Oeuvre* would seem to have been an attempt to weld the disparate art forms into a synthetic, spiritualised, theatrical experience, an act of initiation meant to redeem the decay into which late nineteenth-century theatre had fallen.

Mallarmé's *Notes sur le théâtre*, contributed to the *Revue Indépendante* (1886–7) continued to stress the need for an ideal, symbolic drama; naturalism is deplored, and the formulation of spiritual attitudes, imaginative vision and timeless states of soul are encouraged. Wagner's example is deemed paramount, as is his advocation of Greek drama and the approximation to Catholic Mass in *Parsifal*. The notion of *Mystère* becomes of supreme importance to Mallarmé; the need for collective involvement is also stressed, as Wagner had emphasised the 'völkisch' elements of the new art form. But whereas Wagner had turned to myth, Mallarmé turned for his hero not to a legendary figure but, increasingly, to abstractions, the 'figure que Nul n'est';[20] similarly the preference for poetic drama (Swinburne's *Erechtheus*, for example) would lead to a rejection of the theatrical stage in preference to the drama which is read, this being superior to the one which is acted. The physical theatre, for Mallarmé, would ultimately be rejected – 'le livre' being extolled at the expense of 'le drame'. The emphasis is upon the invisible rather than the visible, the symbolic rather than the actual; to be consistent Mallarmé must play with the idea of reducing utterly the visible to gain a greater inner purity, and it was his distaste for the theatre of his day which led him to posit the superiority of the empty stage over a full one. But his keen sense of the effectiveness of physical theatre saved him from such a sterile impasse, and he sought the interrelation of the arts, beneath the poet's control, to achieve a cultic ceremony. Dance is the source of the poetic atmosphere, as it was for Wagner, who saw the supreme importance of this in ancient theatre, but it is to be de-personalised: the dancer as metaphor and the dance as poem constitute the purest expression of the ideal that art can yield, 'poetry liberated from the contingency of language, symbolizing the elemental gestures of our being'.[21] And from Mallarmé's advocation of a refined, haunting, dematerialised theatre it is but one step towards the creation of symbolic drama whose greatest exponent was Maeterlinck.

A difficulty arises here in any attempt to establish a link between the elusive, reticent and shadowy vagueness of much symbolist theatre and the sheer weight, solidity and monumentality of much Wagnerian stage design. Father to the twentieth century Wagner may well be, but he was also very much a son of the nineteenth, and the furious diatribes against Parisian grand opera conceal frequently a sneaking admiration for grand theatrical effect. Few can have been so familiar with the theatre in all its manifestations, yet Wagner chafed against the restrictions to which he felt his musical vision was subject: none understood better than he the enormous difficulties confronting the realisation of myth upon the nineteenth-century stage. His essay *The Public in Time and Space* (1878) specifically refers to the 'tragedy of the fate of any creative spirit in its submission to the conditions imposed upon its activity by time and space';[22] able to create a new language for his gods and heroes, able to enrich orchestral colouring and finesse as none before him, he nevertheless was forced to translate his music dramas into visual reality encumbered by the accoutrements of the stage of his day. Yet the fact that he built his own theatre based on the form of a Greek amphitheatre and refused to compromise despite apparently insuperable difficulties (how easy to have surrendered and to accept the Markgräfliches Opernhaus) shows a determination to forge something new, something more appropriate, and many instances are recorded of his impatience with conventional stagecraft. Eduard Devrient's reservations concerning the appearance of a ship on the stage during the planned performance of *Tristan und Isolde* in Karlsruhe brought forth Wagner's remark that he had no intention of creating a decorative effect: the ship was of secondary importance, and need merely be hinted at. A superabundance of detail could not, he felt, but detract from the larger, more important pattern in such a drama, which was both mythical and psychological. A tour of inspection of German opera houses undertaken in 1872 brought forth little praise, except for a performance of Gluck's *Orfeo* in Dessau, where little attempt at 'realism' had been made, and the emphasis was upon dream and wonder. He looked forward with dread to the stage designs for the 1876 festival. 'It was one thing for him to construct this colossal drama of land and water and caverns and cloud, of gods and heroes and giants and dwarfs in his own imagination: it was quite another thing to realise it all in terms of steel and wood and stone and canvas':[23] with such richly mimetic music what could be the dramatic purpose of trying to translate the orchestral drama into visual terms? He insisted that the King's pictures of scenes from the *Ring* be painted not by Kaulbach but by Genelli, whose water-colour *Dionysus Taught by the Muses* he greatly admired and who, Wagner felt, would not be concerned with realistic detail and pseudo-historical veracity, but rather with mythical import.[24] To strive for 'visualised musical action' ('ersichtlich gewordene Taten der Musik') was one thing: to be confronted by a ludicrous dragon was another (although Wagner cannot be held responsible for this creature whose neck an English firm chose to dispatch to Beirut). Wagner knew that lighting could achieve much, and was incensed when later productions of *Die Walküre* made the magic fire effect more important than anything else. (It is interesting that Albert Schweitzer should look back with longing to the comparative simplicity of the early *Ring* settings, whereas later – in 1913 – the realistic settings seemed the sole *raisons d'être* of the whole performance.) Finally, *à propos* the realisation of *Parsifal*, Wagner made his famous statement concerning the 'invisible theatre' for which he longed: 'I cannot stand all this costume and grease-paint business! And when I consider how these figures such as Kundry will have to be masqueraded – I immediately think of these repulsive artists' carnivals, and, after having invented the invisible orchestra I would like to create the invisible theatre.'[25]

An invisible theatre, a theatre of allusion, not restricted by the need for historical verisimilitude, a theatre, as Adolphe Appia knew, in which light was an 'agent actif' able to transmit musical sense – symbolist theatre is surely anticipated here. (Appia, incidentally, in his *La Mise en scéne du drame wagnérien* of 1895 and *Music and Stage Production* of 1899, dedicated to Houston Stewart Chamberlain as the only man who understood Appia's intentions, strove for a totally new approach to Wagner's work, and anticipated by sixty years the Bayreuth productions of Wieland Wagner; Appia had submitted designs to Bayreuth which were meant to capture the essential atmosphere, leaving the rest to the music, the singer and the audience's imagination, but they were rejected by Cosima despite Chamberlain's recommendations.) It was Aurélien Lugné-Poe who established the *Théâtre de l'Oeuvre* as the temple of symbolist drama: closely associated with Mallarmé, Lugné-Poe hailed the genius of Maeterlinck and saw in the Belgian writer the precursor of a new theatrical mentality. A meeting with Villiers de l'Isle-Adam, most fervent Wagnerian, had had far-reaching effects for Maeterlinck; Villiers read to him sections of his recently composed *Axël* in Paris in 1886, and Maeterlinck returned to Ghent determined to become a writer. Charles van Lerberghe's *Les Flaireurs* (1889), with its evocation of ill-defined terror and its mingling of the natural and the supernatural, pointed the way for Maeterlinck, whose first play, *La Princesse Maleine*, dates from the same year. In this early work the tone is set for much that will be found in Maeterlinck – a brooding sense of mystery prevails, where the characters are passive victims of incomprehensible forces. Allegory, romance and fairy-tale predominate: the setting of *La Princesse Maleine* is a northern land in a vaguely medieval period, a land of forests and water whose king is senile. The evil Queen Anne of Jutland dominates the doddering king, who agrees to the murder of his son's betrothed: Maleine is a helpless victim who is finally strangled. Symbols of water, moonlight, castle and tower predominate, and the haunting atmosphere of menace is sustained throughout. The sick king of a doomed country brings Amfortas to mind (or Titurel), while his crumbling realm is reminiscent of the atmosphere prevailing in Edgar Allan Poe, particularly *The Fall of the House of Usher*; Queen Anne is an Ortrud figure, but there is no Lohengrin to redeem the stricken Maleine. The characters are never clearly defined, they resemble shadows: they scarcely comprehend their situation and are essentially passive, as are the protagonists of the death-dramas *L'Intruse* (1890), *Les Aveugles* and *Les Sept Princesses* (1891).

The ease with which so many of Maeterlinck's characters slip into death has been frequently remarked, and similarities to Wagner abound: many of his characters die spontaneously, dispensing with external agencies, for death, as Peter Conrad writes, 'is not the agonizing renunciation of physical existence but a blithe migration from one spiritual state into another'.[26] Death, as well as being a metaphor for sex, can also become a metaphor for a condition of abstraction into which Elsa, Elisabeth, Isolde and the immolated Brünnhilde all retire. Wagner may be deemed to be totally original here, in allowing his characters to die into what has been termed an 'intellectual synthesis', ceasing to exist once their work as ideas is over, as Tannhäuser and Kundry demonstrate. (In the novel it is E. M. Forster who is much indebted to Wagner here: the abrupt terminations of the lives of certain of his characters show that he has learned from Wagner that characters are disposable and may be sacrificed for reasons of symmetry and aesthetic satisfaction.) Maeterlinck's nebulous creations recall Wagner's in that they are not so much persons as spirits, conditions or elements. For Wagner it is the music, not the drama, which explains the tangled emotions of Isolde and her relationship with Tristan, and which demonstrates Kundry's different incarnations. The obsessive quality of many of Wagner's characters means that communication between them is impossible, and these characters tend towards static inactivity despite the apparently hectic stance. Isolde on her couch and Tristan on his pallet – the relationship between them is scarcely dramatic in the conventional sense, but musical and internal. It is the past which hangs like an enormous weight over many of Wagner's creations; recollections of childhood usurp the time when action is called for, as Isolde thinks of her mother when preparing the draught, and Siegfried of his when crouched over Brünnhilde. It is in order to learn the fate of his mother that Parsifal, as Peter Conrad explains, suffers Kundry's polluted kiss; retrospection, obsession, trance and a morbid stasis predominate in Wagner, and the world of Maeterlinck is unthinkable without him.

Wagner's famous Beethoven essay saw music as 'the manifestation of the deepest vision of the essence of the world',[27] an expression of inner states which is more poetic than dramatic: the figures of a resulting 'music drama' are emanations rather than fully realised characters. Music's ability to convey trance-like states of suspension is stressed by Wagner here, and one of his most astute readers and students, Vsyevolod Meyerhold, rightly compared his characters to the figures in the frescoes of Puvis de Chavannes. 'Wagner's dramas', Meyerhold insisted, 'were composed from within. His most profound inspiration was drawn from this "eternal god" and poured into the creation of the inner content of his works, the libretto and the musical score. The external output, the form of the drama . . . remained uninspired by any god.'[28] Meyerhold knew Appia's *Music and Stage Production*; more important, he knew his Wagner and insisted, in 1937, that he had studied every score and read every word of the theoretical writings, ten volumes of them, which he had copiously annotated.[29] Meyerhold had been overwhelmed in his youth by Wagner's achievement and never ceased to return to the composer in an attempt to define his own position, to reinforce his reaction against Stanislavski's naturalism and his own predilection for Maeterlinck, Verhaeren and Przybyszewski. Like Appia he rejected most of the conventional staging of Wagner's work; his famous production of *Tristan und Isolde* in the Tsarist Opera in 1909 exemplified his belief that the world of the soul can only be expressed through music, and that 'the mere contemplation of real foliage on the stage would be as flagrantly tactless as illustrating Edgar Allan Poe'.[30] Wagner's immersion in the spiritual world of his heroes, his preference for myth and legend greatly impressed Meyerhold who insisted on a stylised drama, as his production of *La Mort de Tintagiles* made evident; his ideal theatre, the 'total work of art' was to employ 'plastic movement' to convey emotional states as Wagner had employed the orchestra. For words alone cannot say everything, this Meyerhold knew, and for him the essence of human relationships is determined by gestures, poses, glances and silences. 'The world of the soul can express itself only through music: music alone has the power to express fully the world of the soul'[31] – this sentence would not have been out of place in Wagner's Beethoven essay. The need for 'Einfühlung' (empathy) was stressed by both: from Wagner Meyerhold learned of the supremacy of music as an autonomous art, and his emphasis on the objectification of inner experience and of the ego as a magic crystal in which the absolute is in constant play links his name not only with Wagner but also with the expressionist generation. His experimental 'theatre laboratory' in St Petersburg between the years 1913 and 1917 proved the testing ground for many fascinating experiments at which the ten-volume edition of Wagner's theoretical writings doubtless provided both impetus and inspiration.

An age whose main artistic themes were the abnormal cultivation of the self, a guilt-ridden sexuality and a preoccupation with the expression of psychic disturbance was likewise obviously indebted to Wagner: what is of great importance, and what has scarcely been considered, is Wagner's influence on what may be called modernism, or, rather, expressionism, this being the form that modernism took in Germany. (It is also of interest that the so-called *Proclama Futuristica a los Españoles*, devised by one 'Tristan', that is, Gómez de la Serna in 1910, should begin with the impassioned outburst: 'Futurism! Insurrection! Violent onslaught! Festivals with Wagner's music! Modernism! ...')[32] Reference has already been made to the process of internalisation or abstraction which the arts underwent in Europe shortly before the First World War; with the theatre in the vanguard there emerges the idea of the characters fulfilling the function of a musical note or leitmotif, that theme, as it were, which signals an emotional attitude. More explicit references to Strindberg will be found in Chapter Three, but let it be noted here that it is Strindberg who represents in an exemplary form the transition from conventional drama to the theatre of expressionism. He abandoned the dramatic sequence of events for a stream of consciousness technique where the literal embodiments of the leitmotif appear as characters in the guise of human shape. These characters are almost musical themes (and in the preface to *Miss Julie* Strindberg had already stressed that he had left behind the symmetrical constructions associated with French drama and was using material that would later be manipulated like a theme in a musical composition): the begger in *To Damascus*, as Walter Sokel points out,[33] is not a character in the traditional sense of the term but may be called an aspect of the protagonist, an embodiment of his unrealised emotional condition. Going beyond the symbolism of Ibsen and Maeterlinck the expressionist's use of the leitmotif, the containment of character within the aesthetic attribute, made possible to an unprecedented degree the divulgence of inner states and secrets of the soul. The 'characters' in *To Damascus* are all emanations from the mind of the Unknown One, as the phantom creatures called 'little formless fears' of O'Neill's *The Emperor Jones* are externalisations of his terror, and the penitents of Kaiser's *From Morn till Midnight* are representations of the bank-clerk's own transgressions. The 'musicalisation' of theatre, the expression of character and emotional situations by means of symbolic leitmotif enormously enriched European drama, leading to such fascinating experiments as Kandinsky's *The Yellow Sound*, for example, and the hallucinatory tendencies of surrealism. (It was, incidentally, whilst listening to *Lohengrin* as a student in Moscow that Kandinsky first became aware that painting could possess the same power as music: it was Wagner's work which acted as a catalyst, bringing all his colours to life and making him aware of the possibility of non-objective art.)[34]

Stream of consciousness, leitmotif, increasing inwardness – the modern novel must now engage our attention, for the Wagnerian presence looms equally large in this genre. The tendency for the novel to reject definite plot and subject matter, to concentrate on the consciousness of the main character frequently to the exclusion of everything else, the tendency for its sections to be related not by some action but by continual cross-references of symbol and image, which must be related to one another spatially (it was Gurnemanz, it may be remembered, who stressed that *time* had become *space*) provokes a discussion on what is meant by 'musicalisation' and the importance of a leitmotif technique for the advocates of the stream of consciousness or the interior monologue. Attempts to construct novels on fugual or sonata lines are not of interest here, being frequently contrived and bearing only a superficial analogy with music: Philip Quarles, in Aldous

Huxley's *Point Counter Point*, had speculated upon the musicalisation of fiction, but the fugual or simultaneous treatment of events, the complicated shifts and playing off of one incident against another reduces the novel to mere cleverness. Similarly Edouard, in Gide's *Les Faux-Monnayeurs*, had suggested using the 'Art of Fugue' as a model for his fiction and claimed that 'I do not see why that which was possible in music should be deemed impossible in literature'.[35] Likewise the sonata form, the juxtaposition and possible fusing of two contrasting themes, when applied loosely to a work of fiction, tends to become glib and unconvincing: to insist that a piece of writing has a fugual or sonata form says little more than that a theme is expanded textually from its point of focus by a contrapuntal style or that two contrasting themes are juxtaposed, which basically means very little. The use of music in fiction which is of interest here is an off-shoot of French symbolism which was nurtured by Wagner's inspiration: the suspension of the fictional flow in the consciousness of a certain character, and the use of the stream of consciousness, sustained by the leitmotif, is what concerns us. 'The novelist of the future', writes Téodor de Wyzewa in 1895, 'will erect a single consciousness, which he will imbue with life; through it, images will be perceived, themes will be resolved, emotions will be felt. The reader, in the same way as the author, will see everything – inanimate as well as animate – through this unique consciousness, whose life he will experience.'[36]

Wyzewa had been an active contributor to the *Revue Wagnérienne*, but what are of crucial importance here are the remarks of the founder of that remarkable journal, Edouard Dujardin. Dujardin's *Les Lauriers sont coupés*, published in instalments in 1887 and in book form in the following year, was revolutionary in that the reader is suspended in the consciousness of a single character throughout the entire novel: the interior monologue is used for the first time to that extent, and the distinction between poetry and prose is considerably lessened. (Dujardin later claimed to be one of the progenitors of *vers libre*, explaining that the term was first used at a meeting between himself, Laforgue and Houston Stewart Chamberlain in Berlin at the end of March 1886; he would also, of course, produce his *La Légende d'Antonia* in 1891, a trilogy with obvious parallels to Wagner's *Parsifal* which, although a spectacular flop, at least met with Mallarmé's guarded praise and Maeterlinck's more enthusiastic response.) James Joyce read Dujardin's novel in 1902 during a trip to Paris and did, in fact, meet Dujardin some twenty years later. In *Le Monologue intérieur: Son apparition, ses origines, sa place dans l'oeuvre de James Joyce*, published in 1931, Dujardin gives much useful information on the stream of consciousness technique and the need for the leitmotif:

I recently pointed out the analogy – which is generally misunderstood – existing between musical motifs and the short, direct phrases of interior monologue. I am now about to reveal a secret: *Les lauriers sont coupés* was begun with the mad intention of transposing Wagnerian procedures into literary devices. I defined the method in this way: the movement of consciousness is expressed by the incessant thrusts of musical motifs, which attempt to approximate, one after the other, indefinitely and successively, to the 'states' of thought, feeling and sensation.[37]

In the same book Dujardin explains: 'The majority of critics have compared inner monologue to every variety of thing, to film, to the wireless, to radiography, and even to the diving bell: no one has yet, at least to my knowledge, pointed out the analogy – or shall we say kinship – between those short successive phrases and musical motifs such as Richard Wagner has used.'[38] Closer study of what the leitmotif can achieve is appropriate here, for this is the most consistent contribution of music to fiction, a device most suitable to literature because it was originally a *literary* device taken over by music – by Wagner above all. The novels employing the stream of consciousness technique rely upon the use of the leitmotif, for the recurrence of certain themes is a characteristic of these novels, and the leitmotifs provide points of orientation. The great modern novels, like the Wagnerian music dramas, achieve their vastness with an economy of means, an ever-developing web of cross-references and an interweaving of images and phrases. Epic prose composition may now be regarded as an interlocking of themes, a musical complex of associations.

As Melvin Friedman explains, a genuine leitmotif in literature is easy to locate but difficult to define: it is either a repeated group of words or a mere verbal formula.[39] In interior monologue the leitmotifs are usually staccato thrusts, frequently having no meaning out of context. Their shortness means that they can easily be recalled to the mind of the reader when they recur; the associations are programmatic, since a leitmotif must refer to something beyond the tones or words which it contains. It has been called the inevitable handmaid of the interior monologue technique of the stream of consciousness novel because, if not carefully controlled, the dangerous facility of this method lends itself all too easily to a complete disregard for literary values. A contrivance is needed to relieve the uninterrupted flow of thought, a contrivance delicately interwoven into the pattern of the monologue, indicating direction and modification in a manner which is not too obtrusive. It must make an *emotional* impact, and here it is Wagner's example that is of importance, for his continual transformation of existing motifs into new ones, conveying a sense of progressive emotional and psychological development, immeasurably enriched the potential of language.

The novel reaches the richness and subtlety of poetry itself; the attempt to capture the actual flow of thoughts which cross the consciousness of the fictional character moves necessarily towards poetry in the interplay of images and symbols and in the delicacy of allusion; the musical translation of moods into major and minor keys encourages the emotional intensification and the psychological finesse. To return to the leitmotif and Dujardin's use of it: little phrases, sometimes no longer than two or three words, are repeated throughout the inner monologues of Daniel Prince, fictional centre of *Les Lauriers sont coupés*, and establish cross-connections in which old sensations are renewed, often wistfully and, indeed, not without a hint of irony. With James Joyce the stream of consciousness technique reaches its finest flowering, but Joyce will be our concern in later chapters. In the hands of a master like Proust (who may be located within the stream of consciousness tradition although refusing to compromise indirect statement in the style of the narrator by mixing it with direct quotations from the mind of the character) the leitmotif is employed with a subtlety and a complexity hitherto unknown: *A la recherche du temps perdu* is, in a sense, a literary counterpart to Wagner's *Ring*, a vast fabric of themes constantly modulating, constantly repeating, constantly cross-referring, until all sense of linear development has been superseded. The narrator is rightly captivated by those insistent, fleeting themes of Wagner which appear, withdraw and return, sometimes distant and even drowsy, almost detached, yet also so near, internal and organic. 'As the spectrum makes visible to us the composition of light, so the harmony of a Wagner . . . enables us to know that essential quality of another person's sensations into which love for another person cannot enter.'[40]

It has been suggested that the whole of the 'overture' to *A la recherche* takes place in the penumbra between sleep and waking, between the subconscious and the conscious, in a region part dream and part reverie: almost all Proust's themes are introduced in the opening phrases and are developed throughout the rest of the *oeuvre*.[41] Vinteuil and his music, however, are approached obliquely, cautiously — but the 'petite phrase' becomes a central motif: its similarity to *Tristan* is commented on at length: 'As I played the passage . . . I could not help murmuring *Tristan* with the smile of an old friend of the family when he discovers a trace of the grandfather in an intonation, a gesture of the grandson who never set eyes on him. And as an old friend then examines a photograph which enables him to gauge the likeness, so in front of Vinteuil's sonata I set up on the music rest the score of *Tristan*.'[42] Friedman explains: 'Like the horn theme in Wagner's *Siegfried*, in which the leitmotiv is first only an interesting and pleasant grouping of sounds but through its connection with Siegfried, who blows the horn, builds up an association so that it comes to represent Siegfried when neither he nor his horn is physically present, Swann's connection with the "petite phrase" gradually becomes a means of identifying both himself and his love affair with Odette.'[43] The fragment of Vinteuil's sonata is used by Proust whenever he wishes to renew the atmosphere of a particular situation: it has a life of its own, passes into the service of the narrator after Swann's death and, transformed into a different musical construction, deserts the image of Odette and connects itself with Albertine. Surely E. M. Forster's description is a valuable one here:

> ... and the little phrase has a life of its own, unconnected with the lives of its auditors, as with the life of the man who composed it ... There are times when the little phrase — from its gloomy inception, through the sonata, into the septet — means everything to the readers. There are times when it means nothing and is forgotten, and this seems to me the function of rhythm in fiction; not to be there all the time like a pattern, but by its lovely waxing and waning to fill us with surprise and freshness and hope.[44]

It may be argued that the 'petite phrase' exists on two planes; firstly it is an *aide memoire*, constructed along lines laid down by Wagner, who made music more than ever the instrument of allusion, association and emphasis. It is composed of clustered associations with other aspects of the narrator's development representing, in miniature, almost the entire work. Large sections of Swann's and Marcel's past are recalled by it, and it touches off a series of reminiscences; it refers, suggestively rather than concretely, to practically every aspect of the book. Its second function is more specifically that of a leitmotif; it is linked to the other musical appearances — the church bells at Combray, the sound of the sea at Balbec, the music of restaurant and salon, and with the narrator's solitary meditations at the piano. The 'petite phrase' is the most suggestive and successful of motifs because of its musical context and its regularity: the reader responds to its reoccurrence with a heightened sensitivity and a greater awareness of the mysterious cross-reference in human existence. *La Prisonnière* is the volume which contains the most overt references to Wagner and his power, but the whole *oeuvre* is steeped in his musical practice; Swann's story may be compared to the Prize Song from *Die Meistersinger*, a demonstration that it was still possible to write an operatic aria or a love story, and other references, not without a sly sense of humour, compare the ringing of a telephone to a theme from *Tristan*,[45] or the sound of sirens during an air raid to the howling of the Valkyries.[46] Humour is also derived from speculations that M. Charlus might well have imagined himself receiving guests to the theme of the Grand March from *Tannhäuser*,[47] and also from the disagreements between the Duc and Duchesse de Guermantes on Wagner's *longueurs* and ostensible tedium, the Duke falling asleep, the Duchess warmly defending *Lohengrin* and *Der fliegende Holländer*.[48] Further, in *Pastiches et Mélanges*, the dismal sound of the car's horn leads the narrator directly to contemplate how the lugubrious may be transformed into the joyful paean; the desolate piping of the shepherd in the last act of *Tristan* giving way to 'the expression of the greatest surge of joy ever to have filled the human soul'.[49] That 'magical suggestiveness of music' which Conrad had discussed in the preface to the *Nigger of the 'Narcissus'* (music which, he added, was 'the art of arts') informs Proust's work at practically every level, and the Wagnerian structure gives coherence, a rich tapestry of interwoven themes and a remarkably enhanced psychological penetration.

   'Apart from the difficulty of changing a musical impression into a literary one, and the tendency to appeal to the literary sense because of the associations of words, there is the further difficulty in the case of music that its scope is much less clearly defined than the scope of the other arts.'[50] Some of the most perceptive statements concerning the relationship between music and literature are to be found in *Impressions at Bayreuth*, written by Virginia Woolf for *The Times* in August 1909. Readers of *The Voyage Out* will also remember Mrs Dalloway's remarks on experiencing *Parsifal* there, the grilling August day, the fat German women in their stuffy high frocks, the dark theatre and the overpowering effect of the music. This novel, Virginia Woolf's first, is constructed along traditional lines (in the same year, 1915, Dorothy Richardson's *Painted Roofs* appeared, that remarkable odyssey through the mind of Miriam Henderson, and a highly technical piece of fiction) and there is little that is experimental; the Wagner references smack of name dropping (as does the *Lohengrin* reference in Richardson's book), although *Tristan* does have an important thematic function. Mrs Dalloway finds the score at Rachel Vinrace's piano, and Rachel later reads a translation of the libretto; she plays the music on board ship where she and Terence Hewet become aware of their love. Her mysterious death seems to bring ultimate fulfilment; it is only then that she achieves union with her lover. A mythical dimension is added to the novel by its references to *Tristan*, but the narrative technique is conventional; *Jacob's Room* (1922) is more interesting in its use of thematic motifs, but *The Waves* (1931) is, to use William Blissett's words, 'the most Wagnerian of all Virginia Woolf's novels because the most despotically organised, the most "composite" in its use of musical and painterly, even sculpturesque and ballet-like effects, and the most pervasively leitmotivistic in its structure and symbolism'.[51] This novel, conceived and composed musically, relegates both character and plot to the background: a pulsating fabric of symbols and motifs, derived incontrovertibly from Wagner, takes precedence. The cyclical structure, the beginning and the end in water, the images of light and burning gold, the arc of fire gleaming on the horizon and the blazing sea derive specifically from Wagner's *Ring des Nibelungen*: to object that these descriptions could refer to any creation myth portraying the coming of light into the darkness of the waters is to forget the prime importance of the *ring* motif in this book. DiGaetani is correct in stressing that the pattern of rings appears, significantly, after the italicised section of the first chapter which portrays the light striking into the water: 'The sun has just appeared over the sea and the first line after the description is: " 'I see a ring,' said Bernard, 'hanging above me. It quivers and hangs in a loop of light.' " This begins a whole series of images of rings, circles and loops.'[52] Rings of gold, of steel, of amethyst, hammered rings, rings of tree-growth, smoke-rings – all these are related to the six characters whose attitude to the world is thereby clarified. Bernard's ring 'hangs in a loop of light', Louis attempts to 'forge a ring of steel' (that is, create poetry), Rhoda refers to Miss Lambert's jewelled ring, Susan to the spiralling song of a lark. As Wagner's ring-leitmotif is capable of infinite modification, so the rings in Virginia Woolf's novel recede and re-emerge with differing degrees of intensity; the basic meaning, what Di Gaetani calls the 'circular concept of life's progression',[53] is central to both works.

Virginia Woolf saw the *Ring* cycle at Covent Garden in 1911 and again in 1913 (*The Years*, published in 1937, is shot through with references to the figure of Siegfried and structured around images of hammering and fire): it was *Parsifal*, however, which remained the quintessential Wagner work for her, and *The Waves* had its mythic hero Percival who is not seen, but whose sudden death, almost as a sacrificial victim, pierces the six characters. 'Yet it is Percival I need; for it is Percival who inspires poetry . . .', 'Now is our festival; now we are together. But without Percival there is no solidity. We are silhouettes, hollow phantoms moving mistily without a background' – thus speak Louis and Neville respectively, and Bernard reinforces the specifically Wagnerian *Parsifal* references by stating, in his final monologue, that the 'wild hunting song'[54] was Percival's music, an allusion to Parsifal's entry in Wagner's music drama and the turbulent music of the huntsman who has just killed the sacred swan. A discussion of the mythical dimensions of the novel belongs properly in Chapter Three: here let it be said that Virginia Woolf, as well as enriching her novels through the Wagner references, imposes a leitmotif pattern upon her experimental fiction; what William Blissett has called 'its enormously subtle use of motifs – their variations, expression, compression, combination, subtle modification, even when apparently identical with previous instances, by key, context and culmulative memory, dramatic and musical'[55] refers to the composer's work, but the novelist has learned her trade by sensitive emulation.

Myth, musicalisation and leitmotif, experiments in the stream of consciousness technique – this chapter must end with a necessarily brief account of the importance of Wagner for Thomas Mann, that European classic most beholden to Wagner's hegemony. Thomas Mann never ceased to acknowledge his indebtedness, and it is of interest for this chapter that he should describe particularly the literary leitmotif and the growing sophistication of its treatment in his hands. In *A Sketch of my Life* he explains, *à propos Tonio Kröger*, that

> Here, perhaps for the first time, I learned to use music to mould my style and form. Here for the first time I grasped the idea of epic prose composition as a thought-texture woven of different themes, as a musically related complex . . . In particular, the linguistic 'leitmotif' was not handled, as in *Buddenbrooks*, purely on an external and naturalistic basis, but was transformed into the lucent realm of the idea and the emotions and therewith lifted from the mechanical into the musical sphere.[56]

Rejecting the 'external' and 'naturalistic', the mechanical use of the leitmotif (Zola had, incidentally, accepted the term 'repetitions' to describe his own use of certain motifs which, he admitted, were somewhat akin to those of Richard Wagner[57]), Thomas Mann insisted on a growth of subtlety in his own use of leitmotifs which intensify the quality of certain feelings by repetition, also increase the symbolic effect of those attributes assigned to certain characters, and which establish a pattern of resonant cross-references. In the Princeton preface to *The Magic Mountain*, written in 1939, Thomas Mann refers to the use of the leitmotif, the 'magic formula which works both ways and links the past with the future, the future with the past. The leitmotif is the technique employed to preserve the inward unity and abiding presentness of the whole at each moment.'[58] The mythical element, the languishing of a Tannhäuser in the 'Zauberberg' or 'Venusberg', that 'Tannhäuser' who is also, in many ways, a guileless fool not unlike Parsifal, learning wisdom through sympathy, is immediately apparent; the musicality of the novel is also seen in Castorp's own guilelessness, making him 'an infinitely malleable musical theme, capable of successive self-transcendence'.[59] As all the persons in the *Ring* may be said to add up to a total humanity, polarised in Licht-Alberich and Schwarz-Alberich, so all the main characters in *The Magic Mountain* may be called experimental parts of the hero. It is not for nothing that Thomas Mann should stress, in his Princeton foreword, that the readers of his vast novel should read it again and note its musical structure, adding that one should know something of music to appreciate it fully.

Thoroughly 'through-composed' in the best Wagnerian tradition are the *Joseph* novels, a tetralogy as vast as Wagner's, a world composed of that vast web of motifs beginning in the depths of the past, that deep well which is the equivalent of Wagner's E flat major triad, out of which a pulsing and resounding cosmos emerges. For Wagner knew – and Proust, and Thomas Mann and, more recently, Günter Grass have learned – that lost time can only be regained from elementary beginnings, that recollection and confirmation are essential, above all recapitulation: the past must be recalled and relived, and hence those passengers of re-statement and retrospection in the *Ring* are as necessary as those tales told in the Joseph novels, those re-statements by Joseph and Jacob. To claim that Thomas Mann turned his back on Wagner during the time of writing his tetralogy is false: he never felt closer to Wagner than at this time, and sought above all to demonstrate that *he* was the heir to that daunting composer rather than the unscrupulous usurpers in Nazi Germany. To argue similarly that Leverkühn's music in *Doktor Faustus* is utterly unlike Wagner's is platitudinous; his stricken nature, 'touched by the woman', brings Amfortas to mind, and his despotic absoluteness is not dissimilar to that of the Bayreuth Meister. Leverkühn summarises modernism, as Nietzsche claimed that Wagner did; the cyclical structure of the novel, together with its supporting leitmotifs and the fearful *Götterdämmerung* of its ending are all too apparent. A novel whose theme is music, whose hero is a musician and whose structure is analogous to a symphony must needs take stock with that tradition of which Wagner was the consummate climax, despite the presence of Schoenberg and Adorno.

Wagner is reported to have claimed: 'My baton will become again the sceptre of the future: it will teach the times to come the path which they will have to take.'[60] Such megalomania might well grate on sensitive ears, but there is much truth in the statement. This chapter has acknowledged that unique impetus which Wagner gave to French symbolism, to the theatre of Mallarmé and Maeterlinck and to the theatrical method of Meyerhold; it sought to detect a link between the musician and the stream of consciousness technique of Dujardin, and the associative use of the leitmotif in Proust, Virginia Woolf and Thomas Mann. That all-pervasive shift towards music, symbolism and, ultimately, abstraction, which German Romanticism inculcated was inherited by Wagner and given a tremendous acceleration: reason enough to admit his importance. But this is only the beginning, for the resurrection of myth in much modern literature and thought also derives from his example: archetypal themes, themes of quest and grail, redemption through love and death by fire have Wagner as their paradigm. This chapter has touched briefly on the mythical: Chapter Three will examine it at greater length. We shall now turn, however, to that bizarre offshoot of symbolism – decadence – to find once more his indelible stamp, for Wagner has been called 'der letzte Pilzling auf dem Dünger der Romantik':[61] the last fungoid growth on the Romantic dunghill nevertheless captivates and enthrals, the limpid effulgence of symbolism giving way to a livid phosphorescence when filtered through the more questionable consequences of his art.

Notes

1 Heinrich Heine, *Lutetia* (20 April 1841) in *Werke und Briefe* (Aufbau). Berlin, 1962, VI, pp. 380–2: 'Für mich ist es ein sehr bedeutungsvoller Umstand, daß Beethoven am Ende seiner Tage taub ward und sogar die unsichtbare Tonwelt keine klingende Realität mehr für ihn hatte. Seine Töne waren nur noch Erinnerungen eines Tones, Gespenster verschollener Klänge, und seine letzten Produktionen tragen an der Stirne ein unheimliches Totenmal.' Wagner, as has been said, tried to copy Heine's witty and satirical style when given the opportunity of earning some additional money by writing articles for French and German periodicals (see Jacobs and Skelton, *Wagner writes from Paris*, London, 1973). The *Pariser Berichte* IV praises Heine's style in glowing terms, and claims that 'never before has a style, emerging so suddenly and with the unexpectedness of a lightning flash, dominated the scene so irresistibly' (*Wagner writes . . .* 161). It was from Heine that Wagner, as he admits in the *Autobiographische Skizze* of 1842, took the idea for the Flying Dutchman; he had met the story in *Aus den Memoiren des Herrn von Schnabelewopski* (1834). Whether or not Heine's 'Jung-Katerverein für Poesiemusik' (*Romanzero*) is a satirical reference to Wagner's music is debatable: see Chapter Four, note 6.
2 Richard Wagner, *Gesammelte Schriften und Dichtungen*, Leipzig, 1871, I. Reprinted in *Richard Wagner Schriften* (ed. Egon Voss), Fischer Taschenbuch, Frankfurt, 1978, pp. 58–9: 'Ich glaube an Gott, Mozart und Beethoven, in Gleichem an ihre Jünger und Apostel; ich glaube an den Heiligen Geist und an die Wahrheit der einen, unteilbaren Kunst; ich glaube, daß diese Kunst von Gott ausgeht und in den Herzen aller erleuchteten Menschen lebt; ich glaube, daß, wer nur ein Mal in den erhabenen Genüssen dieser hohen Kunst schwelgte, für ewig ihr ergeben sein muß und sie nie verleugnen kann; ich glaube, daß Alle durch diese Kunst selig werden, und daß es daher Jedem erlaubt sei, für sie Hungers zu sterben; ich glaube, daß ich durch den Tod hochbeglückt sein werde; ich glaube, daß ich auf Erden ein dissonierender Akkord war, der so gleich durch den Tod herrlich und rein aufgelöset werden wird.'
3 Richard Benz (ed.), *Beethovens Denkmal im Wort*, Munich, 1950, pp. 6, 7 and 9: '. . . und die Welt muß ich verachten, die nicht ahnt, daß Musik höhere Offenbarung ist als alle Weisheit und Philosophie . . .', 'daß Musik der einzige unverkörperte Eingang in eine höhere Welt des Wissens ist . . .', 'So vertritt die Kunst allemal die Gottheit, und das menschliche Verhältnis zu ihr ist Religion . . .'
4 E. T. A. Hoffmann, *Alte und Neue Kirchenmusik* in *Sämtliche Werke*, (ed. Grisebach), 1900, VII, p. 153: 'Keine Kunst geht so ganz und gar aus der inneren

Vergeistigung des Menschen hervor, keine Kunst bedarf nur einzig rein geistiger, ätherischer Mittel, als die Musik.' See also the statement in *Beethovens Instrumentalmusik, op. cit.*, XII, p. 14, where music is called 'die romantischste aller Künste, beinahe möchte man sagen, allein echt romantisch'.

5 Arthur Schopenhauer, *Die Welt als Wille und Vorstellung*, III, paragraph 52, I, p. 346 (in *Gesammelte Werke*, Großherzog Wilhelm Ernst Ausgabe): 'Da unsere Welt nichts Anderes ist als die Erscheinung der Ideen in der Vielheit . . . so ist die Musik, da sie die Ideen übergeht, auch von der erscheinenden Welt ganz unabhängig, ignoriert sie schlechthin, könnte gewissermaaßen, auch wenn die Welt gar nicht wäre, doch bestehen: was von den anderen Künsten sich nicht sagen läßt . . . Die Musik ist aber keineswegs, gleich den anderen Künsten, das Abbild der Ideen; *sondern Abbild des Willens selbst*, dessen Objektivität auch die Ideen sind: deshalb ist eben die Wirkung der Musik so sehr viel mächtiger und eindringlicher als die der anderen Künste, denn diese reden nur vom Schatten, sie aber vom Wesen.' See Ronald Taylor, *The Romantic Tradition in Germany*, London, 1970, for an excellent collection of annotated selections from Wackenroder, Schlegel, Schopenhauer, Wagner *et. al.*. to which I am much indebted.

6 See Walter Sokel's *The Writer in Extremis*, Stanford, Calif., 1958, particularly the second chapter. Sokel traces the philosophical foundations of modernism back to Kant, who destroyed the concept of art as mimesis; absolute art, art as an utterly free creation or as pure design is theoretically conceivable after Kant. Sokel links Kant's aesthetic attributes with Mallarmé's 'la parole essentielle', which is an aesthetic phenomenon, and concludes that Wagner's leitmotif is a similar concept. Wagner expresses the essence of a character or a situation by a sequence of musical notes designed to arouse emotional responses; a character is not analysed in the narrative method, but is contained in the aesthetic attribute, the musical theme, which signals an emotional attitude to the audience. The leitmotif, Sokel persuasively argues, becomes a symbol, one which does not represent a universal idea, but which serves as a function of expression in the work of art.

7 Erich Heller in the *Times Literary Supplement*, 10 October 1975.

8 Richard Wagner, *Gesammelte Schriften und Dichtungen*, Leipzig, 1898, IX, p. 73: 'Aus diesem letzten Grunde der Leiden, mit denen er den Zustand der Begeisterung, in welchem er uns so unaussprechlich entzückt, zu entgelten hat, dürfte uns der Musiker wieder verehrungswürdiger als andere Künstler, ja fast mit einem Anspruch an Heilighaltung erscheinen. Denn seine Kunst verhält sich in Wahrheit zum Komplex aller anderen Künste wie die *Religion* zur *Kirche*.'

9 Lilian Furst, *Counterparts*, London, 1977, p. 113.

10 Edmund Wilson, *Axel's Castle*, New York, 1931, p. 2.

11 Burbidge, P. and Sutton, R. (eds.), *The Wagner Companion*, London, 1979, p. 80.

12 See Cosima Wagner, *Tagebücher*, II, p. 772, where Wagner's pleasure at hearing his wife and daughter play a four-handed reduction of *Götterdämmerung* is

described as being spoilt by the addition of such labels: 'Leider kommen in dieser Ausgabe lauter Andeutungen wie: Wanderlust-Motiv, Unheils-Motiv etc. vor. R. sagt, am Ende glauben die Leute, daß solcher Unsinn auf meine Anregung geschieht!' It was Hans von Wolzogen, in his *Führer durch die Musik zu Richard Wagners Der Ring des Nibelungen* (Leipzig, 1878), who insisted on naming the different themes, and subsequent interpreters of Wagner's music were misled into believing that the disciple had the blessing of the Master. Wagner never used the word 'Leitmotiv', although he did apply the term 'Hauptmotiv' to certain of the musical ideas of *Tristan*. (See also Deryck Cooke, *I Saw the World End, op. cit.*, pp. 38–9.)

13 See William Blissett, 'Thomas Mann, the last Wagnerite'. Reprinted from *The Germanic Review*, February, 1960.

14 Jules Huret, *Enquête sur l'évolution littéraire*, Paris, 1897 (quoted in Furst, *Counterparts*): 'Le symbolisme? ... comprends pas ... ça doit être un mot allemand ... hein? Qu'est-ce que ça peut être bien vouloir dire? Moi, d'ailleurs, je m'en fiche. Quand je souffre, quand je jouis ou quand je pleure, je sais bien que ça n'est pas du symbole. Voyez-vous, toutes ces distinctions-là, c'est de l'allemandisme; qu'est-ce que ça peut faire à un poète ce que Kant, Schopenhauer, Hegel, et d'autres Boches pensent des sentiments humains!'

15 H. M. Block, *Mallarmé and the Symbolist Drama*, Detroit, Mich. 1963, p. 59.

16 Camille Mauclair, *Servitude et grandeur littéraires*, Paris, 1922 p. 225: 'Wagner a été pour nous mieux qu'une passion, une réligion. Par lui nous avons réellement possédé un esprit de mysticisme collectif.'

17 *Revue Wagnérienne*, I, pp. 206–210 (Slatkine reprint, Geneva, 1968), in the section on 'le théâtre spirituel du Livre'.

18 *Revue Wagnérienne, op. cit.*: 'Un drame, lu, paraîtra, aux âmes délicates, plus vivant que le même drame joué, sur un théâtre, par des acteurs vivants ...', in II, p. 104. It was Saint-Saëns who called *Tristan* a 'spectacle dans un fauteuil avec orchestre' (in *Harmonie et Mélodie*, Paris, 1885, p. xi).

19 Block, *op. cit.*, p. 60.

20 Stéphane Mallarmé, *Oeuvres complètes* (Pléiade), p. 545.

21 Block, *op. cit.*, p. 95.

22 In the *Bayreuther Blätter* (ed. Wolzogen), October 1878; reprinted in *Richard Wagner: Ausgewählte Schriften* (ed. Mack), Frankfurt, 1974, p. 236: '... die Tragik im Schicksale des schaffenden Geistes durch seine Unterworfenheit unter die Bedingungen der Zeit und des Raumes für sein Wirken.'

23 Ernest Newman, *The Life of Richard Wagner*, Cambridge, 1976, IV, p. 470.

24 See Curt von Westernhagen's essay, 'Das Bühnenbild. Vision/Vorschrift/Verwirklichung' in Wieland Wagner (ed.), *Richard Wagner und das neue Bayreuth*, Munich, 1962, p. 197.

25 Quoted Westernhagen, *op. cit.*, p. 194: 'Ach, es graut mir vor allem Kostüm-und Schminke-Wesen! Und wenn ich daran denke, daß diese Gestalten, wie Kundry, nun sollen gemummt werden, fallen mir gleich die ekelhaften Künstlerfeste ein, und nachdem ich das unsichtbare Orchester geschaffen, möchte ich auch das unsichtbare Theater erfinden.' He also suggested slyly to Cosima that Kundry should 'wie eine Tizianische Venus nackt daliegen' (Cosima Wagner, *Tagebücher*, II, p. 657).

26 See his article 'Flight from Enchantment' in the *Times Literary Supplement*, 24 December 1976. Of interest here is Hans Mayer's remark concerning the strange passivity of so many of Wagner's characters. Mayer writes: 'Es gehört zu den Eigentümlichkeiten der Dramaturgie Richard Wagners, daß seine wichtigsten Gestalten niemals eigenbestimmt handeln, sondern immer durch fremde Bestimmung getrieben werden: nach den Plänen eines Gottes, eines dämonischen Verbrechers, durch Trank und Gegentrank, als Gralsritter, ehrenhafte Vasallen und "liebe Sänger" eines mäzenatischen Landesfürsten' (*Richard Wagner: Mitwelt und Nachwelt*, Stuttgart and Zurich, 1978, p. 27). Mayer also points out that, in a work like *Tristan und Isolde*, there is, apart from the great duet in act two, no true communication between the characters. Between Isolde and Brangäne, between Tristan and Kurwenal there are hardly dialogues, more monologues; this is similar to much in Kleist, also Büchner.

27 Richard Wagner, *Gesammelte Schriften und Dichtungen*, Leipzig, 1898, IX, p. 108: '. . . die Offenbarung des innersten Traumbildes vom Wesen der Welt'.

28 In *Meyerhold on Theatre*, trans. and ed. Edward Braun, London, 1969, p. 96.

29 See Marianne Kesting's article 'Gesamtwerk und Totaltheater: Richard Wagner und Meyerhold' in the 1965 *Bayreuth Programmheft*.

30 Meyerhold, *op. cit.*, p. 97. (Did Aleksandr Blok see this performance? The Tristan theme is applied to the poet in Blok's 'The hours pass, the days, the years' – the tearing off of the silken sling, the spurting blood and the febrile pain. See F. D. Reeve, *Aleksandr Blok*, New York, 1962, p. 136).

31 Meyerhold, *op. cit.*, p. 85.

32 Gómez de la Serna, *En Prometeo*, vol. 2, year 3, nr. 20 (1910). The original Spanish runs as follows: '¡Futurismo! ¡Insurrección! ¡Algarada! ¡Festejo con música Wagneriana! ¡Modernismo!' The extent of Wagner's importance to Spanish modernism is described in Pio Baroja's *El árbol de la ciencia* (Alianza Editorial, Madrid, 1976), particularly in the section 'La vida de un estudiante en Madrid': 'Sañudo y sus condiscípulos no hablaban en el café más que de música; de las óperas del Real y, sobre todo, de Wagner. Para ellos, la ciencia, la política, la revolución, España, nada tenía importancia al lado de la música de Wagner. Wagner era el Mesías; Beethoven y Mozart, los precursores . . .' (p. 30). Manuel Machado's *Wagner* sonnet should also be noted.

33 Sokel, *The Writer in Extremis*, particularly the chapter on 'Music and existence'. Gabriel Josipovici, in his *Lessons of Modernism*, London, 1977, suggests another link with expressionism. He is writing about the quintessential expressionistic concept of the scream (with reference particularly to Edvard Munch) and

continues: 'Modern literature and music, and in particular modern drama and music-drama flirt with the scream, but they embody it at their peril. Since Wagner at least composers have been drawn nearer and nearer to the edge, as if to see how near they could get and yet allow their music to survive. Practically every work of the second Viennese school is, we could say, a sublimation of the scream' (p. 178). It is also worth noting that the leader of the Italian Futurists, Filippo Marinetti, insisted on the importance of musicalisation for modernism: 'Il faut détruire la syntaxe en disposant les substantifs au hasard de leur naissance. Il faut employer le verbe à l'infini, il faut orchestrer les images . . .' (quoted in K. Vossler, 'Die neuen Richtungen der italienischen Literatur' in *Die neueren Sprachen*, Marburg, 1925, 2. Beiheft, p. 12).

34 See August Wiedmann, *Romantic Roots in Modern Art*, London, 1979, p. 92.

35 André Gide, *Les Faux-Monnayeurs*, Gallimard, 1925, I, p. 237: 'Ce que je voudrais faire, comprenez-moi, c'est quelque chose qui serait comme *l'Art de la fugue*. Et je ne vois pas pourquoi ce qui fut possible en musique, serait impossible en littérature.'

36 Téodor de Wyzewa, *Nos maîtres: études et portraits littéraires*, Paris, 1895, p. 52: 'Le romancier futur dressera une seule âme, qu'il animera pleinement; par elle seront perçues les images, raisonnés les arguments, senties les émotions. Le lecteur comme l'auteur verra tout, les choses et les âmes, à travers cette âme unique et précise dont il vivra la vie.'

37 Edouard Dujardin, *Le monologue intérieur: Son apparition, ses origines, sa place dans l'oeuvre de James Joyce*, Paris, 1931, pp. 96–7: 'J'indiquais tout à l'heure l'analogie, généralement méconnue, qu'il y a entre les motifs musicaux et les petites phrases directes du monologue intérieur. Je vais livrer un secret: les *Lauriers sont coupés* ont été entrepris avec la folle ambition de transposer dans le domaine littéraire les procédés wagnériens que je me définissais ainsi: − la vie de l'âme exprimée par l'incessante poussée des motifs musicaux venant dire, les uns après les autres, indéfiniment et successivement, les "états" de la pensée, sentiment ou sensation . . .'

38 Dujardin, *op. cit.*, p. 54: 'La plupart des critiques ont comparé le monologue intérieur à toutes sortes de choses, film, T.S.F., radiographie, cloche à plongeur; ils n'ont pas, au moins à ma connaissance, signalé l'analogie, disant la parenté que présentent ces petites phrases successives avec les motifs musicaux tels, par exemple, que les a employés Richard Wagner . . .' Joyce, as is known, knew his Dujardin, and William Blissett claims that 'In *Ulysses* . . . Joyce constructs, as Wagner had done in the *Ring*, a major, an all-inclusive work resting upon carefully placed leitmotifs as upon steel reinforcements. There are more than one hundred and fifty motifs in the book, and of its seven hundred and eighty six pages I have found fewer than fifty without the sounding of at least one.' In 'James Joyce in the smithy of his soul', *James Joyce Today*, Bloomington, Ind., 1966, p. 115.

39 Melvin Friedman, *Stream of Consciousness: a Study in Literary Method*, New

Haven, Conn., 1955. Chapters five and six are especially useful.

40 Proust, *A la recherche du temps perdu* (Pléiade edition, 1954), III, p. 159: 'Comme le spectre extériorise pour nous la composition de la lumière, l'harmonie d'un Wagner ... nous permettent de connaître cette essence qualitative des sensations d'un autre où l'amour pour un autre être ne nous fait pas pénétrer.'

41 J. M. Cocking, 'Proust and Music': a public lecture given in the University of Western Australia, 19 July 1965.

42 Proust, *op. cit.*, III, p. 158: 'En jouant cette mesure ... je ne pus m'empêcher de murmurer *Tristan* avec le sourire qu'a l'ami d'une famille retrouvant quelque chose de l'aïeul dans une intonation, un geste du petit-fils qui ne l'a pas connu. Et comme on regarde alors une photographie qui permet de préciser la ressemblance, par dessus la Sonate de Vinteuil j'installai sur le pupitre la partition de *Tristan*.'

43 Friedman, *op. cit.*, 129.

44 E. M. Forster, *Aspects of the Novel* (ed. Stallybrass), London, 1974, p. 115.

45 Proust, *op. cit.*, II, p. 731.

46 Proust, *op. cit.*, III, p. 758. (Did the producer of the film *Apocalypse Now* know this?)

47 Proust, *op. cit.*, II, p. 649.

48 Proust, *op. cit.*, II, p. 491.

49 Proust, *Pastiches et Mélanges*, p. 99: 'L'expression de la plus prodigieuse attente de félicité qui ait jamais rempli l'âme humaine' (N.R.F. edition).

50 Virginia Woolf, 'Impressions at Bayreuth' (1909), reprinted in *Books and Portraits: Some Further Selections from the Literary and Biographical Writings of Virginia Woolf* (ed. M. Lyon), London, 1977, pp. 18–23.

51 William Blissett, 'Wagnerian fiction in English'; reprinted from *Criticism: a Quarterly for Literature and the Arts*, V, No. 3, 1963, p. 259.

52 J. DiGaetani, *Richard Wagner and the Modern British Novel*, Cranbury, New Jersey, 1978, p. 119.

53 DiGaetani, *op. cit.*, p. 120.

54 Virginia Woolf, *The Waves*, London, 1976, p. 29 (Louis); p. 87 (Neville); p. 177 (Bernard).

55 Blissett, *op. cit.*, p. 259.

56 Thomas Mann, *Gesammelte Werke*, Frankfurt, 1960, XI, pp. 115–16: 'Hier wohl zum erstenmal wußte ich die Musik stil-und formbildend in meine Produktion hineinwirken zu lassen. Die epische Prosakomposition war hier zum erstenmal als ein geistiges Themengewebe, als musikalischer Beziehungskomplex verstanden.' See also XIII, pp. 117–18: '... Nur daß dort [i.e. in *Tonio Kröger*] das verbale Leitmotiv nicht mehr wie in *Buddenbrooks* als formales Darstellungsmittel benutzt ist, sondern einen weniger mechanischen, musikalischeren Charakter annimmt und danach strebt, die Gefühlsbewegung und die Idee zu spiegeln.'

57 See E. K. Brown, *Rhythm in the Novel*, Toronto, 1950, p. 28.

58 Thomas Mann's Princeton foreword to *Der Zauberberg*: '... das Leitmotiv, die vor- und zurückdeutende magische Formel, die das Mittel ist, seiner inneren Gesamtheit in jedem Augenblick Präsenz zu verleihen.'

59 William Blisset, 'Thomas Mann, the last Wagnerite', in *The Germanic Review*, February 1960, p. 59.

60 See Glasenapp, *Das Leben Richard Wagners*, Berlin, 1905–12, IV, p. 199: 'Mein Taktstock wird noch einmal das Zepter der Zukunft werden, er wird die Zeiten lehren, welchen Gang sie zu nehmen haben.' The path towards musicalisation, abstraction and obscurity in modern literature is certainly indicated: literature, after Wagner, will increasingly attempt to emulate his orchestration. In an informal radio talk (6 October 1980) Anthony Burgess pointed out that Gerard Manley Hopkins's 'The wreck of the Deutschland' (written, incidentally, in the year of Wagner's triumph, 1876) is one of the first attempts to musicalise or 'Wagnerise' an experience in English: the rhythms and vocabulary Hopkins uses approximate to the crash of chords and whistling woodwind of the Wagnerian orchestra. Again, when the sea is invoked, it seems appropriate – even obligatory – to refer to Wagner, to his elemental physicality. The most 'musical' composition of the twentieth century in English, *Finnegans Wake*, is suffused with Wagnerian puns and patterns, as Chapter Four will point out. The despotic baton will indeed, as this book strives to show, call forth an amazing range of responses, from a self-laceration akin to that described in Grimm's *Der Jude im Dorn* to the transfiguration of Georgiana Carpenter.

61 Max Nordau (i.e. Max Simon Südfeld), *Entartung*, Berlin, 1892, I, p. 344: '... der letzte Pilzling auf dem Dünger der Romantik.'

2

WAGNER *and* DECADENCE

'Wagner est une névrose'
Nietzsche, 1888

'Renoir's portrait, painted in Palermo in 1882, shows the face decomposed and drained of colour, the eyes rheumy and lips pursed in sickly connoisseurship of sensation; the head is surrounded by an impressionistic blizzard of streaks and daubs, threatening a dissolution of form ... It is not Wotan's head, but Alberich's, feverish, obsessive and expiring.'[1] The portrait is that of Richard Wagner who, two days before the sitting, on 13 January 1882, had finished the score of *Parsifal*. It is this work above all, with its highly questionable fusion of Christian mysticism and blatant sexuality, its holy grail and gaping wound, its imagery of spear and chalice, its incense, castration, flower-maidens and cult of blood, which led Nietzsche to damn Richard Wagner as 'décadent', as 'une névrose'. Far from representing a break with his previous *oeuvre*, Wagner's last work may be seen as a continuation of themes, frequently morbid, which are found as early as *Tannhäuser*. The sultry religiosity of *Parsifal*, the death-intoxicated eroticism of *Tristan und Isolde* and the glorification of incest in *Die Walküre* could not fail to enrapture and appal, and it is those 'decadent' aspects of Wagner's work, and their literary manifestations, which this chapter will attempt to discuss. In vain might Max Nordau in his sensational castigation of degeneracy reject Wagner's music as immoral and harmful to the senses, and denounce the composer as a purveyor of sadistic delights, going so far as to claim that he might well have been a sex-murderer had he not been able to sublimate his erotic urges:[2] the Master of Bayreuth remained the paradigm, the godly dispenser of ultimate *frissons*, the magus who had created his own temple of art, and the supreme fount of unheard-of emotional excesses. Refinement and intoxication, voluptuous yearning and headiness, a world 'in love with both death and beauty'[3] – Thomas Mann thus described the cluster of associations that Richard Wagner's name brought forth, seeing in that artist the most perfect example of European *fin de siècle*. Wagner and Poe: an unusual juxtaposition, but one which Thomas Mann suggested with sensitivity and acumen – the name of Baudelaire immediately asserts itself here, one of the earliest and most perceptive writers on Wagner. It is with Baudelaire and *Tannhäuser* that this chapter will begin, for it is this work, together with *Tristan und Isolde* and *Parsifal*, which would fire the imagination of a whole generation of *poètes maudits*.

On 25 January 1860 Wagner conducted the first of his three Paris concerts, giving excerpts from *Tannhäuser, Lohengrin,* the overture to *Der fliegende Holländer* and the prelude to *Tristan und Isolde*; he repeated the concerts on 1 and 8 February and gathered a circle of admirers around him, including, among others, Saint-Saëns, Charles Gounod, Gustave Doré and Catulle Mendès. These would form, in 1861, the nucleus of the *Revue fantaisiste,* with its ardent championship of Wagner, but also, more importantly, would prepare the way for the idolatry of the *Revue Wagnérienne.* After the concerts, on 17 February, Baudelaire wrote an enthusiastic letter to Wagner explaining that 'I owe you the greatest musical joy that I have ever experienced', and, further, 'It seemed that I myself had written this music'.[4] The poet of *Les Fleurs du mal* sensed that here in Wagner was an artist capable of overwhelming, indeed overpowering his audience: the poem 'La musique' with its line 'La musique souvent me prend comme une mer!' seemed to describe perfectly that forceful ravishing. Listening to *Der fliegende Holländer,* Baudelaire experienced Wagner's music as an infinite, tempestuous art, submerging and ecstatic. Erotic associations are undeniable here and, writing about the Grand March from *Tannhäuser* and the Wedding March from *Lohengrin,* Baudelaire continued to equate that music with voluptuousness and sensual abandonment: 'I often experienced a bizarre sensation, namely a feeling of pride and joy at knowing, and feeling, myself ravished and flooded – a truly sensual voluptuousness was experienced which resembled flying, or tossing in the sea . . .'[5] The poet felt that he was raped by this music, that he was hovering, or floundering in deep waters: only a total surrender was possible. He gave no address to his letter, but Wagner knew how to seek him out, and invited him to his Wednesday evening soirées; it was Baudelaire who, one year later, leapt to Wagner's defence after the scandalous uproar surrounding the performances of *Tannhäuser* on 13, 18 and 25 March in the Opéra.

The essay *Richard Wagner et Tannhäuser à Paris* (1861) is indispensable in any attempt to recapture the thrill, the exhilaration and the full force of the Wagnerian explosion. The Paris version of the overture, with the rapturous bacchanal, was felt to reproduce the moans and cries, the yearnings and ecstasies of passionate abandonment: 'Languidness and febrile delights, delights fraught with anguish, incessant twists and turns towards that voluptuousness which promises to slake, but which never extinguishes, thirst; furious palpitations of the heart and the senses, imperious demands of the flesh – the complete onomatopoeic dictionary of love is heard here.'[6] The whole 'onomatopoeic dictionary of love', as well as a desire for religious salvation, Baudelaire writes, are strangely fused in this music; even more fascinating and disturbing is the proximity of savagery and sexual love, the almost inevitable juxtaposition of the delights of the flesh and the delights of crime: 'The diabolical titillations of an ill-defined love are soon succeeded by allurements, by vertigo, cries of triumph, moans of gratitude, and then by ferocious howls, by the victim's reproaches and the blasphemous hosannas of the sacrificers; it would seem as if barbarism would always take its place in the drama of love and that carnal joy would, by its satanic and inevitable logic, lead to the delights of crime . . .'[7] The sadism which Baudelaire observed in the transports of love and which he felt that Wagner's music so well portrayed, as well as the prurient dallying with thoughts of religious salvation during sexual abandonment would, some twenty years later, excite the generation of the 'décadents'; those esoteric worlds which the symbolists had explored will give way to realms both bizarre and perverse where Wagner would reign as hierophant and magus.

It was Baudelaire who determined the reception of Wagner in France: Gérard de Nerval had written on *Lohengrin* (the Weimar performance of 1850), and Léon Leroy and the Comtesse de Gasparin were others who sought to describe the new music, but Baudelaire's insights above all inspired the contributors to the *Revue Wagnérienne* to clarify their own artistic canons *sub specie Wagneri*. This amazing journal, which was founded in 1885 and which survived for two and a half years, was not, as was mentioned in Chapter One, an academic organ which sought an objective appraisal of Wagner but rather one which used his name as a touchstone or a magic cipher by which contributors sought to uncover recondite worlds. Mallarmé's *Richard Wagner: rêverie d'un poëte français* (8 August 1885) which wove around Wagner's achievement a fabric of speculation concerning an Absolute Theatre has already been mentioned; it might be argued that Mallarmé must surely be out of place in a discussion of literary decadence, although Huysmans, in *A rebours*, hailed him as the favourite poet of des Esseintes and claimed: 'Literary decadence, irreparably affected in its organism, weakened by the age of its ideas and exhausted by the excesses of its syntax, was, in fact, exemplified by Mallarmé.'[8] Suffice it that the famous 'Hommage à Wagner' be noted here, that poem of subtlety, complexity and ellipsis which extols Wagner as that deity whose dazzling vision, hardly realisable in this world, transcended the base and the mundane in its glorious epiphany.[9] The same number of the *Revue Wagnérienne* published Verlaine's 'Parsifal' sonnet, made famous by that line with its memorable hiatus: 'Et, ô ces voix d'enfants chantant dans la coupole . . .'[10] which T. S. Eliot would later quote in *The Waste Land*. Edouard Dujardin's 'Amfortas' is a symbolist concoction *à la* Mallarmé, but what is important here is Huysman's *Ouverture de Tannhäuser*, an attempt to render in prose the impact of that outrageous Paris version which Baudelaire had heard in 1861. Huysmans had given no description of Wagner in *A rebours*, but here the omission is made good; Wagner is equated with a decadent eroticism which would have thrilled even the jaded appetites of des Esseintes:

> Suddenly in this musical scene, in this fluid and fantastic site, the orchestra bursts forth and paints with a few pronounced and brilliant passages which shake us to the very depths of our being a heraldic melody – the approach of Tannhäuser. The shadows spread rays of light, and the swirling clouds assume the forms of rearing haunches, of swelling breasts, throbbing and distended; the blue avalanches of space throng with naked forms, with cries of desire and appeals to lustfulness, with outbursts of the carnal life beyond, pouring from the orchestra: and above the sinuous wall of nymphs who faint and swoon Venus arises, but no longer the antique Venus, the Aphrodite of old, whose immaculate form made men and gods bray as beasts during pagan orgies, but a Christian Venus, if such sin against nature and such coupling of words were possible! . . . It is the incarnation of the Spirit of Evil, the effigy of omnipotent luxuriousness, the image of an irresistible and magnificent female satan which levels its delicious and baleful weapons, ceaselessly on the watch for Christian souls . . .[11]

Eroticism spiced with sin, the ultimate *frisson* being the knowledge of damnation, a revelling in forbidden delights: a piece of typical *fin de siècle* impudicity is given here, where it seems as though Huysmans had found in Wagner the archpriest of satanism. The equations of sinful sexuality with a perverse yearning for redemption is very much of its time; the heady fusion of self-indulgence and self-mortification, the white lily and the purple orchids, the Madonna and whore topos, certainly derives from the Elisabeth–Venus juxtaposition in Wagner's opera, but French decadence drove it to extraordinary lengths. Pierre Louÿs (who had, in a letter to Debussy written at the end of the 1890s, reminded the composer that 'I simply said to you that Wagner was the greatest man who ever lived. I didn't say that he was God himself, but I was tempted . . .'[12]) wrote his own *Ouverture de Tannhäuser* where it is difficult to differentiate the powers of Venus from those of Elisabeth or even the Virgin Mary; Joséphin Péladan's novel *Pomone* likewise tells of a composer who desires that his forty-year-old wife should acquire more original sexual response and holds Elisabeth as an example: 'Elisabeth, wife of the Minnesänger, followed her lover along the paths of passion, not even distinguishing whether or not Venus had been the teacher.'[13] The pure Elisabeth would seem to have learned much from Tannhäuser's sojourn in the Venusberg; despite Strindberg's championship, indeed apotheosis of Péladan as the supreme prophet of 'Germanic' profundity and Wagnerian sublimity, Péladan's effusions, particularly in *La Victoire du mari* (1889), with its description of the boat of mother-of-pearl, the Knights of Monsalvat and the magic fire, seem meretricious and ultimately unconvincing.

Such vagaries are, however, the exception rather than the rule; the treatment of the *Tannhäuser* material elsewhere is content to remain within a traditional portrayal of the spirit-flesh dichotomy. Arthur Holitscher's novel *The Poisoned Well* is worth mentioning here: the heroine, a lascivious widow by the name of Désirée Wilmoth (with echoes of 'Melmoth' perhaps) lives a life greatly reminiscent of that of des Esseintes and, in a gigantic greenhouse, has created a garden based, apparently, on that of the second act of *Parsifal*. The greenhouse topos was a favourite one amongst *fin de siècle* writers: the deliberately unnatural creation of exotic blooms, particularly orchids, provided the imagery of many of the poems of this time, and it is appropriate that one of the Wesendonck-Lieder should bear the title 'Im Treibhaus'. (Wagner himself had admitted: 'I can, indeed must, live only in a sort of cloud. Being solely a man of art, I can only lead an artificial life . . . Quite artificial, and I must cut myself off from the atmosphere of reality like a tropical flower in a conservatory.'[14]) To seduce the young poet Sebastian Sasse, Désirée Wilmoth appears in provocative poses and stages of undress; naked, she embraces marble statues and does all in her power to excite the somewhat languid young man. His reactions are, unfortunately for her, those of an aesthete rather than a lover, and she is drawn to lubricious productions of *Tannhäuser* (which she organises herself) to overcome his lassitude: 'For a considerable time now she was concerned with the problem of how to replace the very stilted dances which one saw in the theatres in the Venusberg scene of *Tannhäuser* with more appropriate ones, ones which approximated more closely to the abandoned beauty of the music, wild ones, lustful ones which, however, would not harm the sacred delights of the pagan cult of the senses.'[15] The 'onomatopoeic dictionary of love' which Baudelaire had heard in the music forty years before is meant to act as an aphrodisiac to animate the blasé reactions of Sasse; Thomas Mann, who ostensibly had used Holitscher as a model for the decadent Detlev Spinell in his own story *Tristan*, will employ a similar motif in *Wälsungenblut* where it is act one of *Die Walküre*, as we shall see, which serves as the stimulus. The orgiastic and frenzied bacchanal in Aschenbach's dream, occurring immediately before his moral collapse in *Der Tod in Venedig* could also be mentioned in this context; the *mons veneris*, however, is replaced by 'the obscene symbol, gigantic, wooden', a grotesque metamorphosis of Tannhäuser's staff.

In England the Tannhäuser-motif proved to be especially fruitful: Edward Robert Bulwer-Lytton (son of the author of *Rienzi*) collaborated with his fellow-diplomat Julian Fane after seeing a performance of the opera in Vienna on a *Tannhäuser or the Battle of the Bards* which was published under Bulwer Lytton's pseudonym Owen Meredith in 1868.[16] The theme is treated in Tennysonian fashion and cannot match Swinburne's version in *Laus Veneris*. Swinburne had been led to Wagner by Baudelaire: he had reviewed the latter's *Les Fleurs du mal* in the *Spectator* in 1862 and in the following year had received from Baudelaire a copy of *Richard Wagner et Tannhäuser à Paris*.[17] The hint of sadism in Swinburne (the 'crushed grape' image) is closer to the French example than the somewhat genteel English treatment; Theodore William Wratislaw, however, who left an education at Rugby to write for *The Yellow Book* and *The Savoy*, does provide a more demonic 'Black Venus of the nether gulfs of Hell', whose caresses are 'fierce and swift and deep'. Her adversary is a pallid figure, the 'Maid who canst love and canst for love forgive – O far seen phantom of Elizabeth!'[18] Oscar Wilde, who probably knew only the *Tannhäuser* overture, yet who was undoubtedly impressed by the Huysmans paraphrase in the *Revue Wagnérienne*, describes how his young hero in *The Picture of Dorian Gray* sat 'either alone or with Sir Henry, listening in a rapt pleasure to *Tannhäuser*, and seeing in the prelude to that great work of art a presentation of the tragedy of his own soul',[19] a reference, presumably, to his own sensuality and excessive promiscuity. (It is perhaps interesting that Siegfried Wagner visited Wilde in 1892 and was impressed by his wit and charm, although he later rejected out of hand the Wilde–Strauss *Salome*, a work unthinkable without his father's example.) In E. F. ('Dodo') Benson's novel *The Rubicon* (1894) the theme of dualism is apparent, 'the war between the lower, bestial side of man and something which mankind itself has declared to be higher – the pure, steadfast soul'. Again it is the prelude to *Tannhäuser* which fascinates and convulses: the hero, Reggie, is invited by Lady Eva Hayes, a femme fatale with obvious desires on the young man, to listen in her box to this work:

> The slow, deep notes of the 'Pilgrims' March' rose and fell, walking steadfastly in perilous place, weary, yet undismayed. Then followed the strange chromatic passage of transition, without which even Wagner did not dare to show us the other side of the picture, and then the great animal, which has lain as if asleep, began to stir; its heart beat with the life of its waking moments, and it started up. The violins shivered and smiled and laughed as Venusberg came in sight; they rose and fell, as the march before had done, but rising higher and laughing more triumphantly with each fall – careless, heedless, infinitely beautiful . . .[20]

It is during the height of the bacchanal that the helpless Reggie becomes enlightened as to Lady Eva's intentions: 'The riot was at its height, the triumph of Venus and her train seemed complete, when suddenly Reggie started up. He stood at his full height a moment, watching the curtain rise on Venusberg. "I see, I see," he cried. Then he turned to Eva. "You are a wicked woman," he said, and the next moment the door of the box closed behind him.'²¹ It is not easy to sympathise with Reggie's predicament; the son of Archbishop Benson knew his Wagner (certainly *Tannhäuser*, also *Die Walküre*, for he was commissioned in 1903 to weave a fanciful romance around this music drama), but his imagination was not forceful enough to enable him to recreate Wagner's astonishing work. Mention should perhaps also be made of Maurice Baring's autobiographical novel *C*: like Bulwer Lytton, Baring had been a diplomat; he had travelled widely in Germany and had also visited Bayreuth. The hero of his novel recalls the violent electric shock of a *Tannhäuser* performance in Hanover, an experience which he describes as being similar to witnessing a Swinburne poem in action; a performance of *Tristan und Isolde* in Frankfurt likewise intoxicates the young man who capitulates utterly before the oceanic ecstasy and the stifling twilight of that work.

It is a relief now to turn to the delightful absurdities of Aubrey Beardsley; Beardsley's Wagner drawings are, of course, well known, particularly the rather ambiguous 'Siegfried' which Beardsley gave to Edward Burne-Jones to hang in his drawing room, and 'The Wagnerites', which established Beardsley's reputation in France. Our interest here, however, is with *Under the Hill*, an amusing transposition of Wagner's theme into a Rococo setting, a *galanterie* of witty and preposterous obscenity. The original version, *Venus and Tannhäuser*, took Baudelaire's poem 'La géante' to grotesque extremes of pornotopia: the landscape of hills, woods, chasms, and moist clefts being an obvious masturbation fantasy. *Under the Hill*, more diverting in its fey improprieties, was left incomplete at Beardsley's death; certain sections (chapters one, two, three and seven, and most of chapter five) had already appeared in *The Savoy*, accompanied by drawings. (The manuscript was printed privately in 1907, again in 1927 and reached a wider public with the Olympia Press edition of 1959.) The 'Chevalier Tannhäuser,' more eighteenth-century wit than medieval ministrel, arrives at the court of Venus, whose companions and servants are a typical gallery of Beardsley monstrosities; Venus herself is a charming coquette. The chevalier, excited by amatory perfumes within an elegant pavillion, thrusts himself upon the goddess: 'Her frail chemise and dear little drawers were torn and moist, and clung transparently about her, and all her body was nervous and responsive. Her closed thighs seemed like a vast replica of the little bijou she had between them; the beautiful tétons du derrière were firm as a plump virgin's cheek, and promised a joy as profound as the mystery of the Rue Vendôme, and the minor chevelure, just profuse enough, curled as prettily as the hair upon a cherub's head . . .'[22] After waking next morning the chevalier reads in bed, of all things, the score of *Das Rheingold*:

> Making a pulpit of his knees he propped up the opera before him and turned over the pages with a loving hand, and found it delicious to attack Wagner's brilliant comedy with the cool head of the morning. Once more he was ravished with the beauty and wit of the opening scene; the mystery of its prelude that seems to come up from the very mud of the Rhine, and to be as ancient, the abominable primitive wantonness of the music that follows the talk and movements of the Rhine-maidens, the black, hateful sounds in Alberich's love-making and the flowing melody of the river of legends . . .[23]

A drawing of the 'Third Tableau of *Das Rheingold*' was added to the story, and Beardsley explains:

> But it was the third tableau that he applauded most that morning, the scene where Loge, like some flamboyant primeval Scapin, practises his cunning upon Alberich. The feverish insistent ringing of the hammers at the forge, the dry staccato restlessness of Mime, the ceaseless coming and going of the troop of Nibelungs, drawn hither and thither like a flock of terror-stricken and infernal sheep, Alberich's savage activity and metamorphoses, and Loge's rapid, flaming, tonguelike movements, make the tableau the least reposeful, most troubled and confusing thing in the whole range of opera. How the Chevalier rejoiced in the extravagant monstrous poetry, the heated melodrama, and splendid agitation of it all![24]

The description is a pertinent one, but Beardsley does not remain too long in this earnest manner; the chevalier rises at eleven, slips off a charming nightdress and, after posing before a long mirror, steps into his bath with his servant boys, an obvious variation on the opening scene of that music drama which he had just been studying:

> 'Splash me a little!' he cried, and the boys teased him with water and quite excited him. He chased the prettiest of them and bit his fesses, and kissed him upon the perineum till the dear fellow banded like a carmelite, and its little bald topknot looked like a great pink pearl under the water. As the boy seemed anxious to take up the active attitude, Tannhäuser graciously descended to the passive – a generous trait that won him the complete affections of his valets de bain, or pretty fish, as he liked to call them, because they loved to swim between his legs . . .[25]

To speculate upon the reactions of the editors of the *Revue Wagnérienne*, not to speak of the *Bayreuther Blätter*, to these frivolities is indeed diverting, but it is obvious that Beardsley's Tannhäuser, with his 'dear little coat of pigeon rose silk that hung loosely about his hips, and showed off the jut of his behind to perfection; trousers of black lace in flounces, falling – almost like a petticoat – as far as the knee; and a delicate chemise of white muslin, spangled with gold and profusely pleated',[26] would be more appropriate to the *Folies Bergères* than to the *Festspielhaus*; the Wagnerian explosion was such that even this *feu de joie* was ignited.

Aubrey Beardsley's 'The Wagnerites' has already been mentioned; it was sketched from memory after a visit to the Paris Opera in 1893 to see *Tristan und Isolde*, and the name of the music drama is to be seen in the bottom of the right-hand corner of the drawing. If Wagner was the musician who meant most to the decadents (Beardsley, it is reported, confessed to two great passions in his lifetime – one was for Wagner's music, the other for 'fine raiment'[27]), then *Tristan und Isolde*, with its fusion of eroticism and extinction, its yearning, swooning chromaticism, its link with legend and its ultimate modernity, even excelled *Tannhäuser* in its ability to provoke and inspire. The fusion of love and death, the juxtaposition of fecund night and arid day, is a Romantic notion to be found most forcibly in Novalis; it is entirely in keeping that the *fin de siècle* writers, in their rejection of utilitarianism, materialism and vulgar progress, should have turned to *Tristan und Isolde* as an escape into voluptuous morbidity. The orgasmic implications of a 'love-death' would also provide the decadents with much material: although Wagner's reading of Schopenhauer provided much of the philosophical substratum of the music drama it should not be forgotten that Schopenhauer's concept of the abnegation of the will, of the futile round of human existence, was modified by Wagner to suit his own aims. In a letter to Mathilde Wesendonck, written in Venice on 1 December 1858, Wagner disarmingly claims that he has re-read 'friend Schopenhauer's masterpiece' and felt moved to correct certain details of his system. 'It is a question, in fact, of proving that there *is* a sacred path towards the complete pacification of the will – a path recognised by none of the philosophers, not even Sch[openhauer] – and this is through love, and certainly not an abstract love of humanity, but real love, a love which springs from sexuality, the attraction of man and woman.'[28] The way of salvation which leads to the perfect appeasement of the will is not through renunciation, but self-indulgence in absolute abandonment: a post-coital 'death' is implied here. In a letter to Schopenhauer, drafted but not sent, Wagner refers to a certain section in the latter's 'The metaphysics of sexual love' (in *The World as*

Will and Idea), where Schopenhauer could not account for the communal suicide of lovers, and offers an explanation: stressing that sexual love was 'a holy path towards the will's self-knowledge and self-denial'[29] he implies that a sexual climax accompanied by physical death would be the ultimate consummation. At the moment of highest ecstasy, and at the point of death itself, the Romantic imagination had glimpsed the infinite; the more prurient writers at the end of the nineteenth century would explore more dubious variations, Arthur Holitscher in his *Of Lust and Death*, for instance, and Horacio Quiroga in his *Tales of Love, Madness and Death*, particularly 'La muerte de Isolde'.

Wagner himself was under no illusions as to the powerful expressiveness of *Tristan und Isolde*, as a letter from Venice to Mathilde Wesendonck (8 December 1858) quite clearly shows: 'I have been working since yesterday with *Tristan* again. I am still in the middle of the second act – but – what music it is! I could spend my whole life just working on this music. Oh, it is deep and beautiful and the most sublime miracles fit so easily into the meaning of it all.'[30] Four months later, from Lucerne, he continues: 'Child! This Tristan will be something terrible! This last act!!! I fear that the opera will be forbidden, unless bad performances do not parody the whole thing – only mediocre performances can save me! Absolutely perfect ones will make people insane . . .'[31] The first performance of the music drama, on 10 June 1865, the enormous controversy, bewilderment and final recognition that the work marked a watershed in musical history need no further description here: our concern is with the undeniable echoes of Wagner's masterpiece not only in the minor decadents but also in Thomas Mann, George Moore, Gabriele d'Annunzio and, in a subsequent chapter, Eliot, Lawrence and Conrad. Even Nietzsche was pierced by this music; shortly before his mental collapse acrimony, malice and hyperbole fade, and memories of *Tristan* transfigure even his loneliness: 'Yet I am still looking today for a work of such dangerous fascination as *Tristan* – and I look through all the arts in vain. The world is poor indeed for the man who has never been sick enough for this "infernal voluptuousness": it is permitted – it is even demanded – that we apply mystical formulae here . . .'[32] Nietzsche, the self-styled 'decadent' and also the most astute critic of decadence, saw in Wagner the greatest danger, yet also the source of joy that transcended all scruples and reservations.

It is in Thomas Mann that the most skilful evocation of the entrancement exerted by *Tristan und Isolde* is found, the nervous exhaustion and shimmering morbidity of that music providing an inevitable accompaniment to the physical decline of the members of the house of Buddenbrook. In the presence of the seven-year-old Hanno the organist Edmund Pfühl rejects the music of Wagner, and particularly *that* music drama, as immoral and degenerate: 'This is chaos, anarchy, blasphemy, madness! A perfumed fog, shot through with lightning! It is the end of all morality in art! I shall not play it!'[33] But the boy has heard and, intrigued, he yearns for that music, and finally succumbs to its intoxication; the music of Richard Wagner increasingly dominates his life, making him strained, over-excitable and unable to concentrate on practical matters. His own musical compositions are sustained by Wagnerian motifs; one particular piece calls forth an ecstasy which is almost an orgasm, the delayed resolution *à la Tristan* increasing to an unheard-of perturbation the bliss of the final climax. Having reached puberty, and showing many signs of physical degeneration, Hanno completely surrenders to the music which had become an indispensable drug, and it is the *Tristan* music particularly (Thomas Mann speaks of 'a swooning and an agonizing blurring of one key and another', a 'fervent and supplicating tune emerging in the woodwind' and 'horns which summoned to parting'[34]) which seals his fate. This music, a dissolute orgy of sound, causes a feverish collapse: 'He was very pale. There was no more strength in his knees, and his eyes were burning. He went into the adjoining room, stretched himself out on the chaise-longue and lay there for a time, motionless.'[35] Hanno's sickness and death follow shortly afterwards, yet the naturalistic details of the symptoms of typhoid fever do not blind the reader to the inference that it was the Wagnerian delirium which drew a willing victim to his grave.

Two years after completing *Buddenbrooks – Verfall einer Familie* Thomas Mann published the novella *Tristan*, a short narrative imbued with the author's inimitable irony but which again invokes and paraphrases Wagner in a way which betrays the author's sincere devotion to the composer and that particular work. There are obvious echoes of Wagner's 'Wahnfried' in the name of the sanatorium where the action takes place; the aesthete Spinell (the name is significant), a delicious parody of Arthur Holitscher, seems again a typical product of decadence, a grotesque figure of fun in many ways, but his love of Wagner is something that his creator cannot simply lampoon. As in *Tristan und Isolde* the lovers are left together whilst King Mark and his courtiers go on a hunting party, so in Thomas Mann's story it is Gabriele Klöterjahn and Detlev Spinell who stay behind; in the gathering dusk it is she who lights the candles and plays the piano against her doctor's orders, first a Chopin nocturne and then the prelude to that music drama. Inevitably the music of the second act is played, and Thomas Mann portrays without irony the effect of that music and those words, the enraptured celebration of love, night and death, and quotes Wagner verbatim and in paraphrase:

Whoever has gazed in love into the night of death and into its sweet mystery, to him there will remain during the meaningless delusion of light a single longing, a yearning to return to sacred night, to night eternal and true, where all things become one ... O sink upon them, night of love, grant them that oblivion for which they yearn, enfold them totally with thy joy and redeem them from the world of deception and of parting. Look, the last torch is extinguished. Thought and fancy have sunk in holy twilight, which is spread above the torments of folly and which redeems the world. Then, when delusion has faded, when my eyes close in ecstasy − that from which the deception of day has excluded me, that which opposed my yearning with never-ending torment − then, o miracle of fulfilment, even then − I am the world . . .[36]

Seldom has the young Thomas Mann allowed himself such rhapsodic, almost self-indulgent prose: it is this music which ravishes the two and ultimately causes Gabriele's death. The intensely hymnlike fervour of the language perfectly reflects the power of Wagner's music, and the high earnestness of the tone is interrupted only by the amusing references to the effect that the music has upon one Rätin Spatz (indigestion) and by the entry of Frau Höhlenrauch, wife of a vicar, who had brought nineteen children into the world and was incapable of thinking a single thought any more (a most telling confrontation, this, between the will's perfect tool, in Schopenhauer's terms, and those lovers who followed the path suggested by Wagner in his 'correction' of Schopenhauer − abandonment and obliteration).

The lovers at the keyboard with an open score of *Tristan und Isolde* is a situation which, to the English reader, immediately suggests George Moore's *Evelyn Innes*, a novel first published in 1898, three years before *Buddenbrooks*. Moore's *Hail and Farewell* trilogy is a rich storehouse of references to Wagner, some of which will be dealt with in Chapter Four: here let it be said that Moore, by 1898, had outgrown the naturalism of *Esther Waters* and chosen to explore the mysteries of music and religion in his subsequent novels, with *Evelyn Innes* describing above all the impact of Wagner's art. (American fiction could point to Willa Cather's *The Song of the Lark*, written some seventeen years after *Evelyn Innes*: Thea Kronborg's passage from Moonstone, Colorado, to the Metropolitan Opera provides an analogous situation.) As in *Buddenbrooks* a contrast is drawn between the music of the polyphonic masters of earlier centuries and that of Wagnerian excess: Evelyn's father, organist at St Joseph's, Southwark, collector and renovator of such instruments as the viola d'amore and the virginals, is portrayed as a man whose main desire is to restore liturgical chants and to check the spread of Romantic developments. Sir Owen Asher, however, convinced and passionate Wagnerian, wealthy and indifferent to bourgeois morality, hears Evelyn's voice and insists that she sing the great

Wagner roles, particularly Isolde and Kundry. It is the music of *Tristan und Isolde* which enthrals Evelyn, and Sir Owen, connoisseur and seducer, knows full well the effect that this work above all would have on the young girl. Rather surprisingly, it is upon a harpsichord that he plays excerpts from the notorious second act:

> And while they waited for tea, Evelyn lay back in a wicker chair thinking. He had said that life without love was a desert, and many times the conversation trembled on the edge of a personal avowal, and now he was playing love music out of *Tristan* on the harpsichord. The gnawing creeping sensuality of the phrase brought little shudders into her flesh; all life seemed dissolved into a dim tremor and rustling of blood; vague colour floated into her eyes, and there were moments when she could hardly restrain herself from jumping to her feet and begging of him to stop . . .[37]

Sir Owen, however, is no mere debauchee: his liaison with Evelyn is not simply erotic gratification, but a genuine belief that she could, given the right conditions, sing at Bayreuth itself. 'He saw himself taking her home from the theatre at night in the brougham. In the next instant they were in the train going to Bayreuth. In the next he saw her as Kundry rush on to the stage . . .'[38] Evelyn succumbs to Sir Owen and serves the Wagnerian cause, achieving fame and adulation in the major roles; chapter eight in the book opens with her speculations on her past life, where she saw herself as Elisabeth (*Tannhäuser*) who had been superseded by a passionate Isolde. The morbidity of that music drama, however, evades her, and she sees in Isolde's love a life-enhancing ecstasy: 'In the second act Tristan lives through her. She is the will to live; and if she ultimately consents to follow him into the shadowy land, it is for love of him. But of his desire for death she understands nothing; all through the duet it is she who desires to quench this desire with kisses . . .'[39] When singing the part of Isolde she thinks of her relationship with Sir Owen; when kneeling as a penitent Brünnhilde at the feet of Wotan in act three of *Die Walküre* it is of her father that she thinks, and the actual reconciliation with him is informed and suffused by that great scene in Wagner's work. 'She knelt at her father's or at Wotan's feet — she could not distinguish; all limitations had been razed. She was *the* daughter at *the* father's feet . . .'[40] (It is even with the music of the 'Lied' from act one of *Die Walküre*, the famous 'Winterstürme wichen dem Wonnemond', that she appeals to her father to forgive.) But the *Tristan* music (and the references to the *Wesendonck-Lieder* which grew out of it) penetrates Evelyn's every nerve and fibre: 'Eternal Night, oh lovely Night, the holy night of love . . .':[41] that exquisite passage which Gabriele Klöterjahn had played in the gathering dusk of the sanatorium reverberates through Evelyn's blood; the black pearls which Sir Owen had given her for her role as Isolde remain her most precious possession. Yet the intolerable psychological strains imposed by the conflicting demands of conscience and father on the one hand and lover and Wagner on the other, together with her reservations (encouraged by a young friend Ulick Dean) about the propriety and 'spirituality' of *Parsifal*, cause Evelyn to withdraw from Wagner and ultimately find solace in the Catholic Church, that almost obligatory haven for the exhausted souls of the 1890s.

There is no 'Liebestod' in Evelyn Innes; Carlotta Peel, heroine of Arnold Bennett's *Sacred and Profane Love* (1905) does die, but somewhat bathetically of appendicitis in Paris after swallowing strawberry pips. (The pianist Diaz is no Tristan, but redemption of sorts is achieved in the Five Towns Hotel opposite Knype railway station.) In this novel also there is a scene at the piano with the familiar music from act two of *Tristan und Isolde* (plus absinthe) and Carlotta explains: 'Enchanted as I was by the rich and complex concourse of melodies which ascended from the piano and swam about our heads, this fluctuating tempest of sound was after all only a background for the emotions to which it gave birth in me . . . The fervour of the music increased, and with it my fever . . . We plunged forward into the love scene itself – the scene in which the miracle of love is solemnized and celebrated.'[42] But these English novels seem pallid indeed when compared with the voluptuous intensity of d'Annunzio's *The Triumph of Death* (1894), which contains the most thrilling evocation of the *Tristan* music in all literature. (It was, of course, d'Annunzio who composed that lofty inscription upon the wall of the Palazzo Vendramin after Wagner's death: 'In this palace/ the souls hear/ the last breath of Richard Wagner/ perpetuating itself like the tide/ which washes the marble beneath.'[43]) Son of a wealthy and degenerate Roman family, Giorgio Aurispa, overwrought and nervous, increasingly unable to attend to the trivia of day-to-day living, flees with his mistress Ippolita Sanzio, a fiercely passionate woman, to a lonely retreat, to live entirely for love; death however, in many guises, accompanies the lovers and shows Giorgio that only in obliteration can highest ecstasy be found. The lovers live for months in a highly charged eroticism, enhanced by superstitions, memories and, most significantly, the score of *Tristan und Isolde*; it is the memory of an overwhelming performance of that work at Bayreuth which never leaves Giorgio:

> Giorgio had forgotten nothing, not even the slightest trivial detail, of this his first pious pilgrimage to that ideal theatre; he could remember every moment of the extraordinary excitement that he had experienced when he saw that temple dedicated to the Highest Art, standing on the gentle hill at the end of the shady

approach. He felt again the solemn impression made by the spacious amphitheatre, with its pillars and arches, and felt once more the mysterious impact made by the hidden orchestra.

In the darkness and silence of the crowded house, in the darkness and ecstatic silence of each soul present a sigh arose from the 'mystical abyss', a moan which rose and fell, a subdued voice which brought the first mournful appeal of solitary desire, the first indistinct forebodings of future anguish. Sigh and moan and voice all rose and swelled from the vagueness of plaint to the sharpness of an imperious cry, with all the pride of dreams, the anguish of superhuman aspirations, the terrible and relentless power of possession . . .[44]

The music, and the desire it conveyed, is described by d'Annunzio as a searing flame, a conflagration bursting from an unknown abyss, a radiant gleam which rises to an unbearable intensity before yielding to the desolate awareness of anguish. As Tristan did when he heard the shepherd's song, so Giorgio too finds in music an immediate revelation of pain and the revelation of the tragic meaning of his own destiny; as the drama was acted out on the stage he felt that no one could penetrate better than he into the symbolic and mythical meaning of the love-potion, and that no one but he could measure the inner depths of *Tristan* in its entirety, this work whose hero had consumed his life. Giorgio's tendency to mythologise his obsession, his extreme and perverse form of that 'Tristanising' in which Wagner himself indulged, becomes more and more apparent; after such memories and with such music in his soul, Giorgio can never return to normal living with all its responsibilities and cares, and he hurls himself with his mistress, locked in a fierce embrace, over a cliff to destruction. This fascinating book, with its pertinent quotation from Nietzsche's *Beyond Good and Evil* at the beginning, ends in Wagnerian rapture and obliteration.

It is obvious that Giorgio's pathological sensitivity, morbidity and brutality are symptoms of decadence; d'Annunzio, here and in *The Flame of Life* (1900) touches on the proximity of aestheticism and degenerate violence which, it could be claimed, prefigures a fascist mentality. Before looking at that novel the Wagner–Venice link must be considered, for *The Flame of Life* may be seen as the ultimate portrayal of that city and of Wagner's relationship with it. A few biographical details may be of use here: on 29 August 1858, Wagner arrived in Venice; on the following day he moved into the Palazzo Giustiniani on the Grand Canal as the sole occupant. Intolerable tensions and difficulties had driven him from Zurich; emotionally drained, in sombre mood, with *Tristan und Isolde* unfinished (and perhaps unfinishable) he would later describe his melancholy feelings and the mood of apprehension ('bange Stimmung') which the sight of the crumbling palaces called forth. The black gondolas and the overcast skies oppressed him, whilst memories of funerals and cholera could not be dispelled:

> The weather had suddenly become somewhat inclement, and the appearance of the
> gondolas themselves had given me a not inconsiderable fright, for as much as I
> had heard about these remarkable vehicles, painted black all over, the actual
> appearance of one in real life gave me an unpleasant surprise, and when I had to
> step under the roof covered with its black cloth nothing else occurred to me except
> the memory of a cholera-scare which I had earlier experienced: I had the distinct
> impression of having to take part in a cortège during times of plague . . .[45]

The call of the gondoliers, and the lugubrious canals, the alternating desire for
oblivion and the intense yearning for Mathilde Wesendonck, the constant threat
from police surveillance and the feelings of isolation, of having pushed his art to
the limits of the hitherto acceptable – all united to form a unique pattern. This was
the setting for the creation of the music of Tristan's second act, that act which, as
we have seen, became the supreme stimulus. It was Nietzsche who described the
'dangerous fascination' and the 'sweet infinity' of that music, that
'voluptuousness of hell' which could only be explained in the terms of the mystic;
it was Venice, he claimed in his very last coherent pages, that was music itself:
'Whenever I look for another word for "music" I am only able to think of the
word "Venice". I cannot differentiate between tears and music – I can only think
of happiness, of the South, with a tremulous shudder . . .'[46] Wagner and Venice:
it is this motif that commands our attention, for themes of beauty, decay and
death cluster round that city more than any other.

The finest example in German literature must necessarily be Thomas Mann's
Death in Venice.[47] This 'complex crystal' was written in 1911, in the year in
which Wagner's *My Life* appeared, and from which the account of his 1858–9
sojourn was quoted. Thomas Mann's visit to the Lido, his reaction to the death of
Gustav Mahler, the literary echoes supplied by Winckelmann, Platen and
George have been sufficiently documented: less well known are the Wagner
allusions. The change of weather, the apprehension experienced when stepping
into a gondola, above all, of course, the theme of plague, of disease as being
somehow the 'objective correlative' of an inner condition – these themes Thomas
Mann may well have met in Wagner's memoirs. (Even the 'black flag' which
Wagner had spoken of in a letter to Liszt, written on 12 December 1854, the
flag of death, is present in Mann's story as the photographer's black cloth,
snapping in the wind.) The sick artist, gazing out at the waters after his soul has
abandoned itself to a vision of beauty, of beauty inseparable from death, seems to
be informed by Wagner's presence; like Wagner, Aschenbach moved from
Bavaria to Venice, and Aschenbach's rejection of 'Wotan's ravens' in favour of

the sea seems a parallel to Wagner's abandoning his work on the *Ring* to write *Tristan und Isolde*. The image of sultry lassitude associated with that city, its lapping water, dilapidated palaces and promise of lubricious adventure seemed to Mann a paradigm of *fin de siècle* aestheticism matched only by the example of Richard Wagner. It is surely no coincidence that it was in the Grand-Hotel des Bains on the Lido that Thomas Mann should have jotted down, partly on hotel notepaper, the following sentence referring to Wagner: 'As a mind, as a character he seems to me dubious – as an artist irresistible, even though he is highly suspect with regard to the nobility, the purity and the wholesomeness of his effects.'[48] Like Nietzsche, Thomas Mann knew that Wagner was 'une névrose'; like Nietzsche he felt a compulsive need to turn time and time again to this phenomenon.

Wagner, Venice, *Tristan* and moral and physical decay – Maurice Barrès's novel *Amori et dolori sacrum: La Mort de Venise* predates Thomas Mann's short story by some nine years and overtly deals with Wagner's stay in the Palazzo Giustiniani. Barrès was, like Nietzsche, a 'decadent' and at the same time its opposite: having passed through the blandishments of *fin de siècle* aestheticism he later adopted a belligerent chauvinism, but Richard Wagner remained of perennial interest. *La Mort de Venise*, dating from 1902, delights in portraying 'les déracinés', those ultra-sophisticated degenerate souls who were drawn inexorably to Venice, sensing that that city above all was their spiritual home. The enervating, fetid atmosphere exhaled by the canals, the rippling reflections on crumbling stone, damp walls and ornate bridges produced that 'volupté de la tristesse' for which tired souls yearned. A perfect fusion is felt between Wagner's music (particularly the *Tristan* music) and that city:

> Standing at the windows of the Giustiniani palace, which Wagner lived in during the winter of 1857 [*sic*] I have often seen floating above nocturnal Venice those fascinating sorceries which gave it its particular character and which provided the mysterious qualities of its genius. When deepest darkness weighs down upon the canals, neither colour nor form appearing, and when the mighty and radiant Church of the Salute itself seems like a ghost, when it is only with difficulty that a silent boat forces the water to form a reflection . . ., then the bewitching city finds its own way of piercing the denseness of night, and from this solemn secret she breathes like a sacred hymn, overwhelming in its desolation and its nostalgia. These are the hours, I know, which knew how to extract from the deep soul of that German the heartrending rhapsodies of Tristan and Isolde . . .[49]

But the references to night, phantoms and yearning give way to more sombre thoughts, those of fever: 'No light – only night itself. For Tristan the night was the realm of love, for the German, Wagner, it was the realm of the inner life and, for Venice, it was the domain of pestilence . . .'[50] Febrile ecstasies and the cult of death – again it is that second act which is singled out by Barrès for particular attention, that apotheosis of longing and death-intoxication: 'Vertigo – the intoxication of high places and extreme emotions! At the height of the waves to which *Tristan* bears us let us recognise that pestilence which rises from the lagoons at night.'[51] The delirious frenzies of *Tristan* and the lingering infections exhaled by the waters of Venice are inseparably linked for Barrès; to Richard Wagner it was given to exemplify perfectly in his music, his life and above all his death the morbid sensuality of that city. George Moore had likewise stressed the affinity which he felt between the feverish intensity of *Tristan* and the haunting atmosphere of Venice; Evelyn puts away the music of the penitent Elisabeth and turns instead to the score of that other music drama, and as she does so, memories of Venice surge into her mind:

> The score slipped from her hands . . . The old walls of the palace, the black and watchful pictures, the watery odours and echoes from the canal had frightened and exhausted her. The persecution of passion in her brain and the fever of passion afloat in her blood waxed, and the minutes became each a separate torture . . . The moon rose out of a sullen sky, and its reflection trailed down the lagoon. Hardly any stars were visible, and everything was extraordinarily still. The houses leaned heavily forward and Evelyn feared she might go mad, and it was through this phantom world of lagoon and autumn mists that a gondola glided . . .'[52]

It seems entirely appropriate that memories of that city should automatically arise when the alarming intensity of *Tristan* overpowered her in her loneliness.

'This cursed Venice, with its languishing moonlights, its atmosphere of some stuffy boudoir, long unused, full of old stuffs and pot-pourri . . .,' this city, 'exhaling, like some great lily, mysterious influences which make the brain swim and the head faint – a moral malaria . . .'[53]: Vernon Lee's novella *A Wicked Voice* (1890) portrays a young Norwegian musician and his struggles in Venice to complete his opera *Ogier the Dane*, an ambitious project, and one inspired by the genius of 'the great master of the future'. This 'great master' is, of course, Wagner, whose 'Music of the Future' (*Zukunftsmusik*) became the rallying cry for the younger generation of musicians. In her essays *Tannhäuser* and *Music and its Lovers* Vernon Lee refers frequently to Wagner, extolling the music of the eighteenth century as 'healthy' and castigating his own as 'degenerate' in true Max Nordau fashion. In *A Wicked Voice* the young Magnus is wasted by a strange and deadly disease, but it is paradoxically a haunting, disembodied voice from the past which destroys his sanity and his will to live, the voice of the brazen, bloated Zaffirino, the description of whose portrait uneasily brings to mind that Renoir portrait referred to at the beginning of this chapter. It would seem that the depravity of the eighteenth century (the century, after all, of the 'divine Marquis') re-asserted itself in this Venetian setting; the dubious nature of the composer of 'Zukunftsmusik', of music both robust and morbid, is likewise acknowledged, and *Ogier the Dane* is never completed. The juxtaposition 'health–morbidity' or 'tradition–modernity' is also firmly established in Franz Werfel's novel *Verdi* where, in a rather unsubtle and over-schematised manner, the essentially vigorous, sturdy and harmonic elements of the music of that composer are contrasted with the heady impurities and chromatic adventurousness of Wagner. The opening of the novel provides yet again a Venetian setting, the performance, on Christmas Eve 1882 of Wagner's youthful C major symphony at the Teatro la Fenice. The description of moonlight and sombre waters is obligatory: more interesting are Werfel's imaginative reconstructions of Verdi's sense of failure *vis-à-vis* the great Master, of his awareness of belonging to an age which seemed almost simple-minded when compared with the subtleties and searing intensities of Wagner's creation. As Verdi's gondola moves silently down the canals, the Italian finds himself close to those which convey Wagner and his entourage, and with bitterness he is forced to contemplate his rival and victor: 'Wagner is sitting on the left hand side, in front of his wife. In the bewitching chiaroscuro of moonlight his head, with its protruding cranium, looks like the pallid and monstrous skull of a gnome: it leans back, and the eyes are closed . . .'[54] Feelings of resentment and envy temporarily blind Verdi, who rises in his gondola, prepared, almost, to attack the sleeping man: 'Beneath the force of this emotional upheaval the Maestro stood up in the gondola. Wagner's monstrous cranium gleamed peacefully. His wife gazed mournfully ahead. And as he stood there, watching the side of the rival gondola almost touch his own in that moonlight which transfigured everything, the thought flashed through his mind: "Near enough to seize!" '[55] Yet this aberration does not last: contrite, confused and ashamed, Verdi sits down again, whilst the Wagner family is carried in silence towards the Palazzo Vendramin. Some seven weeks later, on 14 February 1883, having overcome his feelings of rancour and inadequacy, Verdi announces himself at the Palazzo, only to hear that Richard Wagner had died the day before.

'Richard Wagner is dead! The world seemed diminished in value . . .'[56] This section must now return to and close with d'Annunzio, whose *The Flame of Life* provides the most sumptuous evocation of Venice, and the most moving account of Wagner's death in that city. (As William Blissett has written: 'No book in the realm of Wagner empire is so dominated by the Despot, and no more complete instance is to be found of the phenomenon of Wagnerian nervous strain.'[57]) As well as being a thinly veiled account of the relationship between d'Annunzio and Eleonora Duse, the novel contains an ecstatic portrayal of the influence of Wagner upon the young Stelio Effrena, ardent aesthete and *superuomo*. Those recently returned from Bayreuth describe their experiences, and Stelio is carried away by the glory of Wagner, the gigantic hero. (It is tempting to see d'Annunzio's later plans for the organisation of a 'Bühnenfestspiel' and his intention to grant music and theatre a supreme role in his constitution for Fiume as stemming from Wagner's example). Before Stelio's eyes a vision of Wagner arises, ruthless and imperious:

> And the image of the barbaric creator suddenly came closer, his features became visible, the light blue eyes gleamed beneath the mighty brow and the lips, around which hovered sensuality, pride and scorn, closed tight above the powerful chin. His body, small and bent by age and fame, achieved the same gigantic proportions as his work, and assumed the appearance of a god. His blood poured like a mountain waterfall, his breath beat like the wind in the forests. Suddenly Siegfried's youth invaded him, poured through him, illuminated him as dawn lighting the mists. 'Follow the beating of my heart, obey my instincts, listen to the voice of nature in me – this is my highest, my one and only law!' The heroic motto resounded again, bursting from the depths as the expression of a youthful, powerful will which, in triumph with the laws of the universe, blazed in victory above all obstacles and enmities . . .[58]

The news of Wagner's presence in the Palazzo Vendramin-Calergi releases a flood of images and visions within Stelio; the physical proximity of the creator of the radiant Siegfried and the majestic Brünnhilde, the ravaged Kundry (with whom the actress La Foscarina feels an inner affinity) and the death-intoxicated lovers, agitates and inspires the youthful worshipper. Vulnerable and susceptible, Stelio Effrena cannot rest until he has seen the Palazzo where his idol is resting; but the conqueror, the victorious artist-god before whom emperors, kings and princes had submitted, is touched by death. On the wintry lagoons Stelio and his companions see the Master, together with Cosima and Liszt, enveloped in sombre silence, their white hair and suffering features noble and sublime. The three Northern figures are mythologised by Stelio as Triumphant Genius, Faithful Love and Undying Friendship, and motifs from *Der fliegende Holländer* pass through the young man's mind; yet the Master collapses, and is helped ashore by the adoring acolytes. A few weeks later it is Wagner's coffin that Stelio helps to carry on to a black gondola and across the canals to the railway station; before the lid is closed the sight of the dead man fills the mourners with veneration:

> An indescribable smile lay upon the features of the dead hero, infinite and remote, as a rainbow upon glaciers or the gleaming of the sea, like the radiance around moon and stars. It was too much for their eyes to bear, but their hearts, full of religious awe and terror, felt that they had received the revelation of divine mystery . . .[59]

In this city, almost thirty years previously, Wagner had written to Liszt of the black flag with which, after completing *Tristan und Isolde*, he would drape himself to die; in *The Flame of Life* it is Roman laurels which adorn the coffin which moves towards the frost and snow of Bavaria.

The temple of art and the cult of the hero, aestheticism and victory, death-intoxication and triumph: a disturbing synthesis seems here to prepare the way for that 'aestheticising of politics' which Walter Benjamin would later associate with fascism. (Rilke's sonnet 'Late Autumn in Venice', written shortly after *The Flame of Life*, likewise portrays the arsenal and the fleet of that city, a powerful force rising from the depths, and the ships with their streaming pennants, both radiant and sinister.[60]) It is the fascinating proximity of aestheticsm and fascism which never ceased to preoccupy Thomas Mann, and Wagner would be for him the supreme paradigm. This will be touched upon in Chapter Three; we must now return to our examination of Wagner and literary decadence.

It is *Tannhäuser* and *Tristan und Isolde* which provided so many of *the fin de siècle* writers with inspiration and example, however dubious; the sin which possessed the decadents, however, and which seemed obligatory in any piece of writing which strove to shock is that of incest, and Wagner's *Die Walküre* must now claim our attention. (Well might the unknown author of the article in *The Church Times* of 19 June 1882 castigate act one of that music drama as 'the most infamous scene ever put upon any stage in heathen or in Christian times. It consists of a glorification of incest, mingled with adultery, and the betrayal of the commonest rites of hospitality.'[61]) Brief mention has been made of *Die Walküre* during a discussion of *Evelyn Innes*, but there it was the father–daughter relationship which was important: it is the glorification of the incestuous love between Siegmund and Sieglinde in act one, and the ensuing act of intercourse, which is of greater significance. The most notorious literary twins bearing these names who go to a performance of *Die Walküre*, return and consummate their incestuous love are Siegmund and Sieglinde Aarenhold in Thomas Mann's story *Blood of the Volsungs*, the German title of which is, in fact, the last word of act one of Wagner's drama ('Wälsungenblut'). There is also a grim irony here: whereas in Wagner it is the hero Siegfried who will be the result of this union the reader of Thomas Mann's story is left with no such reassurance.

The short work, dating from 1906 but withheld from publication for many years because of certain objections and reservations on the part of the Pringsheim family (the family of Thomas Mann's wife), tells, in the author's own words, the 'story of two pampered creatures, Jewish twins from the ultrasophisticated West-End of Berlin, whose over-ripe and scornful revelling in isolation takes as its model the primeval act of incest from Wagner's Volsung brother and sister'.[62] (The Jewish element was subsequently made less important by Mann; the baleful attraction which Wagner had for many Jews – Beardsley's *The Wagnerites* leaves no doubt as to the Jewishness of at least one member of the audience – is not a problem to be discussed here.) Spoilt and cosseted, Siegmund Aarenhold leads a life of sterile boredom; his days pass in emptiness and narcissistic self-reflection (again, Beardsley comes to mind in the description of his dressing table with its bottles, perfumes and powder, his 'Empire Spiegel', his pink silk underwear, slippers, and fur-trimmed smoking-jacket). With his twin sister Sieglinde he has an equal partner in elegant, arrogant refinement; her fiancé, the hapless Beckerath, is their equal neither in sartorial nor in intellectual matters. It is he who is the blundering figure, and it is inevitable that the twins, without him, should drive to the Opera to see *Die Walküre*. Aloof, haughty and blasé they watch the performance on the stage and cannot refrain, amidst the consumption of Maraschino cherries, from ironic and condescending remarks on the singers and the orchestra. Enthusiasm of any kind is alien to their sense of snobbish superiority, but Siegmund particularly feels the powerful and surging momentum of Wagner's work; the passionate turmoil of the music excited him, causing doubts and an unsettling self-awareness: 'A work of art! How does one create a work of art? Pain beat in Siegmund's breast, a burning and yearning, something akin to a sweet torment – where? For what? It was all so dark, so wretchedly obscure. He felt two words – creativity, passion. And whilst his temples throbbed with heat there came like a fervent insight to him the knowledge that creativity sprang from passion and again assumed the form of passion . . .'[63] As Wagner's twins had defied Hunding and passed through ecstasy and tribulation, so Siegmund Aarenhold, nervously agitated despite his cool exterior, sinks with his sister on to the rug in stammering agitation; the Wagner parallels are obvious. But whereas Wagner created out of passionate inspiration, it is Siegmund Aarenhold's tragedy that what was probably his first spontaneous act should be one of narcissism and perversion, born of defiance and vindictiveness. It is only Wagner who can stimulate powerful responses within Siegmund, responses which, however, result in an act of meaningless desecration.

That Wagner's music was the catalyst, the aphrodisiac, there can be no doubt: the love duet at the end of act one which leads to joyful recognition and voluptuous abandonment excited even these cynical and sophisticated young people who despised the world and its vulgarity. A more gentle treatment of the theme occurs in Willa Cather's *The Garden Lodge* (1905) where, during a piano recital of the first act of *Die Walküre*, Caroline Noble feels the embrace of Raymond D'Esquerre, her spiritual, if not physical, brother; Siegmund's famous song is skilfully woven into the narration, and the weather likewise plays its part. In Elémir Bourges's *Le Crépuscule des dieux*, written some twenty years before the stories of Willa Cather and Thomas Mann, that music will drive both Hans-Ulric and Christiane, brother and sister, to incest and destruction. There are, however, important differences: Hans-Ulric and Christiane are not twins, and their relationship is normal until external machinations push them into perversion; Wagner's music is used to overthrow these last scions of a princely German house. Hans-Ulric, prone to melancholy and introversion, loving music and poetry, shares much in common with the angelic Christiane, but it is not until they both fall into the clutches of an Italian intriguer that tragedy ensues. Giulia Belcredi, mistress of the Duke of Blankenburg, who lives in exile in Paris, is an accomplished Wagner-singer; she deliberately sets out to destroy Hans-Ulric and Christiane, and seizes upon the idea of forcing them into an incestuous relationship, using *Die Walküre* as the stimulus. The Duke is persuaded to organise an amateur performance of that work with brother and sister in the leading roles; Christiane particularly feels that she increasingly identifies with the role of Sieglinde, and believes that if Wotan had deemed that the mythological twins should be lovers, then she and her brother should follow their example. It is the great love duet which envelops the two, and all barriers fall away:

> Then, as the poem demanded, Hans-Ulric enfolded Christiane in his arms, and he felt her heart beat against his, her heart so full of him. Their voices rose in unison, and were followed by an ecstatic silence . . . An instinct, like a secret impulse, told them when to sing at the given moment, and this music, more and more ardent, more and more devoured by flame and passion, embraced them, intoxicated them; hesitations, scruples, remorse – the two lovers felt an indefinable heaviness lifting from every corner of their souls. They were singing again, all that they had never been able to say – they cried it to each other in this song which became their wedding vow: they were triumphant, they adored, they gasped with the superhuman satiety of their love, their souls interlocked, they were oblivious to everything, lifted in a powerful transport of ecstasy which made them rise above

each other and made them taste a gigantic sense of pride at flaunting their sin before all . . .[64]

The reader is not surprised that after the performance the two dine together, then fall into an incestuous embrace: Hans-Ulric shoots himself afterwards, and Christiane becomes a Carmelite nun.

In Thomas Mann the incestuous intercourse is the climax of the story, an inevitable act which sets the seal on the lives on the Aarenhold twins; in Bourges it is but one disaster, albeit a fearful one, in the history of the house of the Duke of Blankenburg. The very title of the novel, *Le Crépuscule des dieux*, necessarily has a Wagnerian ring, and the composer himself makes a brief appearance near the beginning. It is during a concert conducted by Wagner (the *Tannhäuser* overture is being played, together with certain sections of *Die Walküre*) that news arrives of the invasion by Prussian troops of the Duke's territory; unable to remain, he leaves for exile, having first decorated Wagner with one of his highest orders. Before he departs he enquires of the composer the name of the last part of the *Ring* cycle, and the reply 'C'est le Crépuscule des dieux, monsieur' startles the Duke who, overcome with vertigo, 'stretches himself out on the ottoman, repeating as if in a dream "The twilight of the gods . . . the twilight of the gods . . ." '.[65] The subsequent decline of his whole family, a decline into insanity, incest, suicide, brutality, idiocy and crime seems presaged here; this theme of the degenerate aristocratic line, especially in its more bizarre manifestations, is a favourite one amongst the writers of the period under discussion. The fate of Hans-Ulric and Christiane has already been described; the son Franz is exposed as a criminal; the brutal Otto, after an attempt upon his father's life, ends in a madhouse and Claribel, over sensitive and delicate, dies after a nervous collapse. The end of the dynasty is imminent: over-refinement, morbid sensitivity and Wagner's music have proved its undoing. And immediately the reader thinks of that other princely line, not fictitious but actual and historical, whose young king, enraptured by Wagner's music, fled into a world of make-believe, fairy-tale castles and Wagnerian excess: the house of Wittelsbach and King Ludwig II. That such a king should have adored such a composer provided a fruitful source for any account of wanton aestheticism.

A proliferation of novels, mostly trivial, dealt with the young king's eccentricities, his dream-world suffused by Wagner's music and his death in the Starnbergersee: writers of worth, such as Stefan George, who dedicated his *Algabal* poems to the memory of Ludwig II, saw in him the embodiment of art, an ideal transcending mere politics. Robert de Montesquiou, the literary dandy on whom Huysmans modelled des Esseintes, greets Ludwig in his *Treizième César* as the supreme personification of the aesthetic vision and, in an interior monologue of the drowning king, lets Wagner's creations pass before him at the point of death. One day, the dying monarch knows, 'there will come to raise me up, to lead me to the day with its evening sky, that sky where my friends reign, those enchanted Floramyes, together with giants, dwarfs of the Nibelung, and kings of the Lied, whom Siegfried's little bird cheers without pause . . . .'. The young king knows that his infatuation with Wagner will bring its just rewards: 'For I have deserved well of these mythologies, for my lowness of spirit was only lightened at the subterranean forge of Mime and Alberich; I have taken unto myself that great, strong Father of Eric and Senta, the one who gallops through Ortlinde and swims through Flosshilde, from Elsa to Brünnhilde − that High Priest of word and sonorousness . . .'[66] The king gives himself to the water's embrace, confident that he will live in Wagner, that Wagner, godlike, will ensure his immortality: 'I have said that I am dying: I live as Empedocles did. For ever I shall live! For my name will fuse with your monument, you, Father of Eva, of Sachs, of Walther and of Pogner, you, the prince, the king, the God − Richard Wagner!'[67] A god, then, in Mallarmé and de Montesquiou; in Catulle Mendès's *Le Roi vierge* the figure of 'Hans Hammer' is eruptive, passionate, almost deranged in his creative fury. This curious *roman à clef*, banned in Bavaria when it first appeared (1881), tells of the country of 'Thuringia' (a land of Alpine peaks, apparently, and containing the village of Oberammergau) which is ruled over by the pathological King Friedrich II, the virginal king of the title who, loathing women, falls under the spell of Hans Hammer and devotes his life to beauty, particularly to the creation of an artificial lake across which he is drawn by swans. The king first appears as a young shepherd (there are obvious allusions here to the transformation scene in *Tannhäuser*, also to act three of *Tristan und Isolde*) playing his pipe among the mountain peaks; the scene is idyllic, but his end is grotesque and sombre. Unable to face a senseless reality he sets fire to his castle, castrates himself and is finally crucified during an Oberammergau Passion play.

This novel by Catulle Mendès takes to absurd lengths the doubtless eccentric relationship between Wagner and his young king; 'Hans Hammer' verges upon caricature in his frenzy, rage and attitudinising (see Chapter Four). Demonic in his tirades, seductive in his blandishments, iridescent in his ambiguity, Wagner is seen as the embodiment of all those dubious, questionable and yet hypnotic qualities which the writers of decadence felt to be indispensable in the modern artist. This chapter has looked at the meaning of *Tannhäuser, Tristan und Isolde* and also *Die Walküre* for certain representative writers of *fin de siècle*, and will conclude, as it began, with comments on *Parsifal*. Its ambivalent import has already been noted, as has Verlaine's sonnet; it is again Thomas Mann who is able to describe its controvertible nature with the finest imaginative precision, pointing out that the coupling of art and religion in this 'sex opera of great daring', with theatrical celebration of the eucharist, was symptomatic of a spiritual bankruptcy of the most alarming proportions. This work, appealing as it did to the humble believer *and* the most sophisticated decadent was, for Thomas Mann, a demonstration of that 'doppelte Optik' of which Nietzsche had spoken, that quality in Wagner which made him appeal to the simplest, as well as the most recondite, mentality. In his address *Sufferings and Greatness of Richard Wagner*, given on the fiftieth anniversary of Wagner's death and arguably the most profound analysis of Wagner ever written, Thomas Mann compares the characters of *Parsifal* with the most grotesque imaginings of the Romantics: a castrated magician, a desperate, ambiguous temptress and penitent, subject to cataleptic fits, a love-sick priest, desirous of redemption through a chaste and guileless boy, and this boy himself, a most equivocal hero. (The problematic nature concerning the guardianship of the grail, together with the highly suspect ideal of the purity of the blood, is not our concern here; it is reported that Adolf Hitler claimed: 'I build my religion from *Parsifal*. Divine worship in solemn garb. Only in the robes of the hero can one serve God'.)[68] Nietzsche had not been taken in by such heroism; in a most perceptive statement he had seen that once the grandiloquent gestures of a figure like Kundry had been stripped away, then something resembling Madama Bovary remained, and the other characters looked much like the little Parisian *décadents*, never more than five steps away from the hospital.[69] Nietsche's tone is light and humorous: he delighted in reminding his readers that Parsifal is the father of Lohengrin and invited them to speculate upon that remarkable act of procreation. More serious issues are faced, however, and in *Nietzsche contra Wagner* the work is rejected as perverse, even immoral, in its prurience: '. . . I despise all those who do not experience *Parsifal* as an attack upon morality.'[70] Yet in Monte Carlo Nietzsche heard the prelude to *Parsifal* and, brushing aside his reservations, wondered if Wagner, from a purely aesthetic point of view, had ever written anything better. Wagner's psychological finesse, his skill at synthesising apparently totally disparate states of soul, and his searing intensity convinced Nietzsche utterly of his skill as a craftsman; it was when Wagner spoke of chastity, repentance and redemption that Nietzsche raised his objections, the self-styled 'Antichrist' paradoxically seeing in *Parsifal* the greatest affront to Christianity.

'*Parsifal* was to Ulick a revolting hypocrisy, and Kundry the blot on Wagner's life.'[71] Ulick Dean, in *Evelyn Innes*, attempts, and ultimately succeeds, in dissuading Evelyn from singing that part in Bayreuth. 'In the first act she [Kundry] is a sort of wild witch, not very explicit to any intelligence that probes below the surface. In the second she is a courtesan with black diamonds. In the third, she wears the coarse habit of a penitent, and her waist is tied with a cord; but her repentance goes no further than these external signs . . .' Ulick Dean can believe neither in Kundry's contribution nor in Parsifal's ordination: the guileless fool who killed a swan and refused a kiss with many morbid, suggestive and disagreeable remarks could not be taken seriously. The music of the Flower-maidens, however, was irresistible, as was the ensuing duet: 'Music hardly ever more than a recitative, hardly ever breaking into an air, and yet so beautiful! There the notes merely served to lift the words, to impregnate them with more terrible and subtle meaning; and the subdued harmonies enfolded them in an atmosphere, a sensual mood . . .'[72] But the vulgarly-vaunted Good Friday music was rejected, for Ulick Dean sensed here an insincerity which appalled him: '*Parsifal* . . . is the oilest flattery ever poured down the open throat of a liquorish humanity.'[72] An Elisabeth, an Isolde, a Brünnhilde even, Evelyn could sing, but Ulick Dean's strictures and her own upbringing and religious scruples prevented her from singing in *Parsifal*; it is not as Kundry but as Sister Teresa that Evelyn finds ultimate fulfilment, the true church triumphing over the specious theatricalities of Bayreuth.

It may finally not be too fanciful to claim that John Davidson, who drowned himself in 1909, had Kundry in mind when writing his famous *Ballad of a Nun,* which appeared in the collection *Ballads and Songs* in 1894: the poem is shot through with echoes of *Parsifal* as the nun, torn between the convent and the world, 'half maiden, half ghoul' approached the young man and offers herself to him. Her beauty, however, turns to haggardness and the world turns hollow; she returns to the convent in mournful joy, her last moments made radiant by a vision of the Virgin Mary.[74] (And how frequently we meet the 'jardin des supplices' at this time, the scarlet and white lilies charged with the religious overtones of the wounds of Christ and the immaculate conception, yet also with perverse defloration and wilful sterility.) But Davidson's nun is a pale creation compared with Wagner's Kundry, part Ahasuerus, part Herodias and part Gundryggia—Valkyrie, that hybrid who exemplifies more than any other creature of decadence the tension between sin and saintliness which the writers and artists of the 1880s and 1890s delighted in portraying. That whole gallery of *femmes fatales* described by Mario Praz in *The Romantic Agony* finds in her its most bizarre climax; the 'sex opera' whose first act is traditionally not applauded because its celebration of the mass is believed to elevate the work above stage conventions, ravished the decadents who exulted in Klingsor's necromancy, and who added the chalice motif to their lakes of blood, their sterile gardens and their moon-bathed swans.[75] The Flower-maidens likewise gave rise to the almost ectoplasmic shapes of women who became flowers and plants in much decadent painting, those wandering shadows floating through an opaque mistiness of landscape with outstretched arms and ill-defined faces. (As late as 1939 Julien Gracq, in the preface to *Au château d'Argol*, stressed the infernal elements of *Parsifal*, the oneiric and chthonic realm from which such a work emerges.) And yet the shimmering vision of the grail itself and the purity of the children's voices from on high, as Verlaine and Rubén Darío knew,[76] gave intimations of a realm of beauty beyond the incense and the seductiveness. George Moore saw in Wagner '. . . a Turk lying amidst houris . . . Scent is burning on silver dishes, and through the fumes appeared the subdued colours of embroidered stuffs and the inscrutable traceries of bronze lamps . . .'[77]; to others he appeared as the Redeemer himself. Those last words from *Parsifal*, 'Erlösung dem Erlöser' – redemption to the Redeemer – were inscribed on a wreath placed on Wagner's grave, an inscription whose unique ambiguity seems an entirely fitting token.

Notes

1 Peter Conrad, 'Unmasking the Master', in *Times Literary Supplement*, 23 July 1976. Wagner himself, when he saw the portrait, preferred to liken himself to the embryo of an angel, or else a swallowed oyster (see Cosima Wagner *Tagebücher* II, p. 873).

2 Max Nordau, *Entartung*, Berlin, 1892, I, p. 324. Nordau also denounced the manifestations of French symbolism as 'symptoms of imbecility' (*op. cit.*, p. 198), and claimed that Verlaine was a frightful degenerate with an asymmetrical skull and mongoloid features (*op. cit.*, p. 200); he also drew attention to Mallarmé's ear, claiming that its shape was frequently found amongst criminals and lunatics (*op. cit.*, p. 204).

3 Thomas Mann, *Gesammelte Werke*, Frankfurt, 1960, IX, p. 424: 'Eine farbige und phantastische, tod- und schönheitsliebende Welt abendländischer Hoch-und Spätromantik tut sich auf bei seinem Namen, eine Welt des Pessimismus, der Kennerschaft seltener Rauschgifte und eine Überfeinerung der Sinne . . . In diese Welt ist Richard Wagner hineinzusehen . . .'

4 Charles Baudelaire: see *Richard Wagner: Vues sur la France*, Paris, 1943, 71–2: 'Je vous dois *la plus grande jouissance musicale que j'aie jamais éprouvée* . . . il me semblait que cette musique était *la mienne*.' (I have used this edition because it is a most useful anthology of comments by French writers on Wagner.)

5 Baudelaire, *op. cit.*, p. 72: 'J'ai éprouvé souvent un sentiment d'une nature assez bizarre, c'est l'orgueil et la jouissance de comprendre, de me sentir pénétrer, envahir, volupté vraiment sensuelle, et qui ressemble à celle de monter dans l'air, ou de rouler sur la mer.'

6 Baudelaire, *op. cit.*, p. 89: 'Langueurs, délices mêlées de fièvre et coupées d'angoisses, retours incessants vers une volupté qui promet d'éteindre, mais n'éteint jamais la soif; palpitations furieuses du coeur et des sens, ordres impérieux de la chair, tout le dictionnaire des onomatopées de l'amour se fait entendre ici . . .'

7 Baudelaire, *op. cit.*, p. 89: 'Aux titillations sataniques d'un vague amour succèdent bientôt des entraînements, des éblouissements, des cris de victoire, des gémissements de gratitude, et puis des hurlements de férocité, des reproches de victimes et des hosanna impies de sacrificateurs, comme si la barbarie devait toujours prendre sa place dans le drame de l'amour, et la jouissance charnelle conduire, par une logique satanique inéluctable, aux délices du crime . . .'

8 Huysmans, *A rebours*, Paris, 1961, p. 245: 'En effet, la décadence d'une littérature, irréparablement atteinte dans son organisme, affaiblie par l'âge des idées, épuisée par les excès de la syntaxe . . . s'était incarnée en Mallarmé.

9 Mallarmé, 'Hommage à Wagner'; the poem appeared in the *Revue Wagnérienne* in 1886 and runs as follows:

> Le silence déjà funèbre d'une moire
> Dispose plus qu'un pli seul sur le mobilier
> Que doit un tassement du principal pilier
> Précipiter avec le manque de mémoire.
>
> Notre si vieil ébat triomphal du grimoire,
> Hiéroglyphes dont s'exalte le millier
> A propager de l'aile un frisson familier!
> Enfouissez-le moi plutôt dans une armoire.
>
> Du souriant fracas originel haï
> Entre elles de clartés maîtresses a jailli
> Jusque vers un parvis né pour leur simulacre,
>
> Trompettes tout haut d'or pâmé sur les vélins,
> Le dieu Richard Wagner irradiant un sacre
> Mal tû par l'encre même en sanglots sibyllins.

It is a notoriously difficult poem, and can only be paraphrased thus: 'The already funereal silence of watered silk arranges more than a single fold on the accessories, which a collapse of the main pillar is to reduce to obscurity. Our old triumphal revels taken from the incomprehensible book of spells, those hieroglyphics which the masses exalt to spread a familiar shudder with their wing! Banish these, rather, in a cupboard. From the radiant original uproar which master brilliances hated amongst themselves there has sprung from on high, right to the outer square, created for their image, the trumpets of gold swooning aloud on the vellums, the god Richard Wagner illuminating a consecration hardly kept silent by the ink itself in Sybilline sobs.' The 'main pillar' would seem to be Wagner, whose disappearance and whose apotheosis are celebrated here. The image of watered silk brings to mind Wagner's passion for wearing silk, and also suggests fabrics and draped furniture. The second stanza suggests that something else should be buried, namely the claptrap associated with trivial art. The third stanza tells of a 'smiling fracas' or radiant uproar, that is, Wagner's music, which established masters rejected, but which pours forth into the outer world ('parvis' means a square in front of a cathedral); the final three lines express the idea that Wagner's music is a consecration which is heard even in the silent musical symbols which have been inked on to the score sheet. This music is not trivial, but mysterious, prophetic and tinged with suffering. Wagner's death makes his apotheosis possible, and this in turn enables us to understand his music for what it really is. In this respect 'Hommage à Wagner' is akin to 'Le tombeau d'Edgar Poe', which expresses the view that Poe's death has transformed him into that which he essentially is. (I am grateful to Ronald Rowe for many of the points raised here.)

10 Verlaine, *Richard Wagner: Vues . . .*, *op. cit.*, p. 148.

11 Huysmans, *Revue Wagneriénne*, ed. cit., I, pp. 59–61: 'Soudain, dans ce site musical, dans ce fluide et fantastique site, l'orchestre éclate, peignant en quelques traits décisifs, enlevant de pied en cap, avec le dessin d'une héraldique mélodie, Tannhaeuser qui s'avance; − et les ténèbres s'irradient de lueurs; les volutes des nuées prennent des formes tourmentées de hanches et palpitent avec d'élastiques gonflements de gorges; les bleues avalanches du ciel se peuplent de nudités; des cris de désirs incontenus, des appels de stridentes lubricités, des élans d'au delà charnel, jaillissent de l'orchestre et, au dessus de l'onduleux espalier des nymphes qui défaillent et se pâment, Vénus se lève, mais non plus la Vénus antique, la vieille Aphrodite, dont les impeccables contours firent hennir pendant les séculaires concupiscences du Paganisme, les dieux et les hommes, mais une Vénus . . . chrétienne, si le péché contre nature de cet accouplement de mots était possible! . . . C'est l'incarnation de l'Esprit du Mal, l'effigie de l'omnipotente Luxure, l'image de l'irrésistible et magnifique Satanesse qui braque, sans cesse aux aguets des âmes chrétiennes, ses délicieuses et maléfiques armes.'

12 Pierre Louÿs, Richard Wagner: *Vues . . .*, 186. His *Crépuscule des Nymphes* should also be noted.

13 Joséphin Péladan, *Pomone*, Paris, 1913, p. 145: 'Elisabeth, épouse du minnesinger [sic], suivrait son bien-aimé dans les voies passionnées, sans même distinguer si Vénus a été l'éducatrice.' The self-styled 'Grand-Maître de l'Ordre de la Rose Croix de Temple et du Gral' was not the most reliable exponent of Wagner.

14 Richard Wagner, *Das braune Buch: Tagebuchaufzeichnungen 1865–1882* (ed. Bergfeld), Zurich, 1975, p. 42 and p. 44: 'Ich kann und muß nur in einer Art von Wolke leben. Wie ich einzig Kunstmensch bin, kann ich auch nur ein künstliches Leben führen . . . Ganz künstlich, wie ein tropisches Gewächs im Wintergarten, muß ich mich gegen die Atmosphäre der Wirklichkeit abschließen.'

15 Arthur Holitscher, *Der vergiftete Brunnen*, Munich, 1900, p. 318: 'Sie befaßte sich seit geraumer Zeit mit dem Problem, wie die so überaus studierten Reigen, die man in den Theatern in der Venusbergscene von *Tannhäuser* zu sehen bekommt, durch entsprechendere, der zügellosen Schönheit der Musik näherkommende, wilde, brünstige, jedoch die heilige Anmut des antiken Sinnenkultes nicht verletzende Bewegungsfolgen ersetzt werden können.'

16 Julian Fane, incidentally, had met Wagner and left a record of the meeting with the composer: 'I had lately a delightful evening at Lady B.'s with Wagner. He read us the libretto of his new (seriocomic) opera "The Singers of Nuremberg". The work may also be called a satire on the art-critics of the day. It is full of humour and wit; sparkles with lively versification; and is really rich in thought. He declaimed it admirably, with much histrionic power. I was greatly struck with the man as well as his work.' (See Robert Lytton, *Julian Fane: a Memoir*, London, 1872, p. 136.) Another minor poet who had met Wagner is John Payne (1842–1916), who wrote in his autobiography: 'Wagner's music has always been as much and as essential a part of my life as literature. Although all but untaught ... I have a species of innate gift for music, which enables me to judge and appreciate the strangest and most unconventional compositions and to reproduce upon the piano (without a previous hearing) the most complicated orchestral and other works ... I cannot but feel that my love and practice of music are to be traced everywhere in my verses.' (See his *Autobiography*, Bedford, 1926, pp. 11–12). Payne wrote a 'Sir Floris' as a grail poem, dedicated to Wagner as the author of *Lohengrin* a sonnet entitled 'Bride-Night: Wagner's "Tristan und Isolde" Act II scene 2', and devoted twenty-four stanzas to praise of Wagner in *Songs of Life and Death* (1872).

17 The extent to which Swinburne was thinking of Wagner's *Tannhäuser* whilst writing 'Laus Veneris' is a matter for debate (see Anne Dzamba Sessa, *Richard Wagner and the English*, Cranbury, N.J., 1979, p. 94), but the fact that he *did* write a 'Lohengrin', a 'Tristan' and 'The Death of Richard Wagner' is not unimportant. 'Tristram of Lyonesse' appeared a month after *Tristan und Isolde* was produced in London in 1882. Matthew Arnold's comment might be recalled here; he had written a *Tristan and Iseult* in 1852 and he later maintained that he had 'managed the story better than Wagner' (Dzamba Sessa, *op. cit.*, p. 87). For a note on Swinburne's Wagnerism see the Appendix B in Elliot Zuckerman's *The First Hundred Years of Wagner's 'Tristan'*.

18 Theodore Wratislaw, *Orchids – Poems*, London, 1891, p. 31. Arthur Symons, who edited the *Savoy*, contributed a 'Parsifal' in *Images of Good and Evil* (1889), also a 'Tristan's Song'.

19 Oscar Wilde, *The Works of Oscar Wilde*, London, 1966, p. 107.

20 E. F. Benson, *The Rubicon*, London, 1894, p. 263.

21 Benson, *op. cit.*, p. 264.

22 Aubrey Beardsley, *Under the Hill* (completed by John Glassco), Olympia Press, 1966, p. 50.

23 Beardsley, *op. cit.*, p. 55.

24 Beardsley, *op. cit.*, p. 55–6.

25 Beardsley, *op. cit.*, p. 57.

26 Beardsley, *op. cit.*, p. 57. At the end of his life Beardsley sold most of his books, but kept four volumes of Wagner's writings; he also wished to know whether or not Leonard Smithers had seen volume five. In his room in Mentone he had the photograph taken of Wagner in London, 1877 (see Willi Schuh's unpublished article for the *Programmheft* of 1953).

27 Stanley Weintraub, *Beardsley*, London, 1972, p. 206.

28 Richard Wagner, *Briefe an Mathilde Wesendonck*, Berlin, 1904, p. 79: 'Es handelt sich nämlich darum, den von keinem Philosophen, namentlich auch von Sch. nicht, erkannten Heilsweg zur vollkommenen Beruhigung des Willens durch die Liebe und zwar nicht einer abstracten Menschenliebe, sondern der wirklichen, aus dem Grunde der Geschlechtsliebe, d.h. der Neigung zwischen Mann und Weib keimenden Liebe, nachzuweisen.'

29 See the draft of the letter quoted in the *Bayreuther Blätter*, April 1886, pp. 101–2: '. . . ein Heilsweg zur Selbsterkenntnis und Selbstverneinung des Willens . . .'

30 Richard Wagner, *Briefe an Mathilde Wesendonck*, *op. cit.*, p. 83: 'Seit gestern beschäftige ich mich wieder mit dem Tristan. Ich bin immer noch im zweiten Akte. Aber – was wird das für Musik! Ich könnte mein ganzes Leben nur noch an dieser Musik arbeiten. O, es wird tief und schön, und die erhabensten Wunder fügen sich so geschmeidig dem Sinn . . .'

31 Richard Wagner, *op. cit.*, p. 123: 'Kind! Dieser Tristan wird was *furchtbares*! Dieser letzte Akt!!! Ich fürchte die Oper wird verboten – falls durch schlechte Aufführung nicht das Ganze parodirt wird—: nur mittelmässige Aufführungen können mich retten! Vollständig *gute* müssen die Leute verrückt machen . . .'

32 Nietzsche, *Werke*, II, pp. 1091–2: 'Aber ich suche heute noch nach einem Werke von gleich gefährlicher Faszination, wie der *Tristan* ist – ich suche in allen Künsten vergebens . . . Die Welt ist arm für den, der niemals krank genug für diese "Wollust der Hölle gewesen ist: es ist erlaubt, es ist fast geboten, hier eine Mystiker-Formel anzuwenden . . .'

33 Thomas Mann, *ed. cit.*, I, p. 498: 'Dies ist das Chaos! Dies ist Demagogie, Blasphemie und Wahnwitz! Dies ist ein parfümierter Qualm, in dem es blitzt! Dies ist das Ende aller Moral in der Kunst! Ich spiele es nicht!.'

34 Thomas Mann, *op. cit.*, p. 748: '. . . dieses süße, schmerzliche Hinsinken von einer Tonart in die andere . . .', 'ein inbrünstig und flehentlich hervortretender Gesang des Bläserchores . . .', 'Hörner, die zum Aufbruch riefen.'

35 Thomas Mann, *op. cit.*, p. 750: 'Er war sehr blaß, in seinen Knien war gar keine Kraft, und seine Augen brannten. Er ging ins Nebenzimmer, streckte sich auf der Chaiselongue aus und blieb so lange Zeit, ohne ein Glied zu rühren.'

36 Thomas Mann, *Werke*, *ed. cit.*, VIII, p. 245: 'Wer liebend des Todes Nacht und ihr süßes Geheimnis erschaute, dem blieb im Wahn des Lichtes ein einzig Sehnen, die Sehnsucht hin zur heiligen Nacht, der ewigen, wahren, der einsmachenden . . . O sink hernieder, Nacht der Liebe, gib ihnen jenes Vergessen, das sie ersehnen, umschließe sie ganz mit deiner Wonne und löse sie los von der Welt des Truges und der Trennung. Siehe, die letzte Leuchte verlosch! Denken und Dünken versank in heiliger Dämmerung, die sich welterlösend über des Wahnes Qualen breitet. Dann, wenn das Blendwerk erbleicht, wenn in Entzücken sich mein Auge bricht: das, wovon die Lüge des Tages mich ausschloß, was sie zu unstillbarer Qual meiner Sehnsucht täuschend entgegenstellte – *selbst* dann, o Wunder der Erfüllung! selbst dann bin ich die Welt . . .'

37 George Moore, *Evelyn Innes*, London, 1929, p. 56. (Charles Morgan, the poor man's Moore, describes in terms which are not dissimilar the attempt made by Piers Sparkenbroke to seduce a young girl: he fails, but works at his novel *Tristan and Iseult* instead. He dies from an attack of angina; she tries, unsuccessfully, to commit suicide. See *Sparkenbroke*, 1936.)

38 George Moore, *op. cit.*, p. 61.

39 George Moore, *op. cit.*, p. 117.

40 George Moore, *op. cit.*, p. 163.

41 George Moore, *op. cit.*, p. 226.

42 Arnold Bennett, *Sacred and Profane Love*, London, 1905, pp. 51–2. Margaret Drabble speculates in her book *Arnold Bennett*, London, 1974, pp. 124–5, that Carlotta is meant to be a humorous character; there is much to be said for this, particularly in the descriptions of her reading Herbert Spencer (in secret binding), her insistence on buying a straw hat from the maid to appear respectable after being disgraced in the hotel, and the alacrity with which she leaps into bed with Diaz.

43 Upon the wall is written: 'In questo palagio / l'ultimo spiro di Riccardo Wagner / odono le anime perpetuarsi come la marea / che lamb i marmi.'

44 Gabriele d'Annunzio, *Trionfo della Morte* (Mandadori ed.), 1976, p. 363: 'Giorgio non aveva dimenticato alcun episodio di quel suo primo pellegrinaggio religioso verso il Teatro Ideale; poteva rivivere tutti gli attimi della straordinaria emozione nell'ora in cui aveva scorto su la dolce collina, all'estremità del gran viale arborato, l'edificio sacro alla festa suprema del l'Arte; poteva ricomporre la solennità del vasto anfiteatro cinto di colonne e d'archi, il mistero del Golfo Mistico. – Nell'ombra e nel silenzio dello spazio raccolto, nell'ombra e nel silenzio estatico di tutte le anime, su dall'orchestra invisibile un sospiro saliva, un gemito spirava, una voce sommessa diceva il primo dolente richiamo del desiderio in solitudine, la prima confusa angoscia nel presentimento del suplizio futuro. E quel sospiro e quel gemito e quella voce dall'indefinita sofferenza all'acuita di un impetuoso grido si elevavano dicendo l'orgoglio d'un sogno, l'ansia di un'aspirazione sovrumana, la volontà terribile e implacabile di possedere.'

45 Richard Wagner, *Mein Leben* (Jubiläumsausgabe), Munich, 1963, pp. 664–5: 'Das Wetter war plötzlich etwas unfreundlich geworden, das Aussehen der Gondel selbst hatte mich aufrichtig erschreckt; denn soviel ich auch von diesen eigentümlichen, schwarz in schwarz gefärbten Fahrzeugen gehört hatte, überraschte mich doch der Anblick eines derselben in Natur sehr unangenehm: als ich unter das mit schwarzem Tuch verhängte Dach einzutreten hatte, fiel mir zunächst nichts andres als der Eindruck einer früh überstandenen Cholera-Furcht ein; ich vermeinte entschieden an einem Leichenkondukte in Pestzeiten teilnehmen zu müssen.'

46 Nietzsche, *Werke, ed. cit.*, II, pp. 1092–3: 'Wenn ich ein anderes Wort für Musik suche, so finde ich immer nur das Wort Venedig. Ich weiß keinen Unterschied zwischen Tränen und Musik zu machen – ich weiß das Glück, den Süden nicht ohne Schauder von Furchtsamkeit zu denken.'

47 It was Werner Vortriede who first drew attention to the presence of Wagner in this story: see his article 'Richard Wagners Tod in Venedig' in *Euphorion*, 1958, pp. 378–95.

48 Thomas Mann, *Werke, ed. cit.*, X, p. 841: 'Als Geist, als Charakter schien er mir suspekt, als Künstler unwiderstehlich, wenn auch tieffragwürdig in bezug auf den Adel, die Reinheit und Gesundheit seiner Wirkungen.'

49 Maurice Barrès, *Amori et dolori sacrum: La Mort de Venise*, Paris, 1902, p. 100: 'Bien souvent, aux fenêtres du palais Giustiniani . . . que Wagner habitait durant l'hiver de 1857, j'ai vu flotter sur la Venise nocturne les fascinations qui le déterminèrent et qui furent les moyens mystérieux de son génie. Quand la pire obscurité pèse sur les canaux, qu'il n'est plus de couleur ni d'architecture, et que la puissante et claire Salute semble elle-même un fantôme, quand c'est à peine si le passage d'une barque silencieuse force l'eau à miroiter, . . . la ville enchanteresse trouve moyen tout de même de percer cette nuit accumulée, et de ce secret solennel elle s'exhale comme un hymne écrasant d'aridité et de nostalgie . . . Voilà les heures, j'en suis assuré, qui de la profonde conscience de ce Germain surent extraire les déchirantes incantations de Tristan et d'Isolde . . .'

50 Barrès, *op. cit.*, p. 104: 'Plus de lumière: la nuit. La nuit fait pour Tristan le domaine de l'amour, pour le Germain Wagner, le domaine de la vie intérieure et, pour Venise, le domaine de la flèvre.'

51 Barrès, *op. cit.*, p. 112: 'Vertige, ivresse de hauts lieux et des sentiments extrêmes! A la cime des vagues ou nous mêne *Tristan*, reconnaissons les fièvres qui, la nuit, montent des lagunes . . .'

52 George Moore, *Evelyn Innes, op. cit.*, p. 121.

53 Vernon Lee (i.e. Violet Paget), *Hauntings – Fantastic Stories*, London, 1890, p. 217. I am particularly grateful to Erwin Koppen's *Dekadenter Wagnerismus* (Berlin, 1973) for references to Vernon Lee, whose work I did not know.

54 Franz Werfel, *Verdi: Roman der Oper*, Berlin, 1930, p. 29: 'Wagner sitzt links vor seiner Frau. Sein Haupt mit dem vorgebauchten Schädel, der in der hexenhaft-bösen Schattenverteilung des Mondlichts dem bleichen Riesenschädel eines Gnomen gleicht, dieses Haupt ist nach hinten gelehnt und die Augen sind geschlossen.'

55 Franz Werfel, *op. cit.*, p. 31: 'Unter der Wucht dieser Anwandlung richtete sich der Maestro in der Gondel auf. Unberührt schimmerte Wagners Riesenschädel.

Die Frau (Cosima) sandte trübe Blicke geradeaus. Und wie er so stand, und im ungeheuren, alles verwandelnden Mondlicht den Bord der Nachbargondel die seine fast berühren sah, wollte er denken: "Zum Greifen nah!".'

56 Gabriele d'Annunzio, *Il fuoco* (Mondadori ed.), 1977, p. 333: 'Riccardo Wagner è morto! Il monde parve diminuito di valore.'

57 William Blissett, 'D. H. Lawrence, D'Annunzio, Wagner' in *Wisconsin Studies in Contemporary Literature*, VII, 1962, p. 32.

58 d'Annunzio, *op. cit.*, pp. 137–8: 'E subitamente l'imagine del creatore barbarico si avvicinò, le linee della sua faccia divennero visibili, gli occhi cerulei brillarono sotto la fronte vasta, le labbra si serrarono sul robusto mento armate di sensualità, di superbia e di dispregio. Il suo piccolo corpo incurvato dalla vecchiezza e dalla gloria si sollevò, s'ingigantí a somiglianza della sua opera, assunse l'aspetto di un dio. Il sangue vi corse come torrenti in un monte, il respiro vi alitò come il vento in una foresta. A un tratto, la giovinezza di Siegfried lo invase, vi si sparse, vi rifulse come in una nube l'aurora. "Seguire l'impulso del mio cuore, obbedire al mio istinto, ascoltate la voce della natura in me: ecco la mia suprema unica legge!" La parola eroica vi risonò, erompendo dal profondo, esprimendo la volontà giovine e sana che trionfava di tutti gli ostacoli e di tutti i maleficii, sempre in accordo con la legge dell'Universo.'

59 d'Annunzio, *op. cit.*, p. 338: 'Un infinito sorriso illuminava la faccia dell'eroe prosteso: infinito e distante come l'iride dei ghiacciai, come il bagliore dei mari, come l'alone degli astri. Gli occhi non potevano sostenerlo; ma i cuori, con una meraviglia e con uno spavento che li faceva religiosi, credettero di ricevere la rivelazione di un segreto divino.'

60 R. M. Rilke, *Gesammelte Gedichte*, Frankfurt, 1962, p. 365. The German words are far more impressive: 'strahlend und fatal'.

61 Quoted in Max Moser, *Richard Wagner in der englischen Literatur des XIX Jahrhunderts*, Berne, 1938, p. 19.

62 Thomas Mann, *Werke, ed. cit.*, XI, pp. 558–9: 'die Geschichte zweier Luxuswesen, jüdischer Zwillinge des überfeinerten Berliner Westens . . . deren üppig-spöttisches Einsamkeitspathos sich den Ur-Inzest von Wagners Wälsungen-Geschwisterpaar zum Muster nimmt.'

63 Thomas Mann, *Werke, ed. cit.*, VIII, p. 404: 'Ein Werk! Wie tat man ein Werk? Ein Schmerz war in Siegmunds Brust, ein Brennen oder Zehren, irgend etwas wie eine süße Drangsal – wohin? wonach? Es war so dunkel, so schimpflich unklar. Er fühlte zwei Worte: Schöpfertum . . . Leidenschaft. Und während die Hitze in seinen Schläfen pochte, war es wie ein sehnsüchtiger Einblick, daß das Schöpfertum aus der Leidenschaft kam und wieder die Gestalt der Leidenschaft annahm.'

64 Elémir Bourges, *Le Crépuscule des dieux*, Paris, 1954, p. 107: 'Alors, selon que le veut le poème, Hans-Ulric enlaça Christiane dans ses bras, et il sentait battre contre son coeur, ce coeur plein de lui. Leurs voix s'élevèrent à l'unisson, suivies d'un silence d'extase . . . Un instinct leur donna comme un branle secret, pour s'avancer chanter au moment marqué; et cette musique toujours plus chaude, plus pétrie de flamme et de passion, les embrasait, les enivrait: hésitations, scrupules, remords, les deux amants sentaient je ne sais quoi de lourd qui s'envolait, de toutes les parties de leur âme. Ils chantaient encore; tout ce qu'ils n'avaient jamais pu dire, ils se le criaient par ce chant, qui était leur aveu nuptial; ils triomphaient, ils s'adoraient, ils haletaient de ce rassasiement surhumain de leur amour; et l'âme roulée l'un sur l'autre, soulevés par un transport puissant qui les faisait être au-delà d'eux'mêmes, goûtant un orgueil colossal à soutenir leur crime en face, ils ne se souciaient plus de rien.'

65 Bourges, *op. cit.*, p. 26: 'Le duc . . . s'allongeait sur le divan turc, en répétant, ainsi que dans un rêve: *Le Crépuscule des Dieux*, le *Crépuscule des Dieux* . . .'

66 Robert de Montesquiou, *Les Chauves-souris*, Paris, 1907, pp. 265–6:

> Viendront me soulever pour me conduire au jour
> Du ciel crépusculaire où règnent mes amies,
> Vertes filles du Rhin, magiques Floramyes,
> Les Géants et les Nains Nibelungs, roi du Lied,
> Qu'égaie incessamment l'oiselet de Siegfried!
> Car j'ai bien mérité de ces mythologies;
> Car mes langueurs de spleen n'apparaissent rougies
> Qu'au foyer souterrain de Mime et d'Alberich;
> Car j'ai pris le plus grand, le fort père d'Eric
> Et Senta, qui, d'Elsa jusques à Brunehilde,
> Galope, par Ortlinde, et nage, par Flosshilde;
> Le haut pasteur de verbe et de sonorité . . .

Again, I am indebted to Erwin Koppen for the references to Montesquiou.

67 Montesqiou, *op. cit.*, p. 266:

> J'ai dit, je meurs; je suis vivant, comme Empédocle.
> A jamais! car mon nom fait corps avec ton socle.
> Père d'Eva, de Sachs, de Walter, de Pogner,
> Toi, le Prince, le Roi, le dieu Richard Wagner!

68 Quoted in Joachim Fest, *Hitler*, Frankfurt, 1973, p. 683: 'Aus *Parsifal* baue ich mir meine Religion. Gottesdienst in feierlicher Form . . . Im Heldengewand allein kann man Gott dienen.'

69 Nietzsche, *Werke, ed. cit.*, II, 922–3. Nietzsche also delights in speculating on the proximity of Madame Bovary to certain of the Wagner heroines; Hans Mayer (*Richard Wagner: Mitwelt und Nachwelt*, p. 74) surprisingly places Emma Bovary at Lohengrin's side. Both attempt a reconciliation between vision and normality: both fail. There seems to be here a variation on the artist and society theme: Wapnewski (*Der traurige Gott: Richard Wagner in seinen Helden*, Munich, 1978) insists on this dichotomy in Wagner, seeing that there is latent 'artistry' not only in Walther von Stolzing, where it becomes realised, but also in Tannhäuser, Lohengrin and Parsifal (p. 92). The *aperçus* of Wapnewski and Mayer owe much to Nietzsche here; Mayer, however, is not taken in by 'Senta-Sentimentalität' but sees her again in the gallery of those figures created by Lermontov, Mickiewicz and Musset, restless and belonging neither to the past nor the future, crippled by 'Weltschmerz' (Mayer, p. 189).

70 Nietzsche, *op. cit.*, II, p. 1053: 'Ich verachte jedermann, der den *Parsifal* nicht als Attentat auf die Sittlichkeit empfindet.'

71 George Moore, *Evelyn Innes*, p. 148.

72 George Moore, *op. cit.*, p. 149.

73 George Moore, *op. cit.*, p. 149.

74 R. K. Thornton (ed.), *Poetry of the Nineties*, London, 1970, pp. 197–8.

75 The early poetry of Juan Ramón Jiménez provides many examples of imagery derived from Wagnerian decadence; 'Tropical' is typical in its climate of breathless sensuality and artifice, where sexual climax is reached in a setting of tropical luxuriance and oppressive heat. *A propos* the Herodias–Salome figure, Wagner most certainly read in Jakob Grimm's *Die deutsche Mythologie* (1835) of the punishment of this monstrous female; after attempting to kiss the head and being rebuffed 'die unselige wird in den leeren raum getrieben und schwebt ohn unterlass' (quoted Wapnewski, p. 259).

76 See Rubén Darío, 'Wagneriana' in *Obras completas*, V, Madrid, 1953, pp. 1278–9. There are two poems, 'Lohengrin' and 'Parsifal'.

77 George Moore, *Memoirs of my Dead Life*, London, 1906, p. 294.

3

WAGNER *and* MYTH

'There is always someone – Lohengrin, Walther, Siegfried, Wotan – who can do everything and knock everything down, who can release suffering virtue, punish vice and bring general salvation.'
    Walther Rathenau, 1918

'Albert Rich and his rain reflection sloshed through the puddles after the three giggling fourth-form girls. By God, he would have one of them, which one didn't matter . . . The three maidens laughed in peal after peal, a shrill song of provocative triads as they bounded with girlish grace through the water.'[1] The subliminal indoctrination of the mythological and symbolic content of *Der Ring des Nibelungen* must have been rich indeed for Anthony Burgess to have transposed the opening of *Das Rheingold* to a rainy suburban setting, as T. S. Eliot had felt the need to let the siren song of the Rhinemaidens float over the muddy waters of the Thames. Even that bathing scene, all male though it is, of E. M. Forster's *A Room with a View* is informed by a spiritual or mythological presence which transcends the realistic milieu; references to blood and benediction, to spell and chalice, seem to partake of an order more Germanic than English, as do the 'rainbow bridges' of *Howards End*[2] and other intensely emotional passages in Forster where an almost panic-like sense of euphoria is inevitably described with reference to a situation or character in Wagner. Our task will now be to discern and discuss those mythical and symbolic images present in European literature and thought which are attributable to Wagner's influence: if Chapter Two assessed his meaning for the decadents, so it is now our aim to see Wagner as thaumaturge and creator of powerful mythical impulses. For his music dramas prove to be an enormously fecund source of redolent symbols, a pulsating fabric of inexhaustible richness and complexity which has contributed more than any other artistic expression to that 'return to myth'[3] which is a particular feature of the modern experience.

    The term 'myth' almost immediately brings to mind a fantastic tale involving gods, heroes and supernatural beings, a tale closely related to ritual and to the religious and social order of a people or culture.[4] The world of myth is a dramatic world, a place of actions, forces and conflicting powers: great natural upheavals are interpreted as representing the collision of these energies. Mythical perception is always impregnated with emotional qualities, and whatever is seen or felt is surrounded by a special nimbus, an atmosphere of joy or grief, of anguish, excitement, exultation or fear. On a more sophisticated level it may be claimed that myths are precious psychic revelations, exemplifying a particular existential posture, a means of relating to the universe and of defining a special attitude to the world. Both C. G. Jung and Karl Kerényi have demonstrated the importance of myth as a re-enactment of certain psychic preoccupations: beneath rational thought the mythical world, fed by the emotions, lives and emerges in art, dreams and fantasy. To deny this substratum of fertile symbolism within the psyche means a necessary impoverishment, and it is Wagner's supreme importance that he more than any other artist in the nineteenth century was aware of the fructifying force of myth, of the numinous significance of fire and water, gold, chalice and spear and a host of related images. The hero and his departure into a mysterious world of dangerous forces, the idea of the quest, the theme of the curse, the battle between disaffected subterranean beings and the established order — these mythical images emerge from the psyche as archetypal patterns. And it is none other than Claude Lévi-Strauss who saw Wagner as the father of the structural analysis of myths, going so far as to claim that those strange words of Gurnemanz on time and space (Act 1 of *Parsifal*) were the most profound definition of myth in general.[5] Wagner's exemplary handling of mythical situations and of themes handed down in ancient legends represented a stimulating antidote to jejune naturalism and an urban civilisation: a vast body of literature sprang up after him in which mythical patterns may be to varying degrees displaced or concealed behind ordinary events. In certain examples that we shall quote the myth is transparent, in others it will be disguised, yet still suggesting to the reader a higher or more profound reality.

Wagner is, of course, associated with the sombre turbulence of Nordic legends; it should not be forgotten that it was the ancient Greek world which first captivated his imagination and supplied the focus for his theoretical writing on myth. In the summer of 1847 he experienced an almost mystical revelation on reading Aeschylus; the *Oresteia* particularly overwhelmed him and had a decisive effect on his ideas concerning drama and the theatre. (In later life, in 1880, he arranged for the *Oresteia* to be read on three successive nights, and was transfigured by the intensity of that work, one which he considered to be the supreme *Gesamtkunstwerk*.)[6] In his impassioned *Art and Revolution* (1849) Wagner stressed the paramount need of the modern artist to study the art of ancient Greece, that art which, suffused at every point with myth, was the means by which a people came to terms with its own being. 'The popular art of the Greeks, reaching its climax in tragedy, was the expression of the noblest and most profound elements in the consciousness of a people ... For the Greeks a performance of a tragedy was a religious celebration: on their stage gods had their being, and bestowed their wisdom upon men ...'[7] Being heir to German Romanticism − probably its most favoured beneficiary − Wagner sensed the indispensable quality of a life-sustaining mythology and, being an artist accustomed to thinking in images rather than concepts, he sought this mythology not in German idealist thought, as Friedrich Schlegel had suggested, but in the drama, ritual and poetry of ancient Greece. In *The Work of Art of the Future* (1849) Wagner saw that in ancient Greece actors and audience were one, the artwork being a joint creative activity, a re-enactment and appreciation of those ancient legends which were a self-projection of the people's spiritual essence. 'Tragedy blossomed as long as it was derived from the innermost being of the people, and for as long as the innermost being was truly the essence, a genuine spirit of the people, a *communal* spirit ... The communal celebration of the memory of their communal origin was found in the religious festivals of the Hellenic peoples, that is in the glorification and veneration of gods and heroes, during which these peoples felt themselves to be a communal whole.'[8] It was the people who created art, Wagner wrote, in their beliefs and stories, and in *Opera and Drama* (1850−1) he elaborated on the life-enhancing power of myth, its eternal truth and its insistence on feeling as the basis of all understanding:

> It is only from the Greek vision of life that the true, dramatic artwork can blossom − including even our own present age. It is *myth* which provides the subject matter for this drama, and only from the essence of myth can we understand the Greek art-work and its form which entrances us. The unique thing about myth is that it is true for all time and that its content, condensed to the utmost intensity, is inexhaustible for all time. It was simply the task of the poet to interpret this ... Song is the beginning and end of language, as feeling is the beginning and end of understanding and myth the beginning and end of history.'[9]

It is in this same publication that Wagner, half a century before Freud, insisted upon the importance of the Oedipus myth for an understanding of human behaviour (the themes of father-quest and mother-fixation in his work are vitally important ones), and he also discussed the relationship between Antigone and Creon, a situation which contributed much to the inception of the *Ring*, as did *King Lear*.

Wagner began work on the tetralogy in 1847, that year of intense study of the *Oresteia*, and the Greek influences on the work are undeniable. (The Swiss writer Gottfried Keller warmly recommended Wagner's privately printed *Nibelungen* work to Hermann Hettner in a letter of 16 April 1856, and explained: 'You will find a powerful, typically Germanic poetry here, but one which is ennobled by a sense of antique tragedy.)[10] The speculative first part of Aeschylus's work bears great similarities to *Das Rheingold*, which was originally entitled *The Theft*, (the quarrel between Zeus, the new and ruthless master, and the other gods, as well as the theft of fire by Prometheus, for example); *Prometheus Bound*, with its sea-nymphs, earth-goddess, remote rock and the prophecy that Zeus will desire a female destined to bear a son mightier than his father seems to supply much of the imagery and thematic material of Wagner's tetralogy. The apparent similarities between Brünnhilde and Athene (both warrior-maidens and special favourites of their fathers) are less important than the link between Brünnhilde and Prometheus: both are the offspring of an earth-goddess who has the gift of prophecy (there is no Erda in the Norse–Germanic mythology, although Jakob Grimm, whose *Germanic Mythology* Wagner had studied, postulates 'Erda' as the name of an ancient Germanic earth-goddess, and the *Poetic Edda* speaks of a 'volva' or wise-woman[11]); both defy the ruler of the gods who orders a fire-deity to secure them for an indefinite period of time on a remote crag. Each of the pair befriends a female pursued by the great god; whereas Brünnhilde will be released by Sieglinde's son it will be a descendant of Io who will come to the aid of Prometheus. (There are also striking similarities between the *Ring* and the legend of Jason, Medea and the golden fleece, particularly Grillparzer's version of the story with the curse on the gold, the conquest of Medea and the latter's fearful and destructive jealousy.) In order to make a story of crime and punishment out of the Nordic myths where it is lacking, Wagner imposed the Aeschylean elements upon them, borrowing much from Aeschylus's use of confrontation between characters and the employment of persistent images which he, as a musician, transformed into leitmotifs. It is also interesting to speculate upon the similarities between Zeus's relationship with Semele and that between Lohengrin and Elsa: both women desire to know the identity of their lover, in spite of repeated warnings against this, and both are destroyed when the divine origin of the partner is revealed. Wagner's roots are fed by a rich subliminal realm: both *Germanic Mythology* and the *Oresteia* suggested situations which, when enhanced by his music, would provide prodigiously fruitful stimuli for a future generation of writers as well as musicians.

What is of great importance for this chapter is to assess the impact which Wagner made upon the young Nietzsche, whose *The Birth of Tragedy from the Spirit of Music*, a work conceived and written in the days of the warmest affection between the two men, is of considerable significance. Wagner was delighted to welcome to Tribschen the young professor of classical philology, and long discussions on Greek myth and drama ensued. In *The Birth of Tragedy* Wagner's music drama and Greek art are fused in a remarkable synthesis, and for Nietzsche it was the mystery of the death and rebirth of Dionysus that constituted the essence of all true tragedy, the Apolline principle of form being a secondary phenomenon. Nietzsche sensed that the irresistible torrent of the Wagnerian orchestra represented the very beat and the rhythm of life itself: it represented that which Schopenhauer had called the will, that which the Greeks knew as Dionysian rapture and anguish, and that which a later psychologist would term the id and the unconscious; articulation, differentiation, formulation and clarity rose temporarily over this dark ecstatic flood. Despite Wagner's earlier insistence that his work be regarded as a *Gesamtkunstwerk* where music, word and gesture be taken as equals in importance (a view which, as we have stressed, he would later modify), Nietzsche noted the predominance of the musical element: it was the musical sound which convinces us, whereas the spoken word seems unable satisfactorily to elucidate. In this context Nietzsche also pointed out that the true import of tragic myth similarly never became transparent with sufficient clarity to the Greek poets and thinkers whose language, model of lucidity though it may be, failed to grasp the true weight of mythical meaning. The Greek heroes speak, Nietzsche explains, more superficially than they act, and hence the myth is not able to find its adequate objectification in the spoken word.[12] Nietzsche speaks of 'adäquate Objektivation': it is tempting to translate this as 'objective correlative', and the fact that Nietzsche immediately speaks of Hamlet, who also talks more superficially than he acts, links Nietzsche's meditations on Wagner and his art immediately with T. S. Eliot, whose essay 'Hamlet and his problems' in *The Sacred Wood* (1920) tells of the intractability of the material of Shakespeare's play and formulates that famous phrase to which Wagner seems to stand more or less as godfather.[13]

But *The Birth of Tragedy* not only speaks of Greek drama: it is shot through with Schopenhauer's philosophy and extols *Tristan und Isolde* above all, a work utterly remote from the Greeks (bearing only a superficial resemblance to Euripides's *Hippolytus*) and one which Nietzsche found literally overwhelming in its purely musical effect. The utter desolation of the phrase 'Öd und leer das Meer' struck Nietzsche as being of quintessential anguish, a hollow sigh, he believed, echoing from the heart of existence, an experience whose nihilistic ground achieved an almost metaphysical dimension. In *his* portrayal of spiritual barrenness Eliot found it again appropriate to use Wagner's phrase in the original German: the longing of the sailor for his 'irisch Kind', a longing most poignantly expressed and one, ironically, to be satisfied only in death, is also transposed to *The Waste Land*. The meaning of Eliot's title, together with the theme of the dying king, will concern us later with the discussion of *Parsifal*: here we must consider *Tristan und Isolde*, Wagner's most intensely formulated work, that work, in fact, most commonly held to be the ultimate amongst his music dramas. Chapter Two considered its impact upon the writers of decadence, particularly its second act; here its powerful mythical resonance must be acknowledged. In Wagner's re-creation the ancient Celtic legend, known to him in the version of Gottfried von Strasbourg, became for some an expression of desolate waste, for others a love-story of unprecedented perturbation whose images of yearning, consummation and death-wish impressed themselves with an indelible impact. For Nietzsche and Eliot, as was noted, the depiction of the void and mournful sea was a vision of spiritual waste and affliction; for a man like D. H. Lawrence Wagner's handling of the ancient theme, the dark torrents of sound, the spurting blood and the sombre passion provided the mythical framework against which the human drama might be enacted. Reference has been made to E. M. Forster's need either to refer to Wagnerian *topoi* at moments of panic or intense emotionalism or to write with a magnificence that may be called Wagnerian (when Rickie observes Agnes and Gerald embracing in *The Longest Journey*, for example); with D. H. Lawrence, as with d'Annunzio, more searing and more violent sensations are experienced.

The links between Lawrence and Wagner are particularly close and worthy of study: Lawrence had read, albeit perfunctorily, George Moore, Nietzsche, Otto Weininger and Houston Stewart Chamberlain where Wagner's presence loomed exceedingly large, and Richard Aldington is surely correct in finding 'the essence of Lawrence's beliefs and teachings' in a number of passages from *The Work of Art of the Future*.[14] Lawrence may have read the following passage; if he had not, he would certainly still have endorsed its defence of life and the blood as opposed to the atrophied intellect: 'If conscious, autocratic thought could dominate life fully, if it could usurp the vital impulse and divert it to some other purpose than the great necessity of the absolute claims of life themselves, then Life itself would be dethroned and swallowed up in Science. And, truly, Science, in her overweening arrogance, has dreamed of such a triumph — as witness our tight-reigned state and our modern art: the sexless, barren children of this dream.'[15] Wagner as the provider of mystical, consecrating visions, the forger of great, passionate creatures describable as 'columns of blood', the creator of drowning, oceanic feeling, meant much to Lawrence, and William Blissett's formulation is a neat one: 'In contrast to that other mythmaker, Joyce, who learned from Wagner how to plan and build, Lawrence learned from Wagner how to feel, to sustain feeling, to sustain the flow of feeling.'[16]

Lawrence's years in London enabled him to hear Wagner: his reactions were not always complimentary. '*Tristan* is long, feeble, a bit hysterical, without force or grip . . .' 'On Monday I was up at Covent Garden to hear Siegfried . . . It was good, but did not make any terrific impression on me . . .' 'I love Italian opera – it's all so reckless. Damn Wagner, and his bellowings at fate and death.'[17] Di Gaetani quite plausibly speculates that Lawrence was seeing too much Wagner at this time, frequently in ludicrous performances, and that he was loath to enthuse about what he had seen; [18] the letter to Blanche Jennings (15 December 1908) is less derogatory, however, and links music and blood in a most characteristic manner: 'Surely you know Wagner's operas – *Tannhäuser* and *Lohengrin*. They will run a knowledge of music into your blood better than any criticism.'[19] It was the move to Cornwall which brought the Wagnerian world to the fore: Lawrence's vital interest in myth was quickened in such surroundings and with the pulse of Wagner's music still fresh in his soul. Di Gaetani traces allusions to Wagner in *Witch à la Mode (Die Walküre* and immolation), and *The Primrose Path* (love and death),[20] but these are peripheral indeed when compared with the full-blown Wagnerism of *The Trespasser*. This novel, dating from 1912 and originally called *The Saga of Siegmund*, is as overtly Wagnerian as is *Evelyn Innes*, although for very different reasons: the passionate ecstasy of Siegmund and Helena, a nympholepsis against sea and sky, is directly derived from Wagner the mythmaker, and references to the music dramas abound. The novel is frequently rejected as being to florid, too *chargé*: Virginia Woolf referred to it as a 'hot, scented, overwrought piece of work'[21] and Lawrence himself quoted Ford Madox Ford's comment that it was 'a rotten work of genius'.[22] He did, however, object to comparisons with d'Annunzio's *Trionfo della Morte*, calling the latter 'a sensationalist, nearly always in bad taste, as in that rolling over the edge',[23] but both shared the Wagnerian experience and responded eagerly to his vast, *fortissimo* passages.

The Wagnerian patterns in *The Trespasser* are appropriate as a means of characterisation, to create a musical atmosphere and above all to elevate what might have been a stereotyped story of adultery to grander, more mythic dimensions. Some parallels are forced and unsubtle (the baying of the sheepdog and Fafner and Fasolt, for instance, and the unnecessary comparison between the rhythm of the train and the Ride of the Valkyries).[24] But other passages are most lovely: the rippling sunlight on the sea brings to mind the Rhine-maidens spreading their hair to the sun, and the quality of the sunset is such that the Grail-theme from *Lohengrin* is invoked by Helena. The *Tristan* references are the most telling, however; despite the fact that the hero of the novel is called Siegmund there is much of Tristan in him: he thinks of death even in the moments of intense happiness, and the lugubrious fog-horn seems like the mournful dirge of the shepherd in act three of Wagner's work. The pattern of light and darkness, sun and moon – and also water – are charged with mythical significance: the dreaded return to domesticity, and Helena's departure for Cornwall, causes an acute relapse in Siegmund, a febrile anguish which presages his death. Alone amidst the grey-green emptiness of the far west of England Helena can only think of Siegmund in the context of Wagner's harrowing music; at Tintagel, Lawrence writes, 'she found that the cave was exactly, almost identically, the same as the Walhalla scene in *Walküre*; in the second place, *Tristan* was here, in the tragic country filled with the flowers of a late Cornish summer, an everlasting reality . . . Helena forever hummed fragments of *Tristan*. As she stood on the rocks she sang, in her little, half-articulate way, bits of Isolde's love, bits of Tristan's anguish, to Siegmund . . .'[25] Her return to Siegmund comes too late; there is in Lawrence, however, no *Liebestod* but a resigned acceptance of unheroic reality.

Wagner's world, the world of the sagas, great, sweeping and dark, struck a resonant chord within Lawrence at that time immediately preceding the First World War and is juxtaposed, in *The Trespasser*, with the daily round of cramping domesticity, the good-natured bad taste of English suburbia. The elemental world of the music dramas, particularly rock and water, play a considerable part; the sea above all is lovingly portrayed, as is appropriate. The sea plays the role in *The Trespasser* that snow and mountains do in *Women in Love*; it is a place of purification, cleansing and exhilarating metamorphosis. What are the Wagnerian allusions in this later novel, written when Lawrence was at the height of his literary powers? The relationship between love and power dominates this book, and it is, of course, the central theme of Wagner's *Der Ring des Nibelungen*. Gerald Crich is an Alberich figure, whose mastery over the mines is ruthless and unyielding (Ursula Brangwen humorously calls him a 'Nibelung' when she sees him in the water, but her jesting words are perhaps not without significance); the world of mining, of darkness, danger and ruthless activity is portrayed in mythic terms, as is Gerald's new regime, the 'convulsion of death' which follows him. The chapter entitled 'Death and Love' has an undeniably Wagnerian ring, as Di Gaetani insists;[26] Gerald seeks to dominate the sexual responses of Gudrun but only mechanically, and it is the curse of death which Gudrun receives from him: 'Into her he poured all his pent-up darkness and corrosive death . . . And she, subject, received him as a vessel filled with his bitter potion of death.'[27] Gerald's beauty, however, makes him into a Siegfried more than an Alberich: the 'Blutbruderschaft' oath suggested by Rupert Birkin derives from *Götterdämmerung* as, indeed, does the name Gudrun (Gutrune). The self-destructive madness of industrial society seems, for Lawrence, ripe for a holocaust such as is found in the apocalyptic ending of Wagner's tetralogy; Rupert and

Ursula, whose love has a purity and authenticity remote from the selfish sterility of Gerald's, escape the general anathema.

Women in Love was written in its first form, Lawrence claims, in the Tyrol in 1913: it was finished three years later in Cornwall. Some ten years earlier there had appeared in England a novel of epic stature which again elevated the theme of power and possession (and again the possession is of a mine) to mythic levels, and described the terrible failure of love. 'Treasure and love' – these are the last three words of Joseph Conrad's *Nostromo*, a portrayal of the fearful silver mine of San Tomé, 'worked in the early days mostly by means of lashes on the backs of slaves . . .'[28] The way in which this mine became an obsession for Charles Gould is described in a remarkable few sentences, where the image of a wall of metal built up between two human beings seems to derive most aptly from scene four of *Das Rheingold*; it is Mrs Gould who meditates: 'The fate of the San Tomé mine was lying heavy upon her heart. It was a long time now since she had begun to fear it. It had been an idea. She had watched it with misgivings turning into a fetish, and now the fetish had grown into a monstrous and crushing weight. It was as if the inspiration of their early years had left her heart to turn into a wall of silver-bricks, erected by the silent work of evil spirits, between her and her husband . . .'[29] It cannot be doubted that Conrad absorbed Wagnerism as did most of his Edwardian contemporaries, and *Nostromo* contains many echoes; Conrad's friendship with Ford Madox Ford, son of Francis Hueffer and author of *The Nature of a Crime*, must also have brought Wagner's presence very close to him. (Ford Madox Ford, incidentally, gives an amusing report of Conrad's working on *Nostromo* in a Belgian hotel whilst a powerful contralto from Bayreuth shook the flimsy house with her voice. 'Whilst we wrote or groaned on the fourth floor the glasses on the tray jarred together in sympathy with the contralto passages of *Götterdämmerung*.)[30] Like Lawrence, Conrad may be called a mythic novelist, and Di Gaetani puts the point clearly that 'Conrad's artistic imagination naturally saw characters and situations in terms of mythic conflict and in this he is very similar to the German composer, whose operas display the combination of music and myth that Conrad sought in his writing'.[31] The 'operatic' scenes contained in many of Conrad's novels, the desire for effects in his prose that are self-consciously musical plead for a knowledge of and an indebtedness to Wagner, and this is what must now be briefly examined.

Reference has already been made to that famous statement concerning the supremacy of music, found in the preface to *The Nigger of the Narcissus*: specifically alluding to Wagner is the letter to Marguerite Poradowska, written when Conrad was working on *Almayer's Folly*. In this letter (May 1894) Conrad explains: 'I shall soon be sending you the final chapter. It begins with a trio Nina, Dain, Almayer, and finishes in a long solo for Almayer which is almost as long as Wagner's Tristan-solo.'[32] (A further letter to William Blackwood, 31 May 1902, emphasises Conrad's affinity to Wagner; this composer is specifically mentioned, as is Rodin, as a kindred spirit, one closer to Conrad than the great Victorian novelists.) The immolation scene (the burning of the house) and Almayer's longing for oblivion are Wagnerian motifs, and the theme of night, death and water bring *Tristan* forcibly to mind. Most potent is the symbol of the forest, the rank tendrils which 'carried death to their victims in an exulting riot of silent destruction',[33] a baleful magic garden which would not be out of place in the most febrile imaginings of the decadents. The atmosphere of *Tristan* hangs most heavily over *The Lagoon*, a story which is stylised and 'operatic' – musico-dramatic, rather – with its symbolic patterns of light and darkness, mist and water. That Conrad's writing is enriched by these Wagner parallels there can be no doubt: an extra dimension is added which makes the stories more elusive and universal. In *Falk* the sombre silence which surrounds the tugboat captain who longs for peace and domesticity ineluctably suggests the figure of the Flying Dutchman; ironic touches, however, deflate an all too earnest involvement. In *Freya of the Seven Isles* Wagner is specifically referred to: 'Freya would sit down to the piano and play fierce Wagner music in the flicker of blinding flashes, with thunderbolts falling all round, enough to make your hair stand on end';[34] she is very much of the sea, as is the heroine of Ibsen's *Lady from the Sea*, and the water imagery is all important. Subtle and effective are the parallels with *Tristan und Isolde*: the suicide of Jasper Allen is an act which makes the same desperate impact as Tristan's tearing off the bandages. Klingsor's magic garden seems present again in *A Smile of Fortune*, with the scent of the massed flowers, the mysterious woman, the irresistible magnetism which draws the narrator into a net of seduction. The conversation in *Chance* between land and sea people is greatly reminiscent of Wagner's famous simile in *Oper und Drama* where the musician is the artist of the sea, whilst the poet, landlubber, finally enters his vessel.

Mythical reverberations, then, enrich and universalise: the short stories are given a musical nimbus, and the great novels an epic, archetypal quality. The silver of *Nostromo*, the avarice it breeds and the threat to love suggests the tragedy of *Das Rheingold* and is thereby enriched: doom is prophesied by the old woman on her death bed, as those sombre knitters in the *Heart of Darkness*, knitting Norn-like their black wool, hint at a dreadful destiny. Not merely Charles Gould, but Sotillo, Nostromo, Captain Fidanza and his love are cursed by the silver, unable to extricate themselves from the power which it exerts. A similar fatalism prevails in *Victory* (1915), where Axel Heyst (is the Christian name an oblique tribute to Villiers de l'Isle-Adam's famous play?) moves Tristan-like to his own destruction: the three criminals become emissaries from some realm of darkness before which he must capitulate. The ritualistic quality of Lena's death is such that is seems as though Isolde were before us; Di Gaetani[35] stresses that Lena's final vision demonstrates a victory over death, the musical cadences of the prose and the abstract phrases emphasising the affinities with Wagner's masterpiece:

> Over Samburan the thunder had ceased to growl at last, and the world of material forms shuddered no more under the emerging stars. The spirit of the girl which was passing away from under them clung to her triumph, convinced of the reality of her victory over death . . . Exulting, she saw herself extended on the bed, in a black dress, and profoundly at peace; while, stooping over her with a kindly, playful smile, he was ready to lift her up in his firm arms and take her into the sanctuary of his innermost heart — for ever! The flush of rapture flooding her whole being broke out in a smile of innocent, girlish happiness; and with that divine radiance on her lips she breathed her last, triumphant, seeking for his glance in the shades of death . . .[36]

Heyst's self-immolation is an attempt to join the beloved through fire and transformation: nothing remains of the two bodies but ashes, and yet a sense of redemption, of Heyst's redemption through Lena's love, hangs over the book at the end.

Wagner's music is considered to be most powerful when portraying natural grandeur, and many writers know that a reference to Wagner would intensify and enhance their own purple passages. George Moore felt drawn to describe his novel *The Lake* thus: '*Evelyn Innes* is externally musical as *Carmen* is externally Spanish; but the writing of *The Lake* would not be as it is if I had not listened to *Lohengrin* many times . . . the pages in which the agitated priest wanders about a summer lake recall the silver of the prelude. The sun shining on the mist, a voice heard in vibrant supplication is the essence of the prelude . . .'[37] Edward Martyn's plays *The Heather Field* and *Maeve* (1899) abound in river nymphs and gold, music and even a rainbow, and the young heroine (Ishtar Brandès) of James Huneker's *Painted Veils* (1920), when summoned to Bayreuth, experiences music as an erotic inundation: 'Music, the most sensual of the arts, for it tells us of the hidden secrets of sex, immersed her body and soul in a magnetic bath . . .'[38] It is fitting that imaginative literature has stressed the link between Wagner's music and water, for the importance of that element and the legends associated with it cannot be over-emphasised for him. It was after the sea journey through the Baltic that he broke through to his own authentic style, with *Der fliegende Holländer* supplanting the grand opera of *Rienzi*, and it was after the seatrip to La Spezia, stretched out on a couch in his hotel room, that Wagner experienced the sensation of being inundated in rushing waters, that E flat major chord and those surging triads from which the Rhine-maidens would emerge. (An entertaining variation on the lustral quality of water here is an etching by David Hockney of a glass of water standing on a postcard bearing Wagner's portrait: the sadistic aquiline profile', in Peter Conrad's words, 'is refracted by the water, and the repellance of the cruel face washed clean by distortion.'[39]) The association of deep water, eroticism and death was naturally known to the German Romantics, particularly Novalis: Heinrich von Ofterdingen's dream of the caress of gentle waves like the touch of a tender breast, and the description of the water as a solution ('Auflösung') of charming girls may well have been known to Wagner. The bathing of Siegmund and Helena (chapter eight of *The Trespasser*) has unmistakably erotic overtones, and it is also interesting to note that the original prose sketch for *Das Rheingold* writes of 'Wodan (bathing) with the water-nymphs',[40] a draft which Wagner jotted down during hydropathic treatment at Albisbrunn. The link between water, love and death is seen most forcibly in *Der fliegende Holländer*, where it is Senta who finds in the sea and in the arms of the Dutchman her ultimate transfiguration, and *Tristan und Isolde* likewise portrays the love-death against the background of an immensity of sea and sky. It is also remarkable that Wagner should have dreamed of Undine figures a few hours before his death, and that he should have played the Rhine-maidens' lament on the piano, pledging his devotion to these underwater creatures.[41]

In modern German literature the treatment of the themes of water, oblivion and ecstatic fulfilment is found in Hermann Hesse's *Klein and Wagner* (1920). Klein, the 'small man', flees from wife and family to seek a new life: the image of Wagner the musician persistently imposes itself, fused with the memory of a certain Wagner who had killed his entire family. For Klein the name 'Wagner' under which musician and murderer were subsumed, becomes the epitome of freedom, genius, revolt and defiance, guarantor of vast horizons and unheard of adventures. Anticipating the technique he would later use in *Der Steppenwolf*, Hesse allows his hero to enter, in a dream, a theatre called 'Wagner' (or, possibly; 'Lohengrin'), an entry into the subconscious and a journey of self-exploration. 'The theatre with the inscription "Wagner" – was this not himself, was it not the invitation to step into himself, into the mysterious realm of his own true being? For he himself was Wagner – Wagner was the murderer and quarry in him, but Wagner was also the composer, the artist, the genius, the seducer, the tendency to hedonism, sensuality, luxury – Wagner was the collective name for everything oppressed, suppressed, neglected and despised in the former functionary Friedrich Klein.'[42] Unable to bear the dichotomy between 'Klein' and 'Wagner', Friedrich Klein seeks a re-absorbtion into the Whole: on a dark, rainy lake he steps into the water, into death and transfiguration. The process might also be called one of rebirth, for mythology often has recourse to the theme of a descent into or a journey over water, across the sea or along a river; Lohengrin's arrival and Siegfried's Rhine journey may well have this function. But most vividly Isolde's final utterances are remembered, the waves of which she sings and that final ecstatic oblivion. The composer who had indeed died in that city of water, who had dreamed of Undine shortly before his death and whose very last written words, before his pen slipped diagonally across the page, were 'Ecstatic convulsions — love — tragedy'[43] suffuses this story as an indispensable presence.

Klein is not sure whether or not the 'theatre' also bore the name 'Lohengrin', that hero of ancient Germanic legends, the wandering emissary from a higher realm driven, like the Flying Dutchman, to spend but little time in one appointed place. The swan motif becomes of interest here: swans held a curious fascination for Wagner, from the time of *Lohengrin* and the piano piece *Ankunft bei den schwarzen Schwänen (Coming to Black Swans)* to *Parsifal*, and it was entirely fitting that Ludwig II should similarly have venerated this bird. The swan is known, of course, to many mythologies (Leda and the swan, and the swan of Tuonela are but two obvious examples), but Wagner's use of the bird in *Lohengrin* provided a particularly powerful stimulus. These rare, proud and solitary creatures, quietly gliding over dark waters, supplied an emblematic motif in the work of Mallarmé, Rilke, Viélé-Griffin and Rubén Darío; at the turn of the century painters such as Degouve de Nunque and the Berlin Secessionists frequently turned to the swan for inspiration. A work in which both swan and *Tristan* motifs are found is Strindberg's *Svanehvit*, written in the spring of 1901. The play, a 'fairy play' with its castles above the sea, has much of the atmosphere of Maeterlinck, but the parallels with *Tristan* are undeniable: the prince is sent to bring back the maidenly Swanwhite across the sea to marry the king and, having fallen in love with her, is caught in her embrace by the stepmother. Stylistically *Svanehvit* is very close to *Tristan*: the staccato inversions and repetitions, and the fierce concentration of erotic desire are very close in form and in spirit to act two of Wagner's work, particularly when Swanwhite and the prince yearn for flight from the harsh glare of reality into a land of dreams: 'On your arm! — in my bosom! — in your arms! — This is ecstasy — The eternal, without end, without stain — Can we be parted? — Never! — Are you my bride? — Are you my bridegroom? — In the land of dreams — Not here . . .'[44] The prince finds death in the sea, but Swanwhite lies beside him, knowing that the power of love can conquer death itself. Redemption, then, through fierce eroticism — yet also through compassion; compassion, Parsifal's 'Mitleid', can perform miracles, as the stepmother proclaims at the end. Themes of chivalry, of the sword between the lovers, play a considerable part in this play, but more archetypal patterns are also found, the swan, as Jung has written, being frequently a symbol for rebirth in its emergence from dark waters.[45] (In *Parsifal*, it should be remembered, the swan sanctifies the waters of the lake where Amfortas bathes.) *A propos* Jung, it is tempting to speculate upon the extent to which Wagner was aware of the seminal work of C. G. Carus, *Psyche: the Biogeny of the Soul* (1846), which speaks of 'Urbilder', archetypal pictures, in the human consciousness much in the manner of the later Swiss thinker; Carus was court physician in Dresden at the same time that Wagner was court musician there, and contact between the two was by no means impossible. That haunting picture by Caspar David Friedrich, *Swans in the Reeds*, was long held to be by Carus and Wagner, always susceptible to stimuli from painting – Ismael Mengs's copy of Carlo Dolci's *Madonna* which he saw in Aussig, and Titian's *Assumption of the Virgin* in Venice inspired him to continue work on *Tannhäuser* and *Die Meistersinger* respectively – may well have derived from the picture encouragement to work on the *Lohengrin* material which was germinating within him. 'Music', writes Jung, 'certainly has to do with the collective unconsciousness – as the drama does too'; it comes as no surprise when he adds: '– this is evident in Wagner, for example'.[46]

To return to Strindberg, it could possibly be argued that the Swedish dramatist drew upon Nordic and Celtic sources, as did Wagner, and did not, in fact, need the mediating assistance of the German musician; it is well attested, however, that after his 1896 crisis Strindberg turned more and more to music and myth, greatly admiring *Das Rheingold* (particularly Alberich's terrible curse on love, described in the *Legends* of 1897–8) and emulating Wagner in his desire to assimilate music and drama in his late lyrical plays. A further example of Wagnerian alliteration is most noticeable in *A Dream-play*, where objects and dialogue are employed in a reiterating manner that Wagner would doubtless have appreciated. (The gentle music, for example, which is meant to conjure forth waves and winds is greatly reminiscent of the opening song of the Rhine-maidens: 'We, we are the waves – which rock the winds in their cradle to rest – we, we are the winds – which wail and moan – woe – woe – woe ...')[47] Strindberg certainly devoted all his energies to fashion a truly symbolic theatre in the manner of Maeterlinck, but Wagner's influence was similarly potent. In 1902 Strindberg wrote a sketch for a *Flying Dutchman* drama in which the theme of compassion was to have been paramount, but this remained only a plan, and certain comments in the prose works *Gothic Rooms* (1904), *Black Flags* (1907) and *The Blue Book* (1907–9) are not always complimentary towards the composer. (A remark in *Black Flags* is enlightening: 'Wagner brings tones together unnaturally, "against nature", and therefore his music has upon the

innocent mind the effect of something dreadful, unnatural, unhealthy and rotten
. . .'[48]) It may have been Nietzsche's attack on Wagner's music which encouraged
a certain antipathy in Strindberg at this time (Georg Brandes had sent him *The
Wagner Case*), but for Wagner the dramatist and Wagner the mythmaker
Strindberg's remarks are entirely laudatory: the closing comments in the
foreword to *Miss Julie* on the need for a hidden orchestra, a steeply raked
amphitheatre, the removal of boxes and complete darkness during performances
seem to be a description of Bayreuth, and Wagner's example must have left
impressions on Strindberg which were positive and lasting. It may not be without
significance that it is only by seeing a performance of *Die Walküre* that the
student may enter the mysterious house in *The Ghost Sonata*, that place of
ultimate transfiguration and redemption.

And what of the other great Northern master? Unlike Strindberg, who was
profoundly musical, Ibsen lacked a feeling for this art; he did, however, similarly
move towards symbolic worlds in his late plays, to references to mysterious
creatures and forces possessed of an archetypal validity. It is the argument of this
chapter that the great European movement towards myth and symbolism owed
an enormous debt to Wagner's example: the sea trolls and mermaids of *The Lady
from the Sea*, the theme of water and death in *Rosmersholm*, indeed water, sex and
death in *Little Eyolf*, the reference to the Flying Dutchman in *The Wild Duck*,
and to singing metals and dwarfs toiling beneath the earth in *John Gabriel
Borkman* seem to derive from the same poetic and mythical realm as Wagner's
creations, if not directly from them. Pervasive and profound indeed is the
impingement of Wagner on literature; writers such as G. B. Shaw and Thomas
Mann have stressed the parallels between the Norwegian and the German, the
two great masters of psychological exploration and mythical illumination, who
share the technique of condensing a complex sequence of events into a few
symbolic situations played out between two or three characters. The last play of
all, *When We Dead Awaken* (1899), a work as consciously conceived as a final
utterance as *Parsifal*, conveys the poignancy of the past, of the lost radiance of
naive wonder most movingly as Professor Rubek and Irene sit by the stream, the
man remembering the childish games with water-lilies and sorrel leaves, the
woman remembering the transfiguration of these into Lohengrin's boat and the
silver swan. It was, incidentally, James Joyce who commented that Ibsen's last
play, with its theme of death and resurrection, should rank with the greatest of
that author's work, if it be not *the* greatest. Joyce felt most keenly the need for
mythical substructures in his writing: in a lecture on 'Drama and Life', given at
University College, Dublin, in 1900, he announced that 'Every race has made its
own myths and it is in these that early drama often finds an outlet. The author of

Parsifal has recognised this and hence his work is solid as a rock.'[49] In his later work, in *Ulysses* and *Finnegans Wake* above all, Joyce will quote from Wagner extensively, and frequently ironically, as Chapter Four will later describe. From the *Ring* above all, that glittering storehouse, the literary as well as the musical artist can draw material which deepens and enhances: the mythical dimension above all, derived from Wagner, will provide many a modern novelist and playwright with stature by association and comparison. (Another Irishman, George Moore, used the sword-motif, literally printed on the page, to portray the vision of the rebirth of Irish culture: 'It seemed to me that the garden filled with tremendous music, out of which came a phrase glittering like a sword suddenly drawn from its sheath and raised defiantly to the sun.'[50]) Both Norwegian dramatist and his Irish admirer felt drawn to the German magus to reinforce and intensify, the ultimate authority in hierophantic divination.

A remarkable work of Wagner's which gives the 'Schwanenjungfrau' or swan-maiden great prominence is the fragmentary *Wieland der Schmied (Wieland the Smith)* dating from 1849–50; this became widely known when published in Wagner's *Complete Works* and the subsequent 'Volksausgaben'. The work was pushed into the background by the colossal conception of the *Ring*, but certain situations found their way into the greater work – the theft of gold, the magic ring and the destruction of the forge being obvious examples. Wieland the crippled smith is a Nordic version of Vulcan; in Wagner it is Schwanhilde, half swan-maiden, half Valkyrie, who yields to him and attempts to flee with him. The scheming Bathilde, daughter of King Neiding, prevents their union by magic and trickery; Wieland is mutilated but, upon hearing Schwanhilde's voice, forges wings and rises with her into the skies after destroying the forge and burying King Neiding and his men beneath the rubble. Wagner wrote no music for his fragmentary drama; thirty years after his death, in 1913, the composer Kurt Hoessel produced his own opera on the same theme in Berlin. It is reported that Adolf Hitler attempted his own version of Wieland,[51] doubtless seeing the smith as a symbol for Germany, which would rise from privations to glory; Wagner's tribulations in Paris, and his later call for the destruction of that city, fed the morbid imagination of the future Leader who had suffered similar hardships in Vienna. In *The Work of Art of the Future* Wagner certainly extolled the people from which such a legend had sprung, but a writer like Gerhart Hauptmann, in a perceptive remark in the *Marginalie* of 1911, realised that Wagner '. . . is just as Greek as he is German, just as Asiatic as European'. A work such as the *Ring*, Hauptmann sensed, was 'the only one of its kind in the world and perhaps the most puzzling art work of the last millennium',[52] comparable to a massive fragment hurled into the air by a volcanic eruption. His own *Veland*, published in

1925, is a northern world of sombre rock and desolate water; the description of Veland's forge (act two) seems to derive from *Das Rheingold*, but the bestial smith himself, who fascinates the king's daughter by his skill, reminds us forcibly of the monstrous Huhn in Hauptmann's own *And Pippa Dances!* Certain critics have not approved of Hauptmann's rejection of naturalism and his adaptation of myth and legends: Paul Fechter had scathingly castigated the charming *The Sunken Bell* as being 'Richard Wagner in a Silesian setting',[53] whereas the derivative *Lohengrin* and *Parsival* (both dating from 1911–12) were deemed unworthy of mention. Another version of the Wieland theme is Viélé-Griffin's *La Légende ailée de Wieland le forgeron* of 1900, a further example of Wagner's ability to provide the theme of legendary heroism for a writer mentioned previously in connection with swan imagery and *symboliste* aestheticism. Viélé-Griffin passed from misty effulgence to themes of heroism more appropriate to his temperament, and the impetus is not difficult to determine.

The progression from neo-romanticism to myth (whether it be Germanic, Mexican or Greek in Hauptmann's case) is a tendency found most strongly in the work of Paul Claudel. Claudel had shared the Wagner fever of the Mallarmé circle, that sodality which, as André Gide described in his autobiographical *Si le grain ne meurt*, sought music in all things and glorified Wagner above all other gods. In his 1926 essay *Richard Wagner – Rêverie d'un poëte français* (the allusive title is deliberate) Claudel describes his first hearing of *Tristan und Isolde*, an experience which left him radiant and sanctified as though it were his first communion. It is interesting that a writer like Gide should portray both Claudel and Wagner in similar terms: he describes in his diaries the crushing effect of Wagner thus: 'I hold the person and the work of Wagner in horror; my passionate aversion has done nothing but grow since my childhood . . . This amazing genius does not exalt so much as he *crushes*. Germany has perhaps never produced anything at once so great and so barbarous . . .'[54] Claudel in his turn is compared to a steam hammer ('marteau pilon') on two occasions, a man whose work is blunt rather than reticent, overwhelming in the cosmic significance of myth which he employs. It seems beyond doubt that Claudel, in a materialistic and cynical age, was led to myth by Wagner's example; the 1926 essay hails Wagner as a hero, a man whose art dominated the nineteenth century and opened up vast possibilities for the twentieth.[55] 'This is the moment when, alone on the hill at Bayreuth, poised above degenerate Europe, above a Germany bloated with gold and material goods, Richard Wagner gave witness to Christ in sacramental form . . .'[56] Although Claudel's proselytizing tendencies, his devout Catholicism and his belief that Monsalvat was the starting point rather than the goal, all place his work in a different dimension, the undeniable links with

Bayreuth should not be forgotten; such basic themes as the illusion of power, restless yearning and redemptive love betray the presence of Wagner's art, and the expansive assertion and frequently ejaculatory elements in Claudel's style seem also akin to Wagner's own writing.

The first of a long series of characters all bearing the Wagnerian stamp is Simon Agnel, the hero of Claudel's first play *Tête d'or* (1890), a blond world-conqueror drunk with freedom, whose affinity to Wagner's Siegfried is not difficult to discern. There are obvious parallels between the play and Wagner's great tetralogy: Wagner's world ash-tree occurs, for example, as the world oak which must be felled to serve the mortally wounded hero as a resting place. The vanity of power and the reconciling force of love are important motifs for Claudel here: as Siegfried shatters Brünnhilde's father's staff, so Simon banishes the father of the princess from the throne; as Siegfried deceives Brünnhilde, so Simon forces the princess to leave the realm; both Siegfried and Brünnhilde and Simon and the princess are united in an ecstatic *Liebestod*. (It is significant that Claudel should seize on the figure of Erda in the *Ring* and see her as the central symbol of the whole work, a teluric figure who incarnates 'a form of soul or of personality which hides in the very bowels of our planet'[57].) The redemptive power of love had, in Wagner, transfigured the sombre violence of *Götterdämmerung*, and Claudel's work is shot through with this theme: as the Flying Dutchman sought his redemption through Senta, so Pierre de Craon, in *L'Annonce faite à Marie* (1912 — a later version of *La Jeune Fille Violaine* of 1901) needs the merciful love of Violaine to be healed. (Even the restless, tormented Don Rodrigue in *Le Soulier de satin* seems cast in the same mould as Wagner's Dutchman.) In *L'Échange* (1901) Elisabeth and Marthe represent again the purity of love, but sinful desire is portrayed in the figure of Léchy, a Venus greatly reminiscent of Wagner's *Tannhäuser* seductress. In *La Ville* (1903) the fascinating Lâla emerges as a Kundry-temptress who causes the death of Lambert de Besme but who also transfigures and redeems Coeuvre who appears, like Parsifal, in the role of kingly priest. One notable difference, however, is the absence of Klingsor: Lâla is the voice of the earth, not of evil, and the son of Coeuvre and Lâla is destined to rule over the city as an active and radiant priest, not as a mystic. In *Partage de midi*, finally, Wagner's *Tristan und Isolde* undergoes yet another variation: Ysé and Mésa are aware, on the deck of the ship, of the power of physical attraction; in a remote cemetery the two consummate their love and, dying, Mésa finally receives the redemptive embrace of Ysé, a *Liebestod* which seals the final apotheosis of both. But Claudel transcends the death-intoxicated raptures of Wagner's lovers: the direction of *Partage de midi* is towards the light, towards order and ultimate clarity. The last words of the play, 'Man in the glory of August, the conquering spirit in the transfiguration of the South!',[58] are a vindication of Claudel's buoyant faith in divine grace, an energetic Catholicism far removed from Wagner, but nevertheless informed by the mythical foundation which Claudel had learned from him.

'The Christ is sacramental form . . .' Claudel's reference here is obviously to *Parsifal*, and we must now consider the great impetus which Wagner's resusitation of the legend of Parsifal and the holy grail gave to the European imagination at the end of the nineteenth and the beginning of the twentieth century. Chapter Two discussed the fascination which Kundry exerted upon a particular type of mentality, but the concepts of service, a sick king, a charismatic leader and of a mystical elect are of consequence here, together with the powerful symbol of the grail itself. The conception of a 'Bühnenweihfestspiel', a 'stage-dedication-festival-play', originally intended solely for the Bayreuth stage, the atmosphere of hierarchic ritual, of cultic mysteries enacted within sacred vaults fired the imagination of a disaffected generation grown tired of modern urban culture and sterile social reporting. Johannes Schlaf, erstwhile naturalist collaborator with Arno Holz, spoke in 1906 of a new romanticism whose lasting achievements were to be found, paradoxically, not in the lyric but in the drama, and above all in the drama of Richard Wagner. 'The whole of the last century, including the upheavals of its middle years, was suffused by a secret yearning for fulfilment, and for the "blue flower" of Romanticism. Within the sphere of this new realm [Reich] of art, towards which everything is striving, that Romantic principle has achieved a unique and powerful revelation – as pure and unambiguous as the particular conditions of the age allowed – in the work of Richard Wagner.'[59] Writers in Germany such as Ernst Hardt (1876–1947), Eduard Stucken (1865–1936) and above all Karl Vollmoeller (1878–1948), who chose to live in the Palazzo Vendramin where Wagner had died, and who achieved temporary European fame after Max Reinhardt's production of *The Miracle* (1912), all exemplify an esoteric and frequently theatrical fusion of myth, religiosity and aestheticism, and stand very much under the shadow of the Festspielhaus. The fusion of pagan and Christian terminology, the figure of the 'blameless fool', and also the children's voices floating from above ('Et ô ces voix d'enfants chantant dans la coupole!') combined to form a heady atmosphere for souls deprived of orthodox fulfilment, and Wagner's own essay *Religion and Art* (1881) insisted on the duty of art to come to the rescue of religion when the latter ceased to have meaning for the populace.[60] For art, Wagner claimed, was able, through the manipulation of redolent symbols, to communicate the aura of mystery and wonder: Felix von Weingartner's oratorio-opera *The Redemption* is unthinkable without the 'Bühnenweihfestspiel', and the revival of interest in medieval mystery plays, finding its most famous example in Hofmannsthal's *Everyman* (1911) undoubtedly stemmed from the Bayreuth example.[61] The lawyer Lorenz Krapp (who used the more euphonious pseudonym Arno von Walden in his literary pursuits) insisted in 1903 that '*Parsifal*, the "stage-dedication-festival-play" of the pure fool, as Wagner called it, is without doubt the starting point for a new religious art and poetry . . . Through the magic of the "holiest of days, Good Friday", there walks still and solemn the pale figure of our Saviour, bent with sorrows, the crown of thorns on his brow and the purple cloak around his bleeding shoulders . . .'[62] The knights of the grail, the white dove, the celebration of the mass and the transfiguration of Kundry – all struck this poetaster and acolyte with the force of revelation. Likewise Dietrich Eckart, bohemian and colleague of Adolf Hitler in the early Munich days, a man whose only literary claim to fame was a German version of *Peer Gynt*, wrote in fulsome terms of *Parsifal* as 'This Song of Songs of love, this song of sublime love . . .'[63] and claimed it was a work which fused all human aspiration and spiritual longing into a luminous act of faith. *Parsifal* as a new religion? A most Christian work? The similarities between Amfortas and Christ scarcely conceal the differences: Amfortas does not suffer for others, but himself; he rebels against his father, bringing about his death in an almost Oedipan manner (and it is Lévi-Strauss who emphasises the Oedipan world of Klingsor which results from the semi-incestuous mood created in the scene between Parsifal and Kundry: by identifying herself with his mother, Kundry attempts to seduce him.[64]) Similarly the concept of a Christian renewal through the Germanic spirit, the paramount need for the purity of the blood and for an élite dedicated to the highest ideals of service has, with hindsight, a somewhat disturbing ring which Wagner's essay *Heroism and Christianity* does little to dispel: Wagner's attempt to 'redeem the Redeemer' of 'all alexandrian-jewish-roman despotic disfiguration'[65] is scarcely an act of humility. The bizarre obsessions of David Irvine are adumbrated here, the writer who, in *Parsifal and Wagner's Christianity*, longed for the saintly hero who would abolish 'the alloy of egoistic, optimistic Judaism infecting the unselfish pessimism of Christianity'[66] and expunge degenerate insolence from the earth.

The theatre as temple, the stage as a place of cultic ritual – this is what *Parsifal* donated to the European mind at the end of the nineteenth century, a strange offshoot of Wagner's admiration for Greek theatre. For *Parsifal* is the most un-Greek of his works, albeit an allusion in Goethe's *Tasso* may have brought Wagner's attention to the legend of Telephus, son of Hercules, who was wounded by Achilles's spear and could be cured only by the same weapon.[67] Redemptive love, the quest for spiritual transfiguration, the presence of the grail itself – these ancient themes proved most potent, even irresistible to many writers.

Stefan George's cultic plays, called *Weihespiele* (perhaps to recall the description of *Parsifal*) dwell on initiation and dedication; the mystery plays of Reinhard Sorge (*Metanoeite* and *Three Mysteries*), and even the cloudy soul-dramas of the circle around Rudolf Steiner (Alfred Steffen's *The Fall of Antichrist* and *The Souls' Awakening*, for instance) owe much to Wagner's last work. Steiner himself explained that Wagner was fired by an incandescent vision, a vision granted to those alone who knew of the reality of the spiritual life: 'In truth, it was the great idea of a mission which dawned in Wagner's soul, an idea which can only possess, which can only penetrate that personality, that being which feels in itself something of a genuine, spiritual impulse, a profound faith in the reality of the spiritual life.'[68] The links between theosophy and Wagnerism were close: in London the founder and editor of the Wagner journal *The Meister*, William Ashton Ellis, was a theosophist, as was the redoubtable Manchester spinster Miss Horniman, a frequent visitor to Bayreuth and supporter of Ellis's venture.[69] A perusal of the theosophist journals in London, Dublin and New York would show, for example, that far more attention was paid to Richard Wagner than to any other modern artist: the London Theosophical Society, for example, issued five papers on Wagner, one being an interpretation of *Parsifal* (1908)[70] In France Edouard Schuré was also a follower of Rudolf Steiner, and he and the confused Rosicrucian Joséphin Sar Péladan were among the leading French translators and interpreters of Wagner. It is interesting in this context that Christian Morgenstern, a writer not only of humorous verse, should use the image of the chalice to portray his awakening to theosophical enlightenment;[71] Ernst Barlach, a precursor of German expressionism, likewise used the themes of quest, transcendence and mystical 'excarnation' in many of his plays. *The Good Time* is Calvary, Oberammergau and Bayreuth in one, as the critic Herbert Ihering astutely observed,[72] and C. G. Jung's references to Barlach are made *à propos* a discussion of Wagner, particularly the significance of the father figure in his work.[73]

Barlach and Morgenstern are, however, peripheral writers; what are of far greater importance here are the ways in which the archetypal events and symbols of the grail legend, above all such concepts as the waste land, the bleeding lance and the mystic chalice, came to the fore in Jessie Weston's famous *From Ritual to Romance* (1920), that work which inspired the basic symbolism of Eliot's *The Waste Land*. Miss Weston had been associated with *The Meister* since its inception, and wrote her book *Legends of the Wagner Dramas* in 1896; in 1911, during a visit to Bayreuth, she discussed many topics which would find further elucidation in her later, more famous, book where the genius of Wagner is overtly acknowledged. Miss Weston had been responsible for a translation of Wolfram von Eschenbach's masterpiece and from this source (and others) derived the theme of sterility stemming from the wounded king whose genitals had been pierced by a spear. Wagner (perhaps for reasons of stage-craft?) does not state the exact location of Amfortas's wound, although in the prose sketch he wrote for King Ludwig in 1865 he does refer to the wound which Longinus had inflicted in Christ's thigh;[74] Wagner also referred in this sketch to an erect, bleeding lance: 'In front of Anfortas [*sic*] a lance is carried, erect, with bloody tip.'[75] For Miss Weston the grail legends are not necessarily Christian but are associated with ancient fertility rites, and Wagner, although heavily indebted to Christian ritual in *Parsifal*, likewise seems to touch upon more ancient archetypes. It can be claimed that his mythic gaze encompassed the whole world of slain and martyred loveliness, and the most ancient sacrifices are invoked: Adonis slain by the wild boar and Siegfried, whom Hagen claimed had met a similar end; the mutilated Christ, whose side was pierced by a Roman spear, and the dismembered Dionysus. T. S. Eliot's waste land, a desert of meaningless husks and former beliefs, owes much to *From Ritual to Romance*, and it is the Parsifal of Wolfram and Wagner which fed the basic arguments of that book. The mythical method is seen again most vividly in Virginia Woolf, who was discussed in Chapter One; her Percival hearkens back, across the *Waste Land* to *Parsifal*, the wild hunting song and the breaking of bread.

Is too much being claimed for Wagner here? Did not Tennyson and the Pre-Raphaelites do as much to bring medieval ritual and Celtic–Nordic legends to the fore? The opaline haze and undulating sweetness of Tennyson, as well as the creations of the Pre-Raphaelite brethren were indisputably important stimuli, but they lacked of necessity the shattering power of Wagner's *music* which, when combined with a fertile mythopoeic vision, proved irresistible to the late Victorians as well as to the precursors of modernism. A brief discussion of the importance of Wagner for the Pre-Raphaelites might be worthwhile. Franz (or Francis) Hueffer communicated his enthusiasm for Wagner to the London circles by his book on *Richard Wagner and the music of the Future*; he became music critic of the *Times* in 1879 and later married the younger daughter of Ford Madox Brown. William Michael Rossetti married Brown's elder daughter: his more famous brother Dante Gabriel had, as a young man, translated much from German but later professed to dislike anything Teutonic (he also refused to read the proofs of William Morris's *Sigurd*, saying that he really could not take any interest in a man whose parent was a snake.)[76] William Morris had read and greatly esteemed both Tieck and Fouqué, but he was unwilling to betray an enthusiasm for Wagner: he had met Cosima at Dannreuther's house in 1877 (Wagner himself had been detained by rehearsals) but failed to reach any particular understanding with her. He had written his own *The Hill of Venus* in 1869 and it was likely that the imminent production of Wagner's *Ring* in 1876 had spurred him on to complete his own *Siguard the Volsung or the Fall of the Niblungs*. Wagner had, of course, published the text in 1853, and H. Buxton Forman sent Morris his brother's translation of *Die Walküre* in 1873. Without having read it, Morris denounced Wagner as 'inartistic' and expressed his horror at 'the idea of a sandy haired German tenor tweedledeeing over the unspeakable woes of Sigurd, which even the simplest words are not typical enough to express'.[77] It would seem that Morris was jealous of Wagner's success, yet there is much in common between the idealism of the two men, their fruitful interest in medievalism, Nordic mythologies and political activism. To return to *Parsifal*, it is known that Edward Burne-Jones heard a concert performance of the work in the Albert Hall in 1884 and was delighted to realise that Wagner had struck in his music exactly the same tone that he had tried to express in some of his paintings. Wagner and he never met, but George Eliot took Cosima Wagner to his studio, and the two met again two or three times subsequently.[78]

Both Nietzsche and Wagner, it may be claimed, created or re-created in their work powerful mythical images whose purpose was to express redemption: Zarathustra strove to redeem man from inauthentic and life-denying creeds and Wagner's work, particularly the *Ring, Tristan* and *Parsifal*, preaches redemption from the heavy burden of life itself. Roy Pascal described how Schopenhauerian pessimism is, paradoxically, impregnated in Wagner's dramas with an awed veneration of life, how spiritual transcendence is strangely steeped in sensuality.[79] Writing on the prevalence of works in Germany in which the word 'Erlösung' was crucial, he described how Wagner played a unique and fascinating role and was, indeed, elevated to a quasi-divine status. Central to our argument here is the undeniable impetus Wagner gave to what might be called a mythomanic tendency in Germany and elsewhere (but the Germans above all have tended to be a nation of mythopoets or, at least, mythophiles),[80] that desire to see the mythical in place of the historical, and vast forces at work behind human affairs. Those who went to see the *Ring*, the cultured German bourgeoisie above all, found their own mythical self-projection, 'the consciousness of greatness and power, an awed feeling of destiny linking the remote past and the future and enhanced by an anticipation of doom ...'.[81] During the First World War Thomas Mann was led to describe the conflict as being between the spirit of Lohengrin on the one side and the sophistication of international society on the other: given such a choice he knew that he could have no reservations about his support for Germany. It was after Wagner had fallen into the hands of unscrupulous mystagogues that Thomas Mann felt obliged to take stock of the situation, and he speculated upon the ambiguities in Wagner which led him to win over the finest as well as the coarsest mentality, the result being a certain sense of discomfort felt by one section of his admirers in the presence of the other. Hitler had spoken (see Chapter Two) of building his religion upon *Parsifal*; it was also the mythical vastness of the *Ring*, Thomas Mann saw, that could not fail to provide the myth-makers of the Third Reich with ample fare. Gerhart Hauptmann had claimed that such a work as the *Ring* stood by itself, apparently utterly beyond modernity and atavistic in its primitive pathos, a world-poem interlaced with music and prophecy; Thomas Mann likewise, in a letter written during his exile, described the way in which, in that remarkable work, day and night hold colloquy, and the mythical archetypes of man – the fair, blithe, golden-haired, and those who brood in hate, grief and rebellion – engage each other in profound fairy-tale plot. Yet Thomas Mann, linking National Socialism with the mythical, primitive, poetic spirit of Germany, with her inherent lack of political maturity, saw that the enthusiasm which the music of the *Ring* engenders, the sense of grandeur that seizes the listener while hearing it, which is comparable only to the feelings inspired by nature at its noblest, should not make us forget that this work, created and directed 'against civilisation', against the entire culture and society dominant since the Renaissance, emerges from the same roots as did National Socialism. With its 'Wagalaweia' and its alliteration, its mixture of roots in the soil and eyes-towards-the-future, its appeal for a classless society and its mythical-reactionary revolutionism – with all these elements, Thomas Mann argued, it was the exact spiritual forerunner of that metapolitical movement which was then, in 1940, terrorising the world.

In Ernst Bertram's famous book on Nietzsche which appeared in 1918 the memorable statement occurs: 'Everything that happens seeks its image, everything that lives its legend, all that is real its mythical equivalent.'[83] The book is about Wagner as much as about Nietzsche; Bertram's claim that all reality tends towards mythical representation finds, indeed, in the composer a most convincing verification. Mythical perception, as we noted at the beginning of this chapter, is charged with emotion, but the drama which surrounds the clash of archetypal entities finds aesthetic expression in the creation of striking images. The fabrication of these powerful images is fascinating indeed, yet disturbing reverberations arise when myth is manipulated by those seeking a bold, simplistic explanation in place of the given facts of history. (Walter Rathenau's address *An Deutschlands Jugend*, from which the epigraph at the beginning of this chapter was taken, demonstrates the way in which literature and politics became tightly interlocked during the immediate aftermath of the First World War, where the same values obtained, the same misty visions were conjured up, the same longings and hopes being expressed in the same theatrical and vertiginously expectant voice, where Wagnerian heroes are the obvious points of reference.)[84] When the social and the political are deemed to be of secondary importance, and the grand aesthetic spectacle is meant to overwhelm and convince, then that 'aestheticisation of politics' which was briefly referred to in Chapter Two, and which Benjamin saw as the hallmark of fascism, is at hand.[85] The thinking of a man like Hitler was essentially mythical, and his predilection for operatic display, for pomp and ritual, for vast ceremonies and above all the cult of death is characteristic of a mentality which seeks in dilettante aestheticism the masterstroke and the crushing effect. Carl von Ossietzky, writer, journalist and later editor of *Die Weltbühne,* who died in 1938 after interrogation by the Gestapo, succinctly describes the enraptured flight into mythical grandeur which Wagner's music promised: 'In Richard Wagner's work the bourgeois age fled from problematic reality into a mythology that was drowned in music . . . Richard Wagner is still amongst us, a resounding spirit, dedicated to aims which are not artistic ones, but rather to an obfuscation of the mind – an opiate. For the second time in its history Germany is being transformed into a Wagner opera.'[86] Thomas Mann's perceptive essay *Brother Hitler,* written two years before the letter to the editor of *Common Sense* referred to earlier, draws fascinating parallels between Hitler's years as a shabby bohemian outsider, prone to fits of melancholy alternating with wild projects, topor, and resentment, and the attitudes of the outsider-cum-aesthete, unable to achieve success and consequently holding to scorn the acceptable and the norm. The embittered outcast sees all too readily his adversary in archetypal form and himself as the glorious hero, thwarted by powers of darkness; the struggle between fair and dark, between heroism and stunted malevolence is given aesthetic grandeur when contemplated in mythical images enhanced by the tumultuous orchestration of a master composer. What greater contrast could there be between the radiant Siegfried and the nodding, twisted, degenerate Mime, whose potions aimed at destroying him, or between the 'Lichtalb' Wotan and the 'Schwarzalb' Alberich? Hitler's account of his chance meeting with an Eastern Jew on the streets of Vienna after a performance of *Götterdämmerung* demonstrates the vulgarity of his mind, but also affords a keen insight into the effect that that music had upon him. He was, he explains, 'wildly excited' ('wahnsinnig erregt') and felt the juxtaposition between such a figure and the image of the dying Siegfried in the very depths of his being: 'A more irreconcilable contrast cannot possibly be imagined! The magnificent mystery of the dying hero on the one hand and then – this Jewish filth . . .'[87] This contrast became an *idée fixe* and, together with memories of the clash and uproar of *Rienzi* and the mystique of blood-purity derived from *Parsifal,* provided the impetus for monstrous excesses.

'Those things which are forever inaccessible to the real Jew run as follows: *immediacy of Being, the grace of God, the trumpet, the Siegfried-motif, the oak-tree, self-creation, the word: I am!*'[88] Oak tree, trumpet and Siegfried-motif — the bright heroism of the child of nature: these images were meant to convey those essential qualities of the Germanic as opposed to the Jewish, and occur in a most remarkable work, *Sex and Character*, by Otto Weininger, a precocious young Viennese scholar who committed suicide in a flamboyant manner a few months after the publication of the book in 1903. Such was the popularity of *Sex and Character* that it went through eighteen editions before the end of the First World War. The two basic themes of the book are sexuality and Jewishness: of Jewish descent himself, Weininger exemplified to an extreme degree Theodor Lessing's concept of 'Jewish self-hatred', as did Joseph Rubinstein, who took his own life shortly after Wagner's death, unable to accommodate himself to the ways of the world without his Master, and having fruitlessly attempted to live in some sort of communion with the spirit of Wagner in Lucerne. It is not the purpose of this book to assess the vexed question of Wagner and Judaism, but to note in Weininger's work mythical patterns deriving from Wagner's *oeuvre*. Claiming that Wagner was the deepest anti-Semite, Weininger believed that 'his Siegfried was the most *unjewish* notion which could ever be conceived',[89] incomprehensible to the Jew, as were the Pilgrims' Chorus from *Tannhäuser* and the account of the journey to Rome in that same work. (That Hermann Levi, son of the Chief Rabbi of Giessen, should be the first conductor of *Parsifal* is not acknowledged.)[90] The creator of 'the most powerful music in the world' had seen most clearly, according to Weininger, more clearly than anyone else, the meaning of Jewishness, also of sexuality. For *Parsifal*, the 'most profound' piece of writing in world literature (again according to Weininger) contains within it the 'most profound' female character in the whole history of art, namely Kundry, who demonstrates that, like the Jew, woman has no soul, no authentic intrinsic value: 'for the real Jew has, like the woman, no "I", and consequently no meaning.'[91] Kundry perfectly exemplifies this absolute reliance of the woman on the man; it is only through Parsifal that Kundry may be redeemed, Weininger argues, and he continues that woman is, in fact, 'nameless' until 'created' by the male principle. He quotes here the incantation of Klingsor from the beginning of act two to substantiate this, his summoning of the 'Namenlose' amidst incense and necromantic utterances, to be manipulated and controlled by his will. It would seem that Parsifal, Siegfried and Lohengrin, utterly alien from and incomprehensible to the Jewish mentality, represent the highest principles of creativity and authenticity, to which the Woman and the Jew can never aspire.

Chapter Four will contain the refreshing counterblasts of less addicted writers to these turgid and often lurid obfuscations: the unsavoury rodomantade of many of Wagner's later essays finds in *Sex and Character* a fitting testimony.

For Otto Weininger the music-drama *Siegfried* represented all that was highest and most radiant: for Tolstoy it was the supreme example of counterfeit art. Tolstoy's is the most authoritative voice of dissent; in *What is Art?*, 1898, the mythological world which Wagner portrayed is rejected as a sophisticated veneer intermingled with impressive, yet sterile, *coups de théâtre*:

> We have here the sleeping beauty, and nymphs, and subterranean fires, and dwarfs, and battles, and swords, and love, and incest, and a monster, and singing birds: the whole arsenal of the poetic is brought into action . . . And it is this poeticality, imitativeness, effectiveness and interestingness which, thanks to the peculiarities of Wagner's talent and to the advantageous position in which he was placed, are in these productions carried to the highest pitch of perfection, which so act on the spectator, hypnotizing him as one would be hypnotized who listened for several consecutive hours to maniacal ravings pronounced with great oratorical power . . .[92]

The performance of *Siegfried* which Tolstoy saw in Moscow (or, rather, the first two acts which he saw, being unable to sit out the entire work) convinced him that Wagner's art was spurious, even absurd: the 'lights, clouds, moonlight, darkness, magic fires, thunder' which he saw and heard demonstrated, in his opinion, the skill of the stage manager but could not be taken seriously. Tolstoy had, of course, undergone a religious conversion twenty years previously which had led him to reject out of hand not only orthodox belief but also most of the manifestations of European art, including his own works; his dismissal of opera as degenerate artifice and mere sensationalism would not therefore be surprising. But music-drama is castigated as well as the most frivolous of operettas; Bayreuth would, Tolstoy argued, be equally unendurable, a place of fetishism and intolerable pretension: 'Sit in the dark for four days in the company of people who are not quite normal, and through the auditory nerves subject your brain to the strongest action of the sounds best adapted to excite it, and you will no doubt be reduced to an abnormal condition and be enchanted by absurdities.'[93] The attack on music in the *Kreutzer Sonata* is too well known to be discussed here; suffice it for this chapter to say that the sage of Yasnaya Polyana refused to admit that the Wagnerian resurrection of myth and legend was in any way examplary.[94] To dress as a peasant and work in the fields was hardly the best preparation for an understanding of the sybarite of Bayreuth, and the vigorous and popular idiom of Tolstoy's later writing, his striking parables and deliberate economy of style represent a rejection of the grandiose gestures of myth and the fascinating archetypes linked to them.

'Wagner did not quote myths merely as metaphors: beneath his gaze everything becomes mythological . . .'[95] Theodor Adorno's essay of 1952 saw and described Wagner's tendency to revert to archaic pictures, even the apparently historical Nuremberg of *Die Meistersinger* merging into a mythical vision. The spell cast by Wagner was felt throughout the whole range of German society, and the mythologising tendencies prevailed above all: the Kaiser could not refrain from using the thunder-motif from *Das Rheingold* as his motorised signal, and the elderly sturdy hiker with beret, raincoat, beard, stick and eyeglass seemed frequently to be proud of a resemblance to Wotan. (Ludwig Thoma, editor of the satirical journal *Simplicissimus*, delighted in caricaturing the patriotic petit-bourgeois with Wagnerian delusions of grandeur as he strode from his office at the week-end; a paraphrase would run: 'I boldly stride, hoorah, hooray/With buoyant step to face the day . . .'[96]) Both emperor and bourgeois in the Second Reich thrilled to the power of mythical suggestion; the leader of the Third Reich, after a performance of *Die Walküre* in Bayreuth, felt moved to christen the projected destruction of Guernica with the name of that magic fire whose musical representation was flooding his mind. On a more trivial level the bestowal of names derived from Wagner operas demonstrates the unique popularity of these works: Elsas, Sieglindes and Isoldes, Siegfrieds and Tristans, some of whom may have been begotten in a rapturous intoxication after a particularly overpowering performance, were spread throughout Germany and even further afield.[97]

This chapter has, however, attempted to look at literature rather than history and sociology and must now close with a restatement of the main idea. The value of myth, its ability to enhance and fructify, has been recognised above all by C. G. Jung, who stressed the need for great primordial images, going so far, indeed, as to stress their indispensability for sound mental health; writers like Lawrence, Conrad, Eliot, Thomas Mann and a host of others mentioned in this chapter have likewise turned to myth in their works. (It was Hermann Broch who was able to define the position of the modern mythic novelist in his essay *The Mythical Legacy of Poetry* and who extolled myth for its ability to illuminate the inscrutable regions of the psyche and its power to bestow coherence in times of historical dislocation.[98]) It has been the contention of this chapter that the mythic underpinning of many works written in the twentieth century owes an incalculable debt to Wagner's art, where myth and ancient legend were brought to the surface, instinct with symbolic resonance. Wagner's symbolism, suggesting archetypes that lie too deep for rational elucidation, is enhanced by music of unparalleled force of suggestion, music which delights the connoisseur yet also the mystagogue, the former responding to the miraculous reconciliation of opposites, the latter to the blatant crudity of certain effects. It is easy to be lead into the Wagnerian labyrinth, and the darkest regions of the soul may be uncomfortably nurtured by his art. This art, however, remains a triumphant vindication of an audacious dramatic aesthetic; *sub specie Wagneri* the world becomes a more wondrous place, and one listener at least feels grateful that even the rain puddles of drab English suburbia are transfigured by its seductive suggestiveness.

Notes

1 Anthony Burgess, *The Worm and the Ring*, London, 1961, pp. 3 and 4. This novel contains a headmaster called Woolton, a wife Frick (Frederica) and describes the building of a new school into which the teachers process, irradiated by a rainbow. See Geoffrey Aggeler, *Anthony Burgess: The Artist as Novelist*, Alabama, 1979, pp. 58–67 for an analysis of the book.

2 See the opening paragraph of chapter twenty-two of *Howards End*. An article by W. J. Lucas, 'Wagner and Forster', in *Romantic Mythologies* (ed. I. Fletcher), London, 1967, pp. 271–279 deals at length with the Parsifal parallels in *A Room with a View*, but the attempt to make old Mr Emerson into both Titurel *and* Parsifal (with George as Amfortas) is hardly convincing.

3 John White, *Myth and the Modern Novel*, Princeton, N.J., 1971, p. 5.

4 Northrop Frye's glossary to the *Anatomy of Criticism*, Princeton, N.J., 1957, p. 365 gives a lucid description of the terms 'myth' and 'archetype'; Frye suggests that the quest-motif is common to all literatures.

5 See his *Parsifal* article in the 1972 Bayreuth *Programmheft*.

6 I am indebted to Hugh Lloyd-Jones's article on 'Wagner and the Greeks' in the *Times Literary Supplement* (9 January 1976) for many of the points raised here. See also Cosima Wagner, *Tagebücher*, I, p. 871.

7 Richard Wagner, *Gesammelte Schriften und Dichtungen*, Berlin, 1914, III, p. 23: 'Die öffentliche Kunst der Griechen, wie sie in der Tragödie ihren Höhepunkt erreichte, war der Ausdruck des Tiefsten und Edelsten des Volksbewußtseins . . . Dem Griechen war die Aufführung einer Tragödie eine religiöse Feier, auf ihrer Bühne bewegten sich Götter und spendeten den Menschen ihre Weisheit.'

8 Richard Wagner, *op. cit.*, pp. 105 and 131–2: 'Die Blüte der Tragödie dauerte genau so lange, als sie aus dem Geiste des Volkes heraus gedichtet wurde und dieser Geist eben ein wirklicher Volksgeist, nämlich ein *gemeinsamer* war . . . Die gemeinsame Feier der Erinnerung ihrer gemeinschaftlichen Herkunft begingen die hellenischen Stämme in ihren religiösen Festen, d.h. in der Verherrlichung und Verehrung des Gottes oder des Helden, in welchem sie sich als ein gemeinsames Ganzes inbegriffen fühlten.'

9 Richard Wagner, *ed. cit.*, IV, pp. 31, 64 and 69: '... nur der griechischen Weltanschauung konnte bis heute noch das wirkliche Kunstwerk des Dramas entblühen. Stoff dieses Dramas ist aber der *Mythos*, und aus seinem Wesen können wir allein das höchste griechische Kunstwerk und seine uns berückende Form begreifen ... Das Unvergleichliche des Mythos ist, daß er jederzeit wahr und sein Inhalt, bei dichtester Gedrängtheit, für alle Zeiten unerschöpflich ist. Die Aufgabe des Dichters war es nur, ihn zu deuten ... Die Tonsprache ist Anfang und Ende der Wortsprache, wie das Gefühl Anfang und Ende des Verstandes, der Mythos Anfang und Ende der Geschichte.'

10 'Sie werden finden, daß eine gewaltige Poesie, urdeutsch, aber von antik-tragischem Geiste geläutert, darin weht.'

11 See Deryck Cooke, *I Saw the World End*, Oxford, 1979, pp. 226–7.

12 Nietzsche, *Werke, ed. cit.*, I, p. 94.

13 See the article by Noel Lees on 'T. S. Eliot and Nietzsche', in *Notes and Queries*, October 1964.

14 Richard Aldington, *Portrait of a Genius, But ...*, London, 1950, p. 329.

15 Richard Wagner, *ed. cit.*, III, p. 46: 'Würde das bewußte, willkürliche Denken das Leben in Wahrheit vollkommen beherrschen, konnte es sich des Lebenstriebes bemächtigen und ihn nach einer anderen Absicht als der Nothwendigkeit des absoluten Bedürfnisses verwenden, so wäre das Leben selbst verneint um in die Wissenschaft aufzugehen; und in der That hat die Wissenschaft in ihrem überspanntesten Hochmute von solchem Triumphe geträumt, und unser regierter Staat, unsere moderne Kunst sind die geschlechtlosen, unfruchtbaren Kinder dieser Träume.'

16 William Blissett, 'D. H. Lawrence, D'Annunzio, Wagner', in *Wisconsin Studies in Contemporary Literature*, VII, 1966, pp. 21–46.

17 See *Lawrence in Love: Letters to Louise Burrows*, Nottingham, 1968, pp. 44, 149 and 88–9. *A propos* Lawrence's reference to *Tristan* it is interesting to remember his later comment in 'Pornography and Obscenity', where he links the work with *Jane Eyre* and claims that these works were 'much nearer to pornography than is Boccaccio. Wagner and Charlotte Brontë were both in a state where the strongest instincts have collapsed, and sex has become something slightly obscene, to be wallowed in, but despised' (in *Selected Literary Criticism*, ed. Beal, London, 1956, p. 39).

18 John DiGaetani, *Richard Wagner and the Modern British Novel*, Cranbury, N.J., 1978, p. 60.

19 *The Collected Letters of D. H. Lawrence*, London, 1962, I, p. 41.

20 DiGaetani, *op. cit.*, pp. 64–6.

21 Virginia Woolf, *The Moment and other Essays*, London, 1952, p. 79.

22 Lawrence, *Collected Letters, ed. cit.*, I, p. 86.

23 See letter of 11 July 1925.

24 Apparently the Flemish writer Albert Rodenbach did find the rhythm of the train most stimulating, and composed his own *Der Walkuren Rid* on the way home after a Wagner concert in Brussels in 1877. G. Verriest reports: 'It was on the train from Brussels to Louvain that he [Rodenbach], after having been to a Wagner concert, quietly hunched in a corner of the shuddering, rattling carriage, conceived his "Walkuren-Rid" so firmly and completely in image and in word that when he got home he wrote out the mighty poem at one sitting, exactly as it is now printed' (In *Ons leven*, jg. 17, 1905, p. 22).

25 D. H. Lawrence, *The Trespasser* (Phoenix ed.), London, 1976, p. 166. Graham Hough suggests that *The Trespasser* was strongly influenced by *Evelyn Innes*: see *The Dark Sun*, New York, 1957, p. 41.

26 DiGaetani, *op. cit.*, p. 82.

27 D. H. Lawrence, *Women in Love*, London, 1969, p. 337. The urge for power as a substitute for love is a basic theme in Wagner: gold is either accumulated as a result of loneliness (Alberich, Fafner even), or power is sought by one incapable of love (Klingsor). A variation on the theme of money and love is found in L. P. Hartley's *Eustace and Hilary* trilogy; it is Eustace who frequently confuses money and love, no more so than when, in Venice, he misunderstands Nancy Steptoe and offers her a cheque. It is surely no coincidence that her married name is Mrs Alberic.

28 Joseph Conrad, *Nostromo*, London, 1962, p. 52. (See F. R. Karl, *Joseph Conrad, Three Lives: a Biography*, London, 1979, p. 458).

29 Conrad, *op. cit.*, pp. 221–2.

30 Ford Madox Ford, *Joseph Conrad: a Personal Remembrance*, Boston, Mass., 1924, p. 124.

31 DiGaetani, *op. cit.*, p. 27.

32 R. Rapin (ed.), *Lettres de Joseph Conrad à Marguerite Poradowska*, Geneva, 1966, p. 132: 'Je vous enverrai bientôt le dernier Chap.: Il commence avec un trio Nina, Dain, Almayer, et il finit dans un long solo pour Almayer qui est presque aussi long que le Tristan-solo de Wagner.'

33 Conrad, *Almayer's Folly*, London, 1961, p. 165.

34 Conrad, *Freya of the Seven Isles*, in *Twixt Land and Sea*, London, 1966, p. 152.

35 DiGaetani, *op. cit.*, p. 54.

36 Conrad, *Victory*, London, 1967, pp. 406–07. (See Karl, *op. cit.*, p. 268.)

37 George Moore, 'The Nineness in the oneness', *Century Magazine*, LXXVII, 1919, p. 66.

38 James Huneker, *Painted Veils*, London, 1920, p. 59. (Apparently Huneker pawned his overcoat to buy a ticket for *Tristan*: see Zuckerman, p. 161.)

39 See Peter Conrad's article, *Times Literary Supplement*, 10 March 1978.

40 P. Wapnewski, *Der traurige Gott: Richard Wagner in seinen Helden*, Munich, 1978, p. 151: 'Wodan (badend) mit den drei Wassermädchen.'

41 Cosima Wagner, *Tagebücher* II, pp. 1112–13.

42 Hermann Hesse, *Klein und Wagner* in *Der Weg nach Innen*, Berlin, 1931, pp. 313–14: 'Das Theater mit der Aufschrift *Wagner*, war das nicht er selbst, war es

nicht die Aufforderung, in sich selbst einzutreten, in das fremde Land seines wahren Innern? Denn Wagner war er selber – Wagner war der Mörder und Gejagte in ihm, aber Wagner war auch der Komponist, der Künstler, das Genie, der Verführer, die Neigung zu Lebenslust, Sinnenlust, Luxus – Wagner war der Sammelname für alles Unterdrückte, Untergesunkene, zu kurz Gekommene in dem ehemaligen Beamten Friedrich Klein.'

43 Richard Wagner, *Entwürfe, Gedanken, Fragmente*, Leipzig, 1885. See the essay 'Über das Weibliche im Menschlichen', V, p. 129: 'Gleichwohl geht der Prozess der Emancipation des Weibes nur unter ekstatischen Zuckungen vor sich. Liebe – Tragik'.

44 Strindberg, *Svanehvit*, in *Samlade Skrifter* (ed. Lindquist), Stockholm, 1916, XXXVI, p. 170: 'På din arm! / I min famn! / I dina armar! / Detta är saligheten. / Den eviga, utan slut, utan vank! / Kan någon skilja oss? / Ingen! / Är du min brud? / Är du min brudgum? / I drömmarnes land! / Icke här . . .'

45 C. G. Jung, *Symbols of Transformation* (Bollingen Series, 20), New York, 1956, p. 348.

46 Jung, *Letters* (Adler ed.), London, 1973, I, p. 542.

47 Strindberg, *Ett drömspel*, *op. cit.*, p. 300: 'Vi, vi vågorna, / som vagga vindarne / till vila . . . Det är vi, vi vindarne – som vina och vinsla – ve! ve! ve!'

48 See Victor Hallström, *Strindberg och musiken*, Stockholm, 1917, p. 74: 'Wagner sammanför tonor "mot naturen", och däför verkar hans musik på ett ofördärvat sinne som hemsk, naturvidrig, osund, förstörd.'

49 James Joyce, in *The Critical Writings of James Joyce*, New York, 1959, pp. 40–1.

50 George Moore, *Vale*, *op. cit.*, p. 291.

51 Joachim Fest, *Hitler*, *op. cit.*, p. 53.

52 Gerhart Hauptmann, *Sämtliche Werke*, Frankfurt and Berlin, 1963, VI, p. 916. The whole quote is an interesting one and worth repeating: 'Ich sehe Wagners Kunst heute als künstlerisches Urphänomen, stammend aus einer Zeit vor aller deutschen Kunst, auch Musik. Ich bin weit davon entfernt, mich an Richard Wagner deutschtümelnd zu entzücken; denn er ist ebenso griechisch als deutsch, ebenso asiatisch wie europäisch. Ein Werk wie der Ring ist, was Ursprung, Wachstum und Vollendung anlangt, das einzige seiner Art in der Welt und vielleicht das rätselhafteste Kunstgebilde der letzten Jahrtausende. Kultur hat damit nichts zu schaffen, und es hat nichts mit Kultur zu schaffen. Es hat nichts mit dem deutschen Rhein, den germanischen Göttern und den Nibelungen zu schaffen, und alle diese schönen Sachen haben nichts mit ihm zu schaffen. Es hat auch nichts zu tun mit Christentum, obgleich es ganz und gar etwas Offenbartes ist. Wer sie verstehen will, muß nicht in dieser Kunst ertrinken, auch nicht darin schwimmen. Er muß sie als das Große, Ewigfremde willkommen heißen. Man könnte sie gleichnisweise als einen unterirdisch hervorbrechenden kochenden Geysir bezeichnen, der ein unbekanntes glühendes Element emporschleudert aus dem Erdinnern, das die menschliche Seele, die es benetzt, von den Schlacken der letzten

Jahrtausende rein baden und rein brennen kann.'

53 Quoted in Kurt Lothar Tank, *Gerhart Hauptmann in Selbstzeugnissen und Bilddokumenten*, Reinbek/Hamburg, 1959, p. 129.

54 André Gide, *Journal (1889–1939)* (Pléiade), Paris, 1941, p. 259: 'J'ai la personne et l'oeuvre de Wagner en horreur; mon aversion passionnée n'a fait que croître depuis mon enfance . . . Ce prodigieux génie n'exalte pas tant qu'il *n'écrase* . . . L'Allemagne n'a peut-être jamais rien produit à la fois d'aussi grand ni d'aussi barbare.'

55 See Gilbert Gadoffre's article 'Claudel et le héros wagnérien' in *Paul Claudel: Zu seinem 100. Geburtstag* (Ludwigsburger Beiträge zum Problem der deutsch-französischen Beziehungen), Stuttgart, 1968. Also Roger Bauer in *Richard Wagner und das neue Bayreuth*, Munich, 1962, pp. 53–61.

56 Paul Claudel, *Oeuvres complètes*, Paris, 1957, XVI, p. 322: 'C'est le moment où seul sur la colline de Bayreuth au-dessus de l'Europe abaissée, au-dessus de l'Allemagne qui se crève d'or et de bonne chère, Richard Wagner confesse le Christ sous sa forme sacramentelle.'

57 Claudel, *La Légende de Pâkitri* (Pléiade), *Prose*, p. 956: '. . . une espèce d'âme ou de personalité qui se cache aux entrailles de notre planète.'

58 Claudel, *Oeuvres complètes, ed. cit.*, XI, 106: 'L'homme dans la splendeur de l'août, l'Esprit vainqueur dans la transfiguration de Midi!'

59 See *Literarische Manifeste der Jahrhundertwende* (ed. Ruprecht and Bänsch), Stuttgart, 1970, p. 145: 'Das ganze Jahrhundert und alle Stürme seiner Mitte durchzieht heimlich die Sehnsucht nach einer Erfüllung und nach der "blauen Blume". Bis dahin, bereits im Bezirk des neuen Reiches, auf das zunächst alles hinauswollte, jenes romantische Kunstprinzip zu einer ersten machtvollen Offenbarung gelangte, die so rein und deutlich war, wie sie es nach Lage der vorläufigen Umstände überhaupt nur sein konnte: nämlich bei Wagner.'

60 Richard Wagner, 'Religion und Kunst', in *Bayreuther Blätter*, October 1880: 'Man könnte sagen, daß da, wo die Religion künstlich wird, der Kunst es vorbehalten sei den Kern der Religion zu retten, indem sie die mythischen Symbole, welche die erstere im eigentlichen Sinne als wahr geglaubt wissen will, ihrem sinnbildlichen Werte nach erfaßt, um durch ideale Darstellung derselben die in ihnen verborgene tiefe Wahrheit erkennen zu lassen.' A most perceptive article relating to this topic is William Blissett's 'The liturgy of *Parsifal*', *University of Toronto Quarterly*, XLIX, 2, 1979–80, pp. 117–38.

61 Although this book is concerned with Wagner and literature a musical digression might be permitted here. Rutland Boughton's *Music-drama of the Future* (1911), with its title-page of a picture of various pillars (artists) supporting a dome consisting of Shakespeare, Wagner and Beethoven demonstrates the English composer's obsession at that time; Glastonbury was to be the second Bayreuth at which a 'Festival of Music Drama and Mystic Drama' was to take place. Boughton sang in *Parsifal* as well as in his own *Immortal Hour* during the 1914 performances; his collaborator Reginald Buckley planned a vast *Arthur* cycle, much as Josef Holbrooke had with his *Cauldron of Annwyn* trilogy, to be a British *Ring.* To return to literature it is perhaps a pity that John Cowper Powys does not use Wagnerian models in his long description of Arthurian ritual and pageant in *A Glastonbury Romance* (1933); the German students 'whose more patient minds, schooled in Faustian mysteries' saw in the cultic accoutrements 'a symbolic if not metaphysical significance' hail not from Bayreuth, but from Weimar. (See the Picador edition, 1975, p. 567.)

62 *Literarische Manifeste der Jahrhundertwende, op. cit.*, p. 395: 'Der Parsifal, das "Bühnenweihfestspiel" vom reinen Toren, wie Wagner es nannte, ist sicher ein Ausgangspunkt für eine neue religiöse Kunst und Dichtung . . . Durch den Zauber des "allerheiligsten Karfreitags" geht ernst und still die blasse, leidgebückte Gestalt des Heilands, den Dornenreif um die Stirn, den roten Purpurmantel um blutende Schultern.' A pity that Lorenz Krapp did not know of Wagner's statement concerning the figure of Parsifal: 'Ich habe an den Heiland dabei gar nicht gedacht' (Cosima Wagner, *Tagebücher*, II, p. 205).

63 See his essay in the *Handbuch für Festspielbesucher*, Bayreuth, 1924. 'Dies hohe Lied der Liebe, dies Lied der hohen Liebe . . .' The pretentious pun is lost in English.

64 Lévi-Strauss in the *Parsifal Programmheft* of 1972.

65 *Richard Wagner an seine Künstler* (ed. Kloss), Berlin and Leipzig, 1908, II, p. 386: '. . . die Reiningung und Erlösung des Jesus von Nazareth . . . von aller alexandrinisch-jüdäisch-römisch despotischen Verunstaltung.' A statement from the 1938 festival handbook runs as follows: 'Wagner's work teaches us hardness in the figure of Lohengrin . . . through Hans Sachs it teaches us . . . to honour all things German . . . In the *Ring des Nibelungen* it brings to our consciousness with unexampled clarity the terrible seriousness of the racial problem . . . in *Parsifal* it shows us that the only religion Germans can embrace is that of struggle towards a life made divine' (quoted in Geoffrey Skelton: *Wagner and Bayreuth*, London, 1965, p. 144).

66 Quoted in William Blisset, 'Ernest Newman and English Wagnerism', in *Music and Letters*, vol. 40, no. 4, October 1959, p. 313. For a full account of the eccentricities of David Irvine see Anne Dzamba Sessa's *Richard Wagner and the English*, chapter three. The authoress is correct in stating that Irvine's books *A Wagnerian's Midsummer Madness*, *Wagner's Bad Luck* and *The Badness of Wagner's Bad Luck* 'connote a certain impatience, even mild hysteria' (p. 79). His statement concerning Wagner's *Deutsche Kunst und deutsche Politik* of 1867, that is, 'Nothing finer, more conclusive, profounder and yet simpler has appeared from any pen the whole century throughout' (Dzamba Sessa, p. 77) is certainly contentious, as is his support of Wagner's eulogy on the murderer of Kotzebue.

67 In act four scene four: 'Die Dichter sagen uns von einem Speer, / Der eine Wunde, die er selbst geschlagen, / Durch freundliche Berührung heilen kann . . .' Act II of

Schumann's opera *Genoveva* contains the words by Golo: 'Du schlugst die Wunde! Still nun auch das Blut, das strömende des Herzens.'

68 Rudolf Steiner, 'Richard Wagner und die Mystik' in *Die Erkenntnis des Übersinnlichen in unserer Zeit*, Dornach, 1959: 'Wahrhaftig, ein großer Missionsgedanke, der vor Richard Wagners Seele auftauchte, ein Missionsgedanke, den nur eine Persönlichkeit haben konnte, ganz durchdringen konnte, die in sich selber etwas von dem wirklichen geistigen Impuls, die einen tiefen Glauben an die Wahrheit des geistigen Lebens hatte. Diesen tiefen Glauben aber hatte Richard Wagner' (lecture given on 28 March 1907). When Bayreuth becomes Montsalvat and the New Jerusalem anything can happen. An example of Bayreuth as Lourdes occurs in Karl Ritter's war film *Stukas*, in which therapy through music plays a decisive part. A shell-shocked pilot, whose only hope of a cure lies in undergoing a profound experience, actually recovers during the performance in Bayreuth of *Götterdämmerung*.

69 Dzamba Sessa's book *Richard Wagner and the English* gives the cover design of *The Meister* as a frontispiece and describes it thus: 'The theme was the pre-Socratic division of the universe into the four elements – water, earth, air and fire – in the same order as they occurred in the *Ring*. A female figure resembling a mermaid and carrying a shield typified the dual nature of man – animal and material in the lower part of the body, human and spiritual in the upper. Her shield presented on its left the sword of power, *Nothung*, and the Nibelung's ring, the symbol of "self devouring Time"; on the right of the shield was the swan of *Lohengrin*, representing the soul, and the chalice, or vessel of divine reason. Other aspects of the picture included a laurel wreath of victory, a lance – Parsifal's spear – denoting the power of spiritual truth, and the masks of comedy and tragedy. Crossing the entire composition and uniting it was a flamboyant scroll bearing the name of the journal; the flames of the scroll symbolized the purifying power of love' (pp. 39–40). No wonder Shaw recoiled on seeing it.

70 *A propos* theosophical Wagnerism, I cannot resist the following quotation from Alice Leighton Cleather's *H. P. Blavatsky as I Knew Her* (Calcutta, 1923). A. P. Sinnett had, in her opinion, usurped the leadership of the movement and had forced Annie Besant to do his will, and the warring factions among the different theosophists are described in terms of the characters from *Parsifal*: 'Richard Wagner, who had considerable knowledge of magic, gives an exact and terrible illustration of this process [i.e. charlatanry] in his symbolical music-drama *Parsifal*. The plastic elemental female principle is there personified in Kundry. Awake she is the humble serving messenger of the Grail Brotherhood; but unknown to them, the black magician, Klingsor, can throw her into a hypnotic trance and compel her to serve his nefarious ends ... The terrible danger to sensitive and hysterical women of being subjected to this process by an unscrupulous male hypnotiser cannot be exaggerated; and men like Sinnett, who have recourse to such evil practices in the pursuit of their selfish ends are black magicians of the worst description, and are a menace to humanity . . . The whole may be taken as a drama of the Theosophical Society, which may now be said to be under the dominion of Klingsor, and still waiting the coming of its Parsifal who can shatter the vast fabric of psychic illusion.' (See Dzamba Sessa, p. 131.) The new Parsifal was, apparently, due to arrive in 1975.

71 Christian Morgenstern, *Gesammelte Werke*, Munich, 1965, p. 440.

72 Herbert Ihering, *Von Reinhardt bis Brecht*, Hamburg, 1967, p. 302. There are also several Wagner references in Barlach's early play *The Poor Cousin* ('Walküre', 'Lohengrin' and 'Frau Venus'): it is also possible to equate Iver with the Flying Dutchman, and Fräulein Isenbarn's pledge to be true is similar to that of Senta. Barlach's world of mists and phantoms is somewhat akin to Wagner's; I am reminded of Thomas Hardy's remark that Wagner's music was 'weather and ghost music' with its wind and storm effects (see Florence Hardy's *The Life of Thomas Hardy 1840–1928*, New York, 1962, p. 181).

73 C. G. Jung, *Symbols of Transformation*, op. cit., pp. 362–3.

74 Richard Wagner, *Das braune Buch*, op. cit., p. 67: 'Es ist die Lanze, mit welcher einst Longinus des Heilands Schenkel durchstach . . .'

75 Richard Wagner, *Das braune Buch*, op. cit., p. 61: '. . . dem Anfortas wird eine hochaufgerichtete Lanze mit blutiger Spitze nachgetragen.' The sculptor Kietz, incidentally, after reading the *Parsifal* sketch in Wahnfried in 1874 announced to his wife: 'Du kennst ja die Dichtung von Wolfram von Eschenbach, daran darfst du aber nicht denken, es ist etwas ganz anderes, Unsagbares!' (Quoted Wapnewski, p. 200).

76 See A. C. Benson, *Rossetti*, London, 1920.

77 See *Letters of William Morris to Family and Friends,* (ed. Henderson), London, 1950, p. 61.

78 In Ernest Newman, *The Life of Richard Wagner*, Cambridge, 1976, p. 556. Francis Hueffer gives an interesting account of Wagner in Dannreuther's house at this time; he was 'the life and soul of a large and distinguished gathering, including, amongst others, George Eliot and Mr. G. H. Lewes. Madame Wagner, who speaks English perfectly, served as an interpreter, and her conversation with the great English novelist – who took a deep interest in music, although her appreciation of Wagner's music was of a very Platonic kind – was both friendly and animated. "Your husband", remarked George Eliot, with that straightforwardness which was so conspicuous and so lovable in her character, "does not like Jews, my husband is a Jew" ' (*Half a Century of Music in England, 1837–1887*, Philadelphia, Pa., 1889, p. 72). Robert Browning also met Wagner at this time.

79 Roy Pascal, *From Naturalism to Expressionism*, London, 1975, p. 194.

80 With the French as mythoclasts? See Harry Levin, 'Some meanings of myth', in *Daedalus*, spring 1959, p. 228.

81 Roy Pascal, *op. cit.*, p. 93.

82 See the letter written to the editor of *Common Sense* (January 1940), published in *Wagner und unsere Zeit* (ed. Erika Mann), Frankfurt, 1963.

83 Ernst Bertram, *Nietzsche*, Berlin, 1918, p. 6.

84 Walther Rathenau, *An Deutschlands Jugend*, Berlin, 1918, p. 83: 'Es ist kaum einzuschätzen, wie stark die letzte Generation vom Einfluß Richard Wagners gebannt war, und zwar nicht so entscheidend von seiner Musik wie von der Gebärde seiner Figuren, ja seiner Vorstellungen. Vielleicht ist dies nicht ganz richtig: Vielleicht war umgekehrt die Wagnersche Geberde der erfaßte Widerhall – er war ein ebenso großer Hörer wie Töner – des Zeitgefallens. Es ist leicht, eine Gebärde aufzurufen, schwer, sie zu benennen: sie war der Ausdruck einer Art von theatralisch-barbarischem Tugendpomp. Sie wirkt fort in Berliner Denkmälern und Bauten, in den Verkehrsformen und Kultur einzelner Kreise, und wird von vielen als eigentlich deutsch angesehen. Es ist immer jemand da, Lohengrin, Walther, Siegfried, Wotan, der alles kann und alles schlägt, die leidende Tugend erlöst, das Laster züchtigt und allgemeines Heil bringt, und zwar in einer weitausholenden Pose, mit Fanfarenklängen, Beleuchtungseffekt und Tableau. Ein Widerschein dieses Opernwesens zeigt sich in der Politik, selbst in Wortbildungen wie Nibelungentreue. Man wünschte, daß jedesmal von uns das erlösende Wort mit großer Geste gesprochen werde, man wünschte, historische Momente gestellt zu sehen, man wollte, das Schwert klingen und die Standarten rauschen hören . . .' It is also enlightening that the writer and critic Hermann Bahr should have felt moved, during a funeral ceremony organised by his student fraternity in Vienna in March 1883, to call Austria a 'schwerbüßende Kundry, die sehnsüchtig des Erlösers harrt' and to demand of his fellow students the pledge 'nicht eher zu ruhen und rasten, als bis Richard Wagners *heiliges Vermächtnis, der großdeutsche Gedanke, erfüllt sei*'. The authorities were displeased; Bahr was expelled and had to continue his studies in Graz. (See letter to his father, 13 March 1883, quoted in Zelinsky, *Richard Wagner, 1876–1976*, Frankfurt, 1976, p. 51.)

85 Walter Benjamin, *Illuminationen*, Frankfurt, 1961, p. 176.

86 Carl von Ossietzky, in *Die Weltbühne*, vol. 29, nr. 8, 21 February 1933: see *Schriften*, Berlin and Weimar, 1966, II, pp. 128–34: 'In Richard Wagners Werk flüchtet die bürgerliche Aera aus ihrer problemhaften Wirklichkeit in musikumbrausten Mythos . . . Richard Wagner wirkt fort, ein tönendes Gespenst, zu Zwecken beschworen, die mit Kunst nichts mehr zu tun haben, ein Opiat zur Vernebelung der Geister.' Ossietzky could not have known Wagner's statement from *Das braune Buch* (11 September 1865): 'Jetzt begreift mich kein Mensch: ich bin der deutscheste Mensch, *ich bin der deutsche Geist* . . .' (p. 86).

87 Quoted Fest, *Hitler, op. cit.*, p. 684: 'Einen unvereinbareren Gegensatz kann man sich überhaupt nicht denken! Dieses herrliche Mysterium des sterbenden Heros und dieser Judendreck . . .' A further example of the stylisation, or 'Dämonisierung', of the struggle is quoted by John White in *Mythology in the*

Modern Novel: on 20 April 1945, Goebbels referred to the war as a colossal drama: 'Was wir heute erleben, das ist der letzte Akt eines gewaltigen tragischen Dramas, das mit dem 1 August 1914 begann, und das wir Deutschen am 9ten November 1918 gerade in dem Augenblick unterbrachen, als es kurz vor der Entscheidung stand' (p. 154). See also E. H. Gombrich's *Myth and Reality in German War Time Broadcasts*, London, 1970.

88 Otto Weininger, *Geschlecht und Charakter*, 18th ed., Vienna and Leipzig, 1919, p. 434: 'Was dem echten Juden in alle Ewigkeit unzugänglich ist: *das unmittelbare Sein, das Gottesgnadentum, die Trompete, das Siegfriedmotiv, der Eichbaum, die Schöpfung seiner selbst, das Wort: ich bin!*'

89 Weininger, *op. cit.*, p. 404.

90 For a most perceptive study of Hermann Levi and his problematic relationship with Wagner see Peter Gay's *Freud, Jews and other Germans*, Oxford, 1979.

91 Weininger, *op. cit.*, p. 408: '... denn der echte Jude hat, wie das Weib, kein Ich und darum auch keinen Eigenwert.'

92 Tolstoy: *What is Art?* (trans. Aylmer Maude), Oxford, 1950, pp. 214–15.

93 Tolstoy, *op. cit.*, p. 216.

94 Téodor de Wyzewa insisted, however, that if Tolstoy, instead of only hearing 'massacrer à Moscou deux actes de *Siegfried*, avait pu entendre jouer *Parsifal* au théâtre de Bayreuth, peut-être se serait-il forcé de citer Wagner dans sa liste de quelques hommes qui ont tenté un art chrétien supérieur.' See the introduction to the French translation, *Qu'est-ce que l'art?*, Paris, 1898, p. xii.

95 Theodor Adorno, *Versuch über Wagner*, Munich and Zurich, 1964, p. 129: 'Nicht als bloße Metaphern hat Wagner die Mythen zitiert: unter seinem Blick wird alles mythologisch ...'

96 Quoted Adorno, *op. cit.*: 'Ich schreite kühn, hussa joho / mit langem Schritt aus dem Büro ...'

97 For a fictional example of conception after a Wagner performance see Robert Musil, *Der Mann ohne Eigenschaften* (1952 Frisé ed.), p. 713: 'Siegmund ... *ist im Wagner-Rausch gezeugt worden*' (Musil's italics). In actual life the *haute-couture* photographer Erwin Blumenfeld claimed that he was conceived at midnight on 5 May 1896 in Berlin in a carriage that was taking his parents home from the opera after they had just seen *Tristan und Isolde*. As regards the bestowal of Wagner names, the scale encompasses both Reinhard Tristan Heydrich at the one end and the popular veterinary surgeons of the Yorkshire Dales at the other.

98 Hermann Broch, *Dichten und Erkennen*, Essays, I, Zurich, 1955.

PARODY *and* PERSIFLAGE

4

I (*recovering myself with an effort*): Don't you know? Richard Wagner, the great breeder of short horns!
Mr Ryan: Begorra, 'tis strange I never came across him in Ballinasloe...

In the fourth of his *Thoughts out of Season*, written at a most crucial stage of his admiration for all that Wagner stood for, Nietzsche commented that the educated – or, rather, 'educated' – man of his day was only able to parody what he found in Wagner (ruefully adding 'as anything and everything had been parodied');[1] unable to grasp the greatness of Wagner's achievement the lesser spirits tended to vaunt their apparent sophistication and superiority by denigrating the Bayreuth adventure through mockery and cheap journalism. A few years after writing these words Nietzsche himself launched a coruscating attack on the Meister: as a free-thinker ('Freigeist'), even as a buffoon ('Hanswurst') the erstwhile professor of classical philology at Basle delighted in a witty process of deflation and castigation, an attack which, however, became increasingly shrill and querulous, losing much of its humour and betraying more than anything the strictures of a disappointed lover. A guilty conscience is apparent here, an awareness of having derogated and besmirched the former idol, friend and mentor, and Nietzche's mental collapse must be seen as resulting at least partly from an appreciation of Wagner's unique greatness and his own malicious contentiousness. The writers of parody and satire which this chapter will attempt to describe will be mercifully free from Nietzsche's obsessions: geographical and historical distance from *that* powerful egomaniac are essential for a cool, trenchant or jocular assessment of his *oeuvre*.

It would indeed be remarkable if a phenomenon such as Wagner had not called forth parodies, witticisms and caricatures as a refreshing counterblast to excessive Wagnerolatry. When Bayreuth became Montsalvat, when the Meister was elevated to a quasi-divine status (true, the Meister was but an instrument of a metaphysical cause, but to confuse instrument and essence was regarded as an understandable abberation not necessarily to be chastised), then the balance could be restored by regarding him as a 'breeder of short horns in Ballinasloe' (George Moore) as 'Herr Blagner', fond of intemperate diatribe and founder of 'Blagnerismus' (George du Maurier) or as 'St Wagner', at whose shrine Mark

Twain sat, watching a performance of *Parsifal* in which 'there is a hermit called Gurnemanz who stands on the stage in one spot and practises by the hour, while first one and then another character of the cast endures what he can of it and then retires to die'.[2] W. B. Yeats tells of a scholar who would denounce Wagner, then at the height of his popularity, insisting that 'I would rather run ten miles through a bog to escape him':[3] others preferred to stand their ground, cast a clear and sober eye at the tide of mounting gobbledegook and disperse the clouds of incense engendered by an all too fulsome panegyric. This chapter will provide a break from the description of portentous hagiography and will assess that process of debunking which is not only confined to the Anglo-Saxon or Anglo-Irish world, and which will be found in writers of merit as well as in the antics of the horror-comic transvestite Dragula who exclaims that 'Wagner does drain one so!'[4] and in Helmut Qualtinger's *Siggy und Bess oder Swing des Nibelungen*, subtitled 'A teutonic jazz-opera for orchestra plus five pistols'.[5]

The earliest Wagner parody of any substance is *Tannhäuser*, the so-called 'Joke of the future with music that is past it and present day arrangements in three acts' by the Viennese satirist Johann Nestroy, performed on 31 October 1857.[6] This was, in fact, based by Nestroy on a *Tannhäuser* parody by a certain Dr H. Wollheim from Breslau who had published his work three years earlier for a student fraternity. Dr Wollheim based his parody on student songs and flippant Wagner references: 'Heinrich Gottlieb Tannhäuser' is a debauched student from Jena who dallies in the Venusberg tavern, while Venus herself, 'née Schulze', is the 'goddess of love and proprietor of a Bavarian Bierkeller' ('Göttin der Liebe und Inhaberin eines bayerischen Bierkellers'). Other figures appear, for instance Walter von der Viehweide (a substitution of 'Vieh', meaning beast, or cattle, for 'Vogel', bird) who is, amongst other things, a 'Public piles officer' 'Staatshämorrhoidarius' – doubtless from sitting too long on his famous stone – and Wolfram von Dreschenbach ('dreschen' meaning to thrash).[7] Nestroy has condensed Dr Wollheim's parody somewhat and substituted Viennese references for other more local witticisms, but otherwise keeps very close to it: Tannhäuser and Venus are seen eating oysters and drinking champagne in the Venusberg (she is the proprietor of a subterranean 'delicatessen-Keller') and in animated mood our hero is heard to exclaim: 'And so we met – I was your shepherd true/O Venus, you are quite a cockatoo!'[8] Nestroy himself played the part of Landgrave Purzel ('Purzel' means somersault in German), the 'Caricature of a noble huntsman'; Elisabeth's song of greeting to the Hall is reduced to pathetic farce, and Tannhäuser's ecstatic outburst in praise of love becomes: 'Would you, like me, eat fortune by the ton/Go on then – swill and booze in Venusberg!'[9] The final act culminates in Tannhäuser's death ('he puts a nightcap on and expires');[10]

Frau Venus, however, restores both Tannhäuser and Elisabeth to life, and the work ends in general rejoicing. Nestroy — without Dr Wollheim's participation — attempted a *Lohengrin* in 1859 which turned out to be a resounding failure despite the antics of the 'Graugraf', the 'Hinundherrufer' (i.e. 'Heerrufer' or herald) and 'Elsa von Dragant'. This parody relied too much on the success of *Tannhäuser* and has few lines that are witty or even farcical: the most amusing episode is predictably Lohengrin's arrival, pulled by a lamb rather than a swan, whom the hero addresses as 'My lovely sheep' and whom he admonishes: 'Go home now, magic sleep for thee / Be good and patient, dear to me / As I have known no sheep to be . . .'[11] It is said that Wagner enjoyed the *Tannhäuser* parody, which he saw in Vienna; he presented the composer Karl Binder with a tie-pin 'für gutes Amüsement'. It was also in Vienna, in 1861, that Wagner met the dramatist Friedrich Hebbel who was unable to forgive Nestroy for the latter's parody of Hebbel's early play *Judith*, and during a conversation with Wagner which touched on Nestroy Hebbel roundly attacked the satirist, claiming that even a rose, were Nestroy to hold it beneath his nose, would stink hereafter. Whether Wagner concurred is not known, although he did repeat Hebbel's remark to Cosima some eight years later;[12] it should perhaps be noted that Wagner's own fragmentary *Lustspiel*, containing such grotesque characters as Barnabas Kühlewind (prompter), Kaspar Schreiblich (a degenerate student), David Bubes (a producer) and Napoleon Baldachin (the hero) has more than a fleeting similarity to Nestroy.[13]

Six years after the *Lohengrin* parody there appeared in the Schweigerisches Isartheater in Munich, on Tuesday 8 June 1865 a so-called *Tristanderl und Süßholde*, purporting to be a 'dramatic little thing with words without melody, a present-day parody on an opera of the future in three acts, in which all hell breaks loose, including a prelude to a prelude by Richard Waggonmaster and playsmith, as well as a musical dramatiser'.[14] This *Tristan* parody appeared two days before the actual performance of *Tristan und Isolde* in the Hoftheater and drew large crowds; the two authors, Ferdinand Fränkl and H. Rauchenecker, explained that 'The action takes place in primitive times and is at present prepared for anything — partly on land, partly on water, which explains why the text is partly too dry and partly too slippery. Libretti will not be on sale as the text is incomprehensible anyway. Only three performances are envisaged: if the public can stand it and the actors don't die we shall perhaps make other arrangements. For the present the price has been increased in order to make the work more valuable.'[15] (It is indeed tragically ironic that the authors should flippantly speculate upon the possible demise of the actors after such a work: Ludwig Schnorr von Carolsfeld, the original Tristan, died but three weeks after the fourth and final performance on 1

July). The reactions of the press, public and musicians to the opening night of Wagner's music drama have been well documented and are not relevant here; what is of interest is the reaction of a writer like Oskar Panizza (who, incidentally, spent the last years of his life in a mental home in Bayreuth) to the Munich Wagner fever. In 1891 he published his witty 'Pious Ejaculations from Bayreuth' in the journal *Die Gesellschaft*, and delighted in describing the effect of a *Tristan* performance on the audience in the Bavarian capital:

> During the première they rushed out of the theatre after the first act, some flushed with rage because of the insults done to their sense of hearing, and others, yawning widely, rushing into the nearest restaurant; acquaintances who met burst out laughing and spoke of Mozart 'turning in his grave' . . . But things soon took a different turn. If two or three hundred bars of the opera were repeated on the piano or in the concert hall there appeared on the listeners' faces – particularly the ladies' – expressions of solemn devotion, and glazed eyes; limbs stiffened, and all the symptoms of trance became apparent. They all sat like frogs who stared into the setting sun at evening time, oblivious to everything except that little source of light which hypnotised them, and only when the last chords died away did the dream-like state recede . . .[16]

Panizza also quoted a certain Dr. Moreau who insisted that Wagner's music should be banned and all copies of the score and the piano reductions of *Tristan* be destroyed; it should also be noted that Theodor Puschmann, pupil of Eduard Hanslick and lecturer in the history of medicine in the university of Vienna, did, in fact, in his *Richard Wagner, a psychiatric Study*, demand that Wagner be confined to a lunatic asylum. Further witticisms circulating in Munich enjoyed parodying the oddities of Wagner's language; the magazine *Punsch* contained the following conversation between two musicians, Maxl and Sepperl, on a possible rise in salary for having to play *Tristan und Isolde*: '*Maxl*: "Hey, for the *Tristan und Isolde* torment every court musician is going to get fifty dollars rise." *Sepperl*: "Oh! Bliss and shuddering ecstasy!" *Maxl*: "But we ain't got it yet." *Sepperl*: "Not yet? Not yet? Illustrious wish, oh wish beyond delusion!"'[17] The satirical journal *Simplicissimus* will later, in 1898, parody the excesses of *Stabreim* in a similar conversation – unfortunately untranslatable – between two musicians: 'Schabst du Schello, schäbiger Schuft? – Nein, ich goge die Gige, geifernder Gauch . . .',[18] a grotesque piece of repartee which might well have pleased the Meister who did, frequently to the dismay of his disciples, indulge in such absurdities himself.

Writers of the stature of Franz Grillparzer, Paul Heyse, Theodor Fontane and F. Th. Vischer continued the tone of mockery *vis-à-vis* the Wagner problem:

Grillparzer remembered that a Bavarian prince had once been bewitched by Agnes Bernauer, who had been drowned in the Danube for her sorcery, and suggested that if Richard Wagner were not thrown into the Isar, then at least a debtor's prison should be his destiny.[19] (It was also Grillparzer who had coined the name 'Lolo Montez, for Wagner, remembering the charms of the adventuress Lola Montez, whom King Ludwig I had been unable to resist.) In Paul Heyse's *Children of the World* (1873) Graf Gaston is portrayed as a decadent Wagnerian who finds in *Tristan und Isolde,* in its unresolved chromaticism, a unique example of the joys of unrequited love, of eternal longing; at the same time his groping and fumbling with the maidservants seem to betoken a less sublime eroticism. Heyse referred in a letter to Theodor Storm (21 October 1875) to the 'madness of the future with all its horrors' ('Zukuntftswahnsinn mit all seinem Greuel') which was rampant everywhere, and devised a motto to be inscribed on the wall of his house: 'Entrance forbidden to all Bayreuth-pilgrims' (Jedem Bayreuth-Pilger ist der Eintritt verboten').[20] In *L'Adultera* (1880) Theodor Fontane adopts a light, satirical tone when discussing 'der Ritter von Bayreuth'; Kommerzienrat van der Straaten cannot share his wife Melanie's enthusiasm for the new music and refers to Wagner as 'a sorcerer such as never was before. And you pledge your soul's bliss to this Tannhäuser-and-Venusberg man and sing and play him morning, noon and night. Or three times a day, as your pill-box prescribes . . .'[21] It was highly suspect to him, although at least it did give food for animated discussion with Herr Rubehn, who shared his wife's profound devotion. (It is also of interest here that Fontane makes von Innstetten, husband of the heroine of his best known novel *Effi Briest,* a convinced Wagnerian, despite his pedantry and emotional coldness.) In certain letters Fontane displays his usual urbanity when referring to Wagner, and on one occasion rejected wholeheartedly the 'dreadful mixture of drivel, nonsense, incomprehensibility and tastelessness' ('furchtbare Menge der Quasseleien, Albernheiten, Unverständlichkeiten und Geschmacksverirrungen') which Wagner had caused, as well as the total lack of humour associated with Bayreuth (to Karl Zöllner, 13 July 1891). A year before *L'Adultera* appeared Friedrich Theodor Vischer published his eccentric novel *Yet Another*, which contains a delightful Wagner parody; Vischer had, of course, in his *Aesthetics*, published twenty years previously, rejected any such notion as the Wagnerian *Gesamtkunstwerk* as 'modernistic over-excitability' leading to an 'overladen, fantastic theatricality'.[22] Professor at the Polytechnic High School in Zurich, Vischer had, like Gottfried Keller and Johanna Spyri, been a member of the Wagner–Wesendonck circle and had ample opportunity to study Wagner at close quarters. In *Yet Another* a manic druid speaks in rodomontade and bombast about his sublime trilogy, a work of mists and monsters. Sections from the work are performed, and the astonished audience listens to the following incantation: 'Send me, o misty one, / moonlighted twisty one! / send me the tickly / prickly / flickery / crackerly / crickerly / Evil to us! / O Selinur! / Pfisala, pfnisla / Pfeia!'[23] The *Rheingold* 'Wagalaweia' is lampooned here, and Vischer will similarly delight in debunking the Wagnerian *Stabreim* or alliterative technique. (It may indeed have been from Vischer's *Critical Studies* of 1844 that Wagner hit upon the idea of the *Ring*: Vischer's long essay 'Vorschlag zu einer Oper' adumbrates a new, national work of art based on the world of Germanic mythology, a five-act *Nibelungen* drama to be given on two successive evenings.)[24] The druid, invoking the fearful dragon Grippo, lashes singers and musicians into a frenzy of demented activity, and chants the following in an arcane incantation: 'But you, o Grippo! / Grim one and gripping, / Grunting old serpent / Dreadful old dragon! / All that is darkness / Dulling and damming / Pressing the brain down / When the dread Pfnüssel / Grasps us and girds us / Spare the good burgher . . . / Fire now shall flame! / Blood red and jagged / Beats from the bending / Burning great timbers! / . . . Griffolo, Griolo, Grio! / Gruffulu, Grugulu / Gruffu!'[25] The reactions of the audience are described as extreme, ranging from swooning, rage and epiletic fits; it is obvious that Vischer kept a cool and critical eye on 'der Fall Wagner', doubting not only the sincerity of the man but also remaining highly suspicious of the audiences who saw in his work a spiritual panacea.

'D'you know Richard Wagner?' asks the cavalry officer in *Children of the World*, before launching into a sardonic description; Eduard Hanslick, mercilessly lampooned by Wagner as Beckmesser in *Die Meistersinger*, wryly suggested that the Holy Ghost, should it descend in the form of a dove upon the twelve apostles in the modern era, would pose the inevitable question: 'Well, gentlemen, what do *you* think of Richard Wagner?'[26] In the face of the devotional excesses, or confronted by that sense of well-bred dread which the works of Wagner increasingly seemed to bring forth, many writers at the end of the century preferred a droll or satirical response: the Viennese journalist and critic Daniel Spitzer published his *Wagnerians in Love* in 1880 with its composer hero, maliciously called Goldschein, as the adored centre of a group of worshippers and acolytes. Spitzer delighted in portraying the satorial excesses of Goldschein who preferred the costume of sixteenth-century Nuremberg plus Dürer beret (an outfit not dissimilar to that adopted by Wilhelm Busch's Balduin Bärlamm when awaiting divine inspiration); his disciples address each other in overused superlatives and euphoric adjectives ('Highest, most wondrous of Women! Unfortunate woe-man! etc.).[27] Three years previously Spitzer had published some of the so-called 'Putzmacherin' letters (which apparently demonstrated Wagner's predilection for pink female underwear) in the *Neue Freie*

Presse, and an amusing caricature entitled 'Frou Frou Wagner' appeared in *Der Floh* in the June of that year showing Spitzer pricking Wagner, who was lost in the contemplation of silks and brocade, with his pen. Spitzer had also published in the *Neue Freie Presse* of 1877 a delicious *Walküre* review beginning with the words: 'Woe, what weeny welcome was to me, wandering Viennese wanderer, through Wagner's *Walküre* . . .' and ending with the statement: 'We find no other solution to this work except that brother and sister, music and drama, here consummated an incestuous marriage, whereby reason — that poor Hunding — had to fall silent for ever at the scornful gesture of Wotan-Wagner. The Wagnerians were really in transports of delight, and I was delighted too when I transported myself away.[28] A frequent source of amusement was the dichotomy between the overwrought sublimity of Wagner's heroes and heroines and humbler, often more domestic, realities; another Viennese, Peter Altenberg, in his collection of impressionistic sketches entitled *What the Day Brings* (1901) gives a witty description of a wife who casts herself in the role of Senta, longing to 'redeem' her husband who stands before her in his underwear, gargling; of a young man who returns in ecstasy from a performance of *Tristan* and finds his Isolde in the maid, and of a young lady whose raptures at a performance of *Die Walküre* are interrupted by her husband who solicitously offers her coffee-cream chocolates with nut centres.[29] Marital dissension caused by the impact of Wagner's music is humorously described by Robert Musil in his unfinished colossus *The Man without Qualities*: it is here the woman, Clarisse, who abominates the music of Wagner, referring scathingly to its steaming warmth, its thickly brewed consistency, its drug-like influence, and refuses to allow her husband his conjugal rights if he plays a note of it. 'And yet he played Wagner, with a bad conscience, as though it were a schoolboy vice'[30] in an effort to make his home a little less like Zarathustra's cave. More cynical is Frank Wedekind's conversation piece *The Court Singer* written in 1897: Gerardo, the ruthlessly determined Wagnerian *Heldentenor*, is idolised by his public, who see in him the epitome of Romantic idealism. He is, however, quite cold-blooded in his resistance to a love-sick girl, an aged professor and finally a cast-off mistress who shoots herself in his presence. Initial dismay gives way to a feeling of relief on Gerardo's part at the thought that her suicide attempt could only enhance his reputation and, letting the half-dead woman slip to the floor, he rushes from the room, his only comment being: 'I must sing Tristan in Brussels tomorrow evening!'[31]

'Wagner! Mankind's holiest treasure!'[32] The consumptive Mandelstam of Carl Sternheim's comedy *Knickers* (published in 1911) is an absurd figure who can only come to terms with the world through seeing it *sub specie Wagneri*: his furtive desires *vis-à-vis* Luise Maske are transfigured by references to Senta and the Flying Dutchman. The fact that Herr Mandelstam had been prostrate before Frau Maske on the street when her knickers fell about her ankles makes the quotations from *Der fliegende Holländer* grotesquely incongruous: the redemption for which Wagner's hero yearned seems promised in this play by a tantalising glimpse of female underwear. In Sternheim's play *Paul Schippel Esq.* the parallels between *Die Meistersinger von Nürnberg* and the singing contest are appropriate for the parodistic plot; earlier versions of this play contained direct Wagner quotes, and the goldsmith Hicketier is quite overtly referred to as 'Pogner'. The members of the men's vocal group are indeed ironic Mastersingers, and the ludicrous Krey would provide the Beckmesser; Thekla's remarks are close to Eva's, and the images of 'Kranz', 'Bild' and 'Sommeranfang' are used by Sternheim with deliberate parody in mind. As Wagner became an almost national obsession in Germany Sternheim and Heinrich Mann saw that the bourgeoisie above all, intoxicated and flushed by this music (see Chapter Three), seized eagerly upon Wagnerian histrionics and excesses to justify a desire for grandeur. Seven years after the publication of *Knickers*, in November 1918, Heinrich Mann's satirical novel *Man of Straw* circulated freely in Germany; as *Knickers* was meant to be part of a cycle of plays entitled 'From the heroic life of the middle classes', so *Man of Straw* was part of a 'Kaiserreich' trilogy. Both works cut through the pretensions of the bourgeoisie under Wilhelm II, and both used Wagner ironically to demonstrate the abject, furtive and vindictive qualities of certain types of character. In *Man of Straw* the obsequious and pusillanimous bully Diederich Hessling exults in the thundering brass and nationalist fervour of *Lohengrin*; seated in a red velvet upholstered box with his rotund fiancée Guste Daimchen, he feels that Wagner should be played to smite all Liberals, Jews and other degenerates, and cannot help joining in the singing: ' "Protect the honour of the Reich in East and West" – Bravo! As often as he sang these words he stretched out his hand, and the music emphasised it accordingly . . . Diederich wished he could have had such music during his debate on the municipal sewers . . .'[33] The couple in the box, exchanging amorous gropings and sticky chocolates, make fun of the singers; Guste spitefully reminds her betrothed that the blond singer of the role of Elsa was Semitic rather than Germanic, and both are amused at the woolly vest worn by Lohengrin. Hessling's ignorance is obviously lampooned by Mann, particularly his decision to send a telegram to Wagner to congratulate him on such a magnificent work (this approximately thirty years after Wagner's death), but the music itself, the pomp and majesty, the 'Shields and swords, much raucous brass, imperialist fervour, Ha! and Hail! and high-held banners'[34] is felt by the author to emanate from dubious sources and to appeal to questionable sentiments. This description of *Lohengrin* in *Man of Straw*, when juxtaposed with a reference to that opera from Thomas Mann's *Buddenbrooks* or *Little Herr Friedemann*, demonstrates quite clearly the different attitudes towards Wagner and Germany entertained by the two brothers at this time. Thomas Mann could, of course, criticise the shortcomings of a performance in a humorous manner (he had, for instance, described in *Blood of the Volsungs* the pink and chubby Siegmund, and the squat and manic Valkyries), but the music itself could never be ridiculed or rejected, not even during the later period of his ambiguous aversion to Wagner's art. It is, incidentally, with *Lohengrin* still running through his mind that Hessling utters what Heinrich Mann felt were his brother's cultural premises at the time of the First World War: Thomas Mann will, more charitably, put his brother's views into the mouth of an infinitely more agreeable character in *The Magic Mountain*.

Bertolt Brecht delighted in the expression 'Mein lieber Schwan', which he frequently used to ironic effect; the 'Ride of the Valkyries' is parodied in *Drums in the Night*, whilst music from *Tristan* is incongruously heard in *Baal*. Brecht and Wagner — apparently utterly disparate and scarcely to be contained within the same sentence, but united surely by their reforming zeal, by their absolute obsession with theatre and by their insistence upon a fusion of the epic and dramatic modes. In the Weimar Republic a far less reverential approach to Wagner was at least adumbrated, despite the Bayreuth pronouncement that 'Bayreuth is not there for certain hypermodern fashions — this would contradict the spirit of the Works, which are not composed in a cubist-expressionist-dadaistic style'.[35] A thinker as distinguished as Ernst Bloch demanded in his *Legacy of this Age* of 1929 the 'saving of Wagner by means of surrealistic colportage',[36] meaning by 'Kolportage' a technique derived from the penny dreadful, the fun fair and the circus (a 'Brechtian' approach, in fact); such a notion was, of course, entirely unacceptable after 1933. In the February of that year Carl von Ossietzky had the courage to publish his famous article, mentioned in Chapter Three, which attacked among other things Wagner's questionable spirituality in *Parsifal* (the 'brothel atmosphere and the music-hall ballet of the whores — the Klingsor-girls!')[37] as well as the much vaunted 'heroism' and 'sublimity' of Wagner's protagonists: 'these Tristans and Lohengrins with double chin and beer-belly, and on top of this these female singers with their flaxen wigs and their eyes rolling heavenwards, the heaving bosom and wobbling bum emphasised most effectively by a red-bordered primitive German nightdress . . .';[38] but Ossietzky was to pay with his life for these and other attacks upon sacred German institutions and upon that Leader who claimed that it was with a performance of *Rienzi* in Linz that his life's work had begun.[39] It was not until

after the Third Reich had come and gone that attempts were made to treat
Wagner flippantly in literature again, dispelling the incense that had since grown
sulphurous, and mocking with a healthy disrespect. The young Wolfgang
Borchert named him in the same breath as Max Schmeling and Shirley Temple in
The Man Outside (1947), and Günter Grass, in *The Tin Drum* (1959) gave a
droll description of a visit to the famous Zoppoter Waldoper, the so-called
'Bayreuth of the North', at which a performance of *Der fliegende Holländer* was
given. (Grass is strictly speaking incorrect here: his opera ostensibly takes place in
1935, the year when *Tannhäuser* was given at Zoppot, whereas *Der fliegende
Holländer* was not performed there until 1939.) In *Dog Years* (1963) there are
references to Wagner in the Open Forum section where, predictably, excerpts
from *Götterdämmerung* are played, at which Hitler's dog howls mournfully,
before licking a portrait of the Führer. Wagner's love for large Newfoundland
dogs is referred to in a mock serious manner in Arno Schmidt's gigantic *Zettel's
Dream* where Siegfried the voyeur (with Tarnhelm) is also found, as is the
scatological pun on *Götterdämmerung*, translated as 'The Toilet of the Guts'[40] – a
far cry indeed from the virtual deification of Wagner not forty years before and
comparable only to the 'gluttergloomering' and 'Wankyrious thoughts' of
Finnegans Wake.[41]

Satirical writing in England has not, quite naturally, had to contend with the
excesses of Wagneroltry at such close quarters: the political dimension is
mercifully lacking, and a country suspicious of radical solutions and of
mythomania has not suffered the obfuscation in its intellectual life caused by an
addiction to the necromancy of old Klingsor. Well might Wagner have claimed in
an imperious moment that his baton was the sceptre of the future (see the end of
Chapter One): Anglo-Saxon irreverence and a welcome awareness of the absurd
insisted on a mocking counterpoint. Fortunately the fanaticism of David Irvine
(see Chapter Three, note 66), an acolyte who confessed himself infused 'like all
Wagnerians with a desire to carry on the Wagner mission among the slums and
back-ways of the East-end of intelligence,[42] is rare, even among the circle around
The Meister; the reaction in London was far less pious than in Paris and many of
the major German cities. After hearing a performance of *Die Meistersinger* during
the 1882 season John Ruskin was by no means impressed by what he had seen,
and his letter to Lady Burne-Jones is worth quoting at length:

> Of all the bête, clumsy, blundering, boggling, baboon-blooded stuff I ever saw on
> a human stage, that thing last night beat – as far as the story and acting went; and
> of all the affected, sapless, soulless, beginningless, endless, topless, bottomless,
> topsterviest, tuneless, scrannelpipiest, tongs and boniest doggerel of sounds I ever

endured the deadliest of, that eternity of nothing was the deadliest, as the sound went. I was never so relieved . . . in my life, by the stopping of any sound – not excepting railway whistles – as I was by the cessation of the cobbler's bellowing; even the serenader's caricatured twangle was a rest after it. As for the great 'Lied', I never made out where it began or where it ended – except by the fellow's coming off the horse-block . . .[43]

One is reminded of Mark Twain's comment concerning the *longueurs* of *Parsifal* quoted at the beginning of this chapter, also his comment that, although the orchestral playing was exquisite (something that Ruskin could not admire) there came the singing, 'and it does seem to me that nothing can make a Wagner opera absolutely perfect and satisfactory to the untutored ear than to leave out the vocal parts'. Told by the experts that one should not expect 'singing' in a Wagner opera, and that runs, trills and 'Schnorkel' [*sic*] had been discarded, Mark Twain could only remark: 'I don't know what a *schnorkel* is, but now I know it has been left out of these operas I have never missed it so much in all my life.'[44]

Parsifal, the 'Stage Dedication Festival Play' ('Bühnenweihfestspiel', or 'Bühnenwehfestspiel' as Fritz Mauthner suggested in his *Ahasuerus Unknown, or the Thing in itself as Will and Idea*), was first performed in London at Covent Garden in February 1914; in the same year R. C. Trevelyan's *The New Parsifal* made mock of the work by having a certain Percival Smith arrive by aeroplane and attempt to buy the grail for a reasonable sum of money. Smith ('Of the Aero-club and the Travellers' too / You'll find all about me in *Who's Who* . . .')[45] indulges in various absurd adventures and at one point 'de-Wagnerises' himself by jettisoning a miniature score of *Parsifal*, much to the disgust of Wagner, who emerges from an abyss, wrestles with Nietzsche and finally manages to seize the grail before returning to the depths. Percival Smith makes the best of a bad job in true Anglo-Saxon fashion and phlegmatically takes off in his aeroplane for London and the Club. Such flippancy would have been anathema to those authors discussed in Chapter Two, but Beardsley *had* indulged in delightful nonsense in *Under the Hill*, and E. F. Benson's *The Rubicon*, although sincere in the appreciation of the magnetic power of *Tannhäuser*, does adopt a tone of badinage with Lady Eva's advice to Reggie: 'Well, Venusberg is not at all the place for a good young man. There is no propriety of any sort observed there, and they are very lax about etiquette and other things. Never go to Venusberg, Reggie . . . It is said to be very unsettling.'[46] It is doubtless a concert performance of *Tannhäuser*, or possibly *Tristan* or *Parsifal*, that 'one with a fat, wide, hairless face' is watching in Rupert Brooke's poem 'Wagner', written in the Queen's Hall, 1908; the effect of the music is hardly sublime upon one whose 'pendulous stomach hangs a-shaking', who 'heaves from his stomach wheezy sighs', and whose 'little lips are bright with slime.'[47] E. M. Forster's indebtedness to Wagner has been discussed elsewhere, but the obvious humour should also not be overlooked in drawing an incongruous parallel between Wagner's Rhinemaidens and the scene where 'Three gentlemen rotated in the pool breast high, after the fashion of the nymphs in *Götterdämmerung* . . .';[48] the Reverend Beebe particularly seems a most unlikely Undine. Further debunking of *Tannhäuser* is found in Ford Madox Ford's *No More Parades* of 1925, where the daunting Sylvia Tietjens tracks down her husband in Flanders, ironically humming Venusberg music as she delighted in reminding him of the questionable code of morals associated with the barracks of the Queen Mary's Auxiliary Armed Corps. 'Isn't it queer that Venus should be your own? . . . Think of poor Elizabeth!'[49] suggests Sylvia in a tone of undeniable mockery. (As we know, Ford Madox Ford's father was Dr Francis Hueffer, who had contributed much to London musical life by his rather earnest articles on modern music, and who was rewarded by that playful limerick written by W. B. Scott: 'There's a solid fat German called Hueffer / Who at anything funny's a duffer: / To proclaim Schopenhauer / From the top of a tower / Will be the last effort of Hueffer.')[50] In more recent times Anthony Powell's *Venusberg* (1932) provides another faint echo of the Master's music (the names Ortrud and Flosshilde, the ironic Baedeker report on Tannhäuser's dalliance, for example), a further exemplification that myth — and Wagner's *oeuvre* is manifestly myth-creating — is to be adapted to fit modern requirements, a notion expounded at length by the character 'Rheingold' in Alberto Moravia's *Il disprezzo*, translated into English as *A Ghost at Noon* in 1964.

George Moore, most devoted of Irish Wagnerians, made that humorous comment inserted at the beginning of this chapter: amazed that a certain Mr Ryan had not recognised a picture of Wagner which stood on a table at their club, Moore had suggested to the peccant miscreant that the composer was a famous cattle breeder.[51] Moore's great biography *Hail and Farewell* contains a splendid account of a visit to Bayreuth where he was warmly received by Cosima and Siegfried Wagner, and *Evelyn Innes*, as Chapter Two has described, is full of the presence of the Master. (The description of the visit to Bayreuth given in *Ave* also contains a diverting account of a search for a clean lavatory; Moore also describes how 'uncouth women, round in the back as wash-tubs, walked about with frying pans in their hands, great udders floating under blue blouses; and we followed a trail of inferior German cookery up a black slimy staircase . . .')[52] Moore's Irish wit precluded undue and unquestioning adulation; the thought of Wagner as a cattle breeder in Ballinasloe is a ludicrous one, and it is probably with tongue in cheek that Moore compares Piccadilly Circus to Klingsor's magic garden: 'Here, too, are flower maidens, patchuli, jasmine, violet ... The Circus in a sultry summer night under a full moon is very like Klingsor's garden. Come, if you be not Parsifal ...'[53] The siren call certainly tempted Moore, but Yeats was tone deaf, and what of Shaw? Shaw's Wagnerism is a curious phenomenon, and it may seem perverse to discuss it in this chapter. Yet the writer who was observed in the Reading Room of the British Museum 'studying alternately – if not simultaneously – Karl Marx's *Das Kapital* (in French) and an orchestral score of *Tristan und Isolde*'[54] must have had a somewhat quizzical – even quixotic – attitude to Wagner, whose emphasis on heroic myth and Celtic–Germanic legend must have meant very little to him. Shaw had collaborated with William Archer on a play which was to contain a garden scene on the banks of the Rhine, with a capitalist villain, tainted gold and finally a grand gesture of throwing the precious metal back into the river, but little came of it, and Archer quickly extricated himself; the play, in fact, became Shaw's *Widower's Houses*, with the opening scene set in a garden restaurant in Remagen. When Corno di Bassetto first visited Bayreuth he was amused to perceive that 'the chief feature of the Wagner district is a great lunatic asylum'[55] (presumably the one in which Oskar Panizza was to spend the last years of his life); he also outraged pious disciples by objecting to the singer of the part of Gurnemanz, claiming that he howled like a wolf, and astounded the conductor Hermann Levi by offering to sing the part himself. *The Perfect Wagnerite* (1898) seems more intent on proving Wagner was a Shavian and delights in mock-serious descriptions of Alberich ('such dwarfs are common in London'), the gloomy mine ('with ... plenty of clergymen shareholders') and the Tarnhelm ('This helmet is a very common article in our streets, where it generally takes the form of a tall hat').[56] His Fabianism is of no concern here, but it is appropriate that only Siegfried, a destroyer of the old, could have any meaning for him; William Blissett is entirely correct in his statement that 'Wagner is, at least half the time, a poet of the night; with Shaw it is always daylight, and that is why, of all the Wagnerian figures, the solar-hero Siegfried alone shines through his pages'.[57] Shaw admitted that he had cribbed the dying words of Louis Dubedat in *The Doctor's Dilemma* from Wagner's story *Death in Paris* which was quoted at the beginning of this book, although Shaw's death scene is hardly treated with a straight face. The interminable discussion in act three of *Man and Superman* between the statue and the devil relegates the 'German-Polish madman Nietzsche' to heaven: he was 'in a huff' after quarrelling with Wagner over the Life Force and after being castigated by the latter as being a Jew. Passing reference is also made to the *Ring* in the preface to *Back to Methuselah*, and the introduction to *Heartbreak House* cannot help but toy with the thought of the amusing reaction of those horsey and healthy ladies of the English equestrian upper classes at suddenly finding themselves transported to Klingsor's garden.[58] (This play, incidentally, has – perhaps contrary to Shaw's intentions – an almost *Tristan*-like atmosphere in that scene where the Hushabyes await the ending of all things in a sense of almost voluptuous languour.) But ultimately Shaw took very little from Wagner: the hectoring speaker from the Fabian platform must have found the Festspielhaus an infuriaing establishment, worthy of mockery and objurgation rather than sycophancy.

A fantastic and frequently overlooked pendant to Shaw's *The Perfect Wagnerite* is the romantic novel *Prince Hagen* by Upton Sinclair, written in 1901, dramatised for publication at a San Francisco Theatre in 1909, rewritten for private publication and finally re-issued in *Plays of Protest* in 1912. Sinclair was probably familiar with Shaw's interpretation, and his own enthusiasm for Wagner led him to create his own work of fantasy which, in the words of Dennis Welland, is 'an indictment of American business and American society but . . . closer to Grimm than to Marx'.[59] The poet Gerald Isman, camping in a Quebec forest, happens to play the Nibelung-theme on his violin, whereupon the smith Mime appears and conducts him to Nibelheim, by means of a spectacular transformation scene, accompanied by the appropriate music from *Das Rheingold*. Isman agrees to take the unruly 'Prince Hagen' (Sinclair's knowledge of Wagner would seem to be faulty here) back to the modern world, to a good school above all where he might learn better manners and Christian principles. In the second act of the dramatised version Prince Hagen has dropped out of school, but a Tammany Hall orator called Steve O'Hagen has appeared, preaching revolution and destruction: this is Prince Hagen incognito, who is using the Nibelung gold to defeat the affluent, industrial society on its own terms. O'Hagen is unscrupulous and virile, lusting for Gerald's sister Estelle: he acquires the techniques of the capitalists he condemns and believes that wealth will buy Estelle's affections, much as Alberich purchases sexual gratification in Wagner's story. Potential tragedy is avoided by a bill passed through Congress which confiscates Prince Hagen's property: Hagen asks Gerald to play the Wagner theme, whereupon another transformation theme unites him with the Nibelungs. Confused and dramatically weak the play certainly is, but it is an amusing reminder of Upton Sinclair's tendency to admit of fantasy at this stage of his writing and to deal with Shavian situations with Wagner very much in mind.

James Joyce's indebtedness to Wagnerian patterns was touched upon in Chapter Three: here the more ironic references should be noted. Joyce knew his Wagner well, possessing copies of the works (a letter of 29 January 1903 to his mother expresses his need to consult them): he also insisted on attending performances and concerts containing excerpts from Wagner when in Italy, listening, as did Thomas Mann at almost the same time, to recitals in the Piazza Colonna in Rome. Joyce's impish and pungent sense of humour precluded effusions of enthusiastic rapture, and an amusing letter to his brother Stanislaus gives a good example of Joyce's satirical tone:

> I went to the *Dusk of the Gods*. Beside me in the gallery was an elderly man who smelt of garlic. He said it was a colossal opera and that it required great voices. He had heard it in Hamburg. He spoke a few words to me in English, such as, very cold, very good and beautiful. Before me was another man who said that Wagner's music was splendid, but intended only for Germans. It was all intellect: no heart. Every time the horn motive sounded my garlicy friend twisted to me and said confidently: *Adesso viene Sigfrido*. He yawned much during the third act and went away before the last scene. When Brünnhilde brought on the horse, the latter, being unable to sing, evacuated; whereat the funny Italian disyllable flew from end to end of the gallery. There were many spectators who followed the opera with scores and librettos. On the stairs coming away and in the street I heard many people hum correctly and incorrectly the nine notes of the funeral motive. Nothing in the opera moved me. I have heard the funeral march often before. Only when Siegfried dies I responded from the crown of my head to his cry '*O sposa sacra*'. I suppose there are a few men from time to time who really feel an impulse towards Gawd.[60]

Despite his reservations (and yet Siegfried's dying words obviously moved him deeply) Joyce did, as DiGaetani points out,[61] go to another performance some two weeks later (on 1 March 1907); delight in debunking is accompanied by an interest in Wagner, particularly in the Wagnerian resurrection of myth, which the later author of *Ulysses* and *Finnegans Wake* would consider to be unquestionably valuable. 'A painful case', one of the *Dubliners*, a collection finished in 1905, parodistically sites the sterile relationship between Mr Duffy and Mrs Sinico in Chapelizod, the legendary home of Isolde (the 'Chapel d'Iseult'); in *A Portrait of the Artist as a Young Man* the bird-call from Siegfried is ironically used to warn Stephen of the dangers of listening to the blandishments of Cranly, the consequences of which would be spiritual death for him.[62]

Stephen's cane, the 'ashplant' provides a mock heroic motif (for Wotan's spear was cut from the *Weltesche*) which links the earlier work with *Ulysses*: our hero — no Wotan he — flaunts his cane as the 'ash-sword' and, with the famous cry of 'Nothung!' shatters the chandelier in Bella Cohen's brothel. The ironical references to the blood-brotherhood oath from *Götterdämmerung* should also be noted here: Stephen 'extends his hand to her [the prostitute] smiling and chants the air of the blood-oath from the *Dusk of the Gods*: "Hangende Hunger, / Fragende Frau, / Macht uns alle kaput . . ."[63] The absurdity of the situation is apparent: a brothel is hardly the place for the swearing of such an oath and the words, meaningless in themselves, betoken Stephen's befuddled condition. The Wagnerian references tend to deflate our hero's pretentiousness: Wotan as Wanderer frequently strikes the ground with his spear, whereupon thunder growls, but all Stephen can do is damage the light-fittings in a Dublin whorehouse. The antics of modern man seem derisory indeed when compared with mythical archetypes, and Joyce derives obvious humour from the parallel. Bloom also alludes to the Flying Dutchman legend, a gloomy parallel to the wanderings of Ulysses, but the chapter which is manifestly 'musical' and mock-Wagnerian is the so-called 'Sirens' episode. Joyce slyly suggested that the chapter had a specifically fugual structure, and that there was also a quintet which derived from that famous one in act three of *Die Meistersinger*,[64] but a parallel to *Das Rheingold* would seem to be more in keeping. A comprehensive analysis is given in DiGaetani's book; here a few salient points must suffice.

The scene is the Ormond Bar, but the constant references to water and gold, and teasing and laughing, are surely not fortuitous. The opening section is an enumeration of themes to come, among which we read of 'Bronze by gold . . . and gold flushed more . . . gold pinnacled hair . . . the morn is breaking . . . boomed crashing chords . . . low in the dark middle earth . . . embedded ore . . . he gnashed in fury . . . by bronze, by gold, in ocean-green of shadow . . . where gold from afar? . . .' The entry of Bloom into the Ormond Bar will be as if Alberich had appeared in the waters; when the themes are finished the author writes 'Done. Begin!'[65] and the narrative elucidation commences. The two barmaids, Miss Douce and Miss Kennedy (the latter has just returned from the sea with a large sea-shell), with bronze and golden hair respectively, delight in teasing the inmates of the bar, 'in a giggling peal . . . freely their laughter . . . high piercing notes . . .'. Bloom is particularly at risk: 'O greasy eyes! Imagine being married to a man like that . . . With his bit of a beard!' — words which are very similar to Flosshilde's mocking appraisal of Alberich's tousled beard and prickly hair.[66] The mockery of other customers is also a reminder of the Rhinemaidens' later teasing of Siegfried in *Götterdämmerung* whose wife, they claim, may beat him: Undine-like the two barmaids preside over the aquamarine gloom of the Ormond Bar, Miss Douce and Miss Kennedy; 'they pined in depth of ocean shadow . . .', amongst the green bottles, golden whiskey and Bloom as the obvious outsider. The association of woman and water, so frequently found in *Ulysses*, here receives amusing treatment: this book is a comic masterpiece whatever else it may be, and the humorous Wagner-patterns do much to assure its effectiveness in this respect. A deflation of the Wagner cult of the contributors to the *Revue Wagnérienne* may also have prompted Joyce here although, as chapter one explained, he did admire Edouard Dujardin and made the latter's use of the leitmotif his model.

Woman and water, and a comic use of leitmotif and mythical structures are found above all in *Finnegans Wake*, where there are numerous references to Wagner (although more esoteric, distorted and teasing) as well as frequently ludicrous puns on both Wagner's name and on the names of his heroes. 'And I suppose you heard I had a wag on my ears?' The 'wagoner' is found in the company of 'headygabblers, gaingangers and . . . pullers off societies', recalling the giant presences of Ibsen and Wagner at the turn of the century, and for Joyce's own beginnings; the 'wagoner' is again referred to with his 'mudheeldy wheesindonck at their trist in Parisise after tourments of tosend years . . .' What Mathilde Wesendonck would have thought of this remarkable transposition of her name defies speculation: another lady, Mildew Lisa, derives her name from the beginning of Isolde's *Liebestod* ('Mild und leise . . .'). The Mark–Tristan–Isolde triangle moves in and out of identity with the Finn–Dermot–Grania/Arthur–Launcelot–Guinevere/Captain O'Shea–Parnell–Kitty O'Shea pattern: Tristan miraculously appears as the 'attawonder Wehpen, luftcat revol, fairescapading in his natsirt'. The Flying Dutchman is also present in the references to 'sentas, eric' and the 'bugganeering wanderducken' who is, here, redeemed by Senta in a particularly down-to-earth fashion. Parsifal is more difficult to find in the text, but he is also present, as is the redoubtable Miss Weston: 'I was parcifal of my subject', we are told (and there are many such puns, 'purseyfold', 'peacifold', 'pierceful' etc.), and the 'Westend Woman', together with the 'west in quest' adventure surely hints at her presence.[67] *A propos* the pun on Wagner's name ('Wagoner'): Wagner himself was well aware of this and, in his more exalted moments, used a depiction of Ursa Major (sometimes called 'Charles's Wain') as his family crest: disciples would later portray Ursa Major as a hammer, with the composer wielding it to smite the disbelievers.[68] Wagner's own sense of humour is frequently overlooked: Thomas Mann found it difficult to believe that the writer of *Parsifal* could have mockingly designated himself as 'Oberkirchenrat' ('high church dignitary') when sending a copy of the work to Nietzsche. His *pièce d'occasion*, the satirical *Eine Kapitulation* of November 1870, although rejected by Newman as a 'tactless, witless farce, the loutish Teutonic humours of which are ungraced by a single touch of literary finesse',[69] is not simply a vicious and boorish portrayal of the sufferings of the Parisians at the hands of the Prussians; it should be remembered that the capitulation of Paris had not taken place when this 'comedy in the antique manner' was written. It describes, rather, the surrender of German art before the blandishments of French opera and demonstrates Wagner's curiously ambiguous attitude towards that city: although Victor Hugo and Offenbach are lampooned, a stage direction describes the various European ambassadors, together with the directors of the larger German court theatres, joining in a general gallop which hints at the victory of French culture. (The ballet consisting of rats from the sewers who have changed into the ladies of the *corps de ballet* in the scantiest of clothing, directed by Offenbach himself, would not be out of place in the Night-town extravaganza of *Ulysses*.)

Chapter One described the enormous impact made by Wagner's music on French symbolism; it has been claimed by many that the Wagnerian revolution took its roots not in Germany but in France, where at least three generations of French writers and artists were able to absorb and transform the Wagnerian ethos.[70] The *petite musique* of the Second Empire was completely crushed beneath the tidal wave, yet the land of *esprit*, although amazed at the Wagnerian eruption, was not slow to mock and castigate. After Wagner left Paris in 1842 pieces of his work became known in the concert hall and disputes arose between admirers and detractors: the influential Belgian critic François-Joseph Fétis compared Wagner to Max Stirner, the exponent of uncompromising individualism (and another son of Bayreuth), and insisted on claiming that Wagner believed himself to be a god, a deity who worshipped himself as the *fons et origo* of all existence. In September 1859 Wagner returned to Paris, astounded that a customs official at the Gare du Nord should be able to hum a melody from *Tannhäuser* upon learning the identity of the traveller; believing that this functionary was of humble status, Wagner rejoiced that his work had penetrated the consciousness of even the lower orders, and was a little discomposed to learn that the official was, in fact, one Edmund Roche, himself a musician and poet as well as a civil servant in customs and excise.[71] Roche was the first French translator of *Tannhäuser*, and it was the scandal surrounding that work which gave the caricaturists ample scope to display their talents. An amusing *Tannhäuser* parody appeared in the *Journal Amusant* on 13 April 1861 under the title *Le Tanne-aux-airs par Monsieur Vagues-Nerfs* by Michel Noël; a similar parody, *La Tanne aux airs* by Clairville-Barbier, was staged in the Théâtre Dejazet, and *Yameinherr*, by Thibonet and Delacourt, was given in the Variétés, together with Victor Chéris's *Kakophonie der Zukunft*, a work for harps, voices and performing dogs. ('La tanne' in French has the meaning of 'spot' or 'blackhead'; in Germany the most popular pun was 'Tannhäuser — dann heiser,' 'heiser' meaning 'hoarse'.) It was the concept of the 'music of the future' which was the butt of many jokes and cartoons: Wagnerian megalomania, Teutonic nimiety and raucous cacophony were indistinguishable to the Parisian wits who generally exulted at the success of the Jockey Club in forcing Wagner to have *Tannhäuser* withdrawn after only three performances. Yet the claque which booed in 1861 was also booing the Empire, for the work was ordered by Napoleon III at the request of Princess Metternich; the Pasdeloup production of *Rienzi* in 1869 was applauded, for to support Wagner then was a sign of daring modernity. It was also this performance of *Rienzi* which inspired that famous cartoon by André Gill in *L'Eclipse* (18 April 1869) where a demented Wagner, hammer in hand, drives a crotchet with fearful force through an ear-drum.

The Franco-Prussian war and Wagner's virulent francophobia (although, as has been stated, *Eine Kapitulation* refers to the capitulation of German audiences before the frivolity of the French) called forth demands that Wagner's work should be removed from all state-subsidised theatres and a plethora of attacks in the journals and newspapers on Wagnerian 'belligerence'.[72] In 1876 Wagner was portrayed by Henri Meyer in the *Sifflet* capering upon a Prussian spiked helmet bearing the inscription 'Théâtre de Charenton-Bayreuth' (Charenton being a famous lunatic asylum), and when Pasdeloup attempted, in the winter of that year, to perform excerpts from *Götterdämmerung* the uproar was such that even the overture to Weber's *Der Freischütz*, mistakenly believed to be by Wagner, was howled down in execration. The patriots fought bitterly to prevent *Lohengrin* being performed in the Opéra while the symbolists, as we know, saw in Wagner the thaumaturgic composer of ravishing harmonies. Yet before the *Revue Wagnérienne*, in 1881, Catulle Mendès could not refrain from a portrayal of 'Hans Hammer' which does verge upon caricature. Catulle Mendès had been a member of that circle of literary figures which had supported Wagner's art in the Paris concerts of 1860: he had visited Wagner in Tribschen in 1869 together with his wife Judith Gautier (who would have a brief but passionate affair with Wagner in 1876), and also after the Munich performances of *Das Rheingold* and *Die Walküre* in 1870. *Le Roi vierge* was referred to in Chapter Two: here the portrayal of Hans Hammer is of interest. Travelling in mufti the young Prince Frederick of Thuringia spends the night at an inn at Oberammergau and encounters a cosmopolitan group of people including 'l'abbé Glinck' (Liszt), certain ladies including 'Madame Dzalergy' and the 'countess Loukhanof' (i.e. Princess Marie von Kalergis-Mouchanoff) and a 'Gräfin Sternistz' (i.e. Schleinitz). About to retire for the night, Frederick hears the breaking of crockery and turns to observe the perpetrator of this mischief: 'Frederick turned his head and saw one of the company standing, his fists clenched, his face contorted, his cheeks deeply etched with rage like water ruffled by the wind — whilst the wreckage of a pile of plates was scattered all over the table or rolling across the floor up to the skirting board . . .'[73] It is Hans Hammer who is described here, frenetic musician whose work the young prince adores, a man who was 'small, thin, tightly clothed in a long maroon frock-coat, and his frail, yet certainly robust body – which seemed to be tightly packed with springs – trembled convulsively like that of a hysterical woman; but his face, when it was not distorted with rage, could bear a magnificent expression, an expression of pride and serenity.'[74] The grimace of anger does, however, triumph, and Hans Hammer rages against the imbecilities of those around him: 'But music, music is the true German art! The English have Shakespeare, France has Victor Hugo, and Germany has Sebastian Bach, Beethoven and me!'[75] Despairing of the German princes, Hans Hammer praises the acumen of the Emperor of Brazil, one of his fervent admirers, and threatens emigration: Frederick later calls him to Nonnenburg, where he may worship and adore. The raving musician in Catulle Mendès's novel does seem to step from one of the caricatures already mentioned, the *fortissimo vivacissimo* leading to a *finale furioso*.

The year 1891 saw the final rout of the chauvinists with a triumphant performance of *Lohengrin* in the Opéra: the Folies Bergères delighted audiences at same time with a parody entitled *L'Oie en crin* ('The horse-hair goose'). *Parsifal*, of course, was only performed at Bayreuth, and a pilgrimage was necessary to experience this offering. In 1896 Colette visited the temple and, in *Claudine s'en va* (1903) her disenchantment with the town is humorously portrayed. (Her husband, Henri Gauthier-Villars – or Willy – was a fervent admirer of Wagner and remained so even during the first World War.) The narrator, Annie, experiences no religious epiphany at Bayreuth but a fine and dirty drizzle which soils her clothes; she is amazed at the vulgarities of the trinkets sold to tourists and by the general tastelessness of the visitors themselves. Claudine, however, is irrepressible and will not be deterred; meeting Annie at the railway station she brandishes with glee a smoking sausage: 'But Claudine, dishevelled, her boater over one ear, did make me smile when she brandished beneath my nose in the Station square a steaming sausage which she held in her bare hands . . .'[76] Claudine delights in this 'Wagnerwurst' and was amused by the 'sort of postman who had hot sausages in his box of cuir bouilli which he fished out with a fork as if they were snakes'.[77] English ladies, shrieking and eating enormous platefuls of greasy food after *Parsifal*, 'their hats ill adjusted, their admirable hair tied in a disgraceful pleat'[78] do not help to redeem the general banality (Mrs Dalloway was obviously not one of these), and Annie wishes that she were anywhere but in this provincial German town. The Festspielhaus, resembling nothing so much as a gasometer, Annie records, has 'the smell of burned rubber and of damp cellars';[79] the performance of *Das Rheingold* is damned by the blasé Parisians for its lack of intervals, absolutely indispensable in their view for seeing other people and for being seen by them, and the only reaction to *Parsifal* is the objection by an ageing actress that Kundry has the effrontery to flaunt a head-band which she herself had made fashionable some years before. Annie bribes the doorman and achieves her freedom (in a manner not dissimilar to the actual experience recorded by Fontane, who found the smell of damp clothing, the claustrophobic darkness and the general fervour quite intolerable and, feigning faintness, groped past forty devout and disapproving disciples for the door); she returns to her hotel to witness a furtive *affaire*, an ironic counterpoint to the mythical sexual encounters enacted upon the Wagnerian stage. Colette's estrangement from Willy may well have led her to view Bayreuth with cynical eye, but Annie's reservations could certainly have been shared by many a visitor who was not prepared to forgo critical discernment.

The juxtaposition of Valkyrie-like German ladies of ample girth and the slender, sophisticated daughters of France became a common and rather trivial theme at the turn of the century; Barrès's *Au service de l'Allemagne* contains such a contrast, and *Colette Baudoche* elaborates the theme of the beer-swilling German torn between pumpernickel and *Parsifal*.[80] Far more interesting, however, are the reservations felt by Paul Claudel, whose mythomania *à la* Wagner was discussed in Chapter Three. Claudel admitted his enormous indebtedness to Wagner, the Meister, but was also aware of the less sublime moments. The *Rêverie d'un poëte français* speaks of communion and dedication, but 'A gauche' also knows of asphyxiating boredom, interestingly enough at a performance of *Die Meistersinger*: 'The chats between the cobbler and Evchen nearly made me die. We were weeping with exhaustion. And when we had the village fête with these good burghers in their jerkins the colour of red-currants and those pregnant women in orange skirts ... we fled!'[81] 'A droite' must agree that Germanic heroines look vastly pregnant, but charitably suggests that this was the fashion of the times rather than anything specifically Wagnerian: 'It is impossible to understand Wotan and the Valkyries if one does not recall those large women with opulent orbs (the fashion of those days) and these powerful industrialists with blond beards, drinking coffee in a conservatory.'[82] 'A droite' is amused at the thought of Wagner after a *Tristan* performance in Vienna appearing 'very small and thin between two enormous women, wearing his velvet beret and looking just like Mr Punch'[83] (Claudel had earlier, in a letter to Suarès of 16 October 1913, referred to Isolde as an 'eiderdown' into which Tristan could sink), and 'A gauche' replies: 'There was something of the goblin in Wagner, and of the Nibelung, not only of the musician but also of a malicious dwarf.'[84] Further flippancy is detected in a comment of 'A droite' that German inventiveness could doubtless make sausages out of the body of Brünnhilde's horse Grane which would be carried down the Rhine, but it is *Le Poison Wagner*, written after the *Anschluss* of 1938, which contains more lethal debunking. After seeing a performance of *Das Rheingold* Claudel wondered what this 'ratatouille boche' could be said to convey, 'this story both childish and confused', this 'poisoned music, dripping with sauce (we know what the restaurant owners mean when they talk about a sauce being *thick*) which leaves on the palate a taste of liquor and verdigris!'[85] Amongst the uproar of *Götterdämmerung*, the raucous and hysterical brass, Claudel mockingly adopts a suitable note of dread and veneration, only to reduce the tone of one of bathos: 'Pardon! pardon! enough! I've understood, I assure you! Don't make me ill! I'm scared! Look, Walhalla's collapsing! Let me get my umbrella!'[86] – a somewhat inadequate defence against incandescent conflagration, one might have thought. But Claudel is indisputably a Wagnerian *malgré-lui,* and the irreverence and persiflage are but one side of an obsession which would prove of life-long duration. The mockery and condemnation of Wagner is with Claudel the reaction of the guilty lover who must needs castigate lest he be considered too fervid in his praise.

The guilty lover, the traducer who turned again and again to revile the beloved idol – this chapter will end, as it began, with Friedrich Nietzsche, whose apostacy and whose vituperation remain the most witty and the most poignant. 'Wagner's art crushes with the pressure of one hundred atmospheres';[87] to escape the intolerable pressure Nietzsche delighted in imagining Parsifal as a 'student of theology with a grammar-school education (the latter indispensable for *pure foolishness*'[88]) and speculating, as was noted before, on the amazing fact of Parsifal's ability to beget a son: 'Parsifal is Lohengrin's father? How did he manage it!'[89] The heaving bosoms of devoted – even obsessed – female Wagnerians amazed and amused him, as did the moonstruck expressions of young men who sat through the festivals and emerged dazed into the open air. 'Ah, this old robber! He steals our young men, he even steals our wives and drags them into his cave . . . Ah, this old Minotaur!'[90] (Nietzsche's later championship of Bizet is akin to Ezra Pound's rejection of Wagner and preference for Pergolesi: 'Pound expatiated on the supremacy of Pergolesi over Wagner, and began to imitate Wagner with groans and grunts, whistles and catcalls, amid much gesturing and cavorting'; as William Blissett remarks, however, Pound did not attempt to expunge the Wagner references from *The Waste Land*, recognising their rightness).[91] Minotaur, mountebank or madman, the 'snuffling Saxon gnome with his whiz-kid talent and his shabby character'[92] would feed the imagination and the yearnings of the decadents and the spiritually impoverished, but also the talents of the wits and the satirists. Great dramatist that he was,

Wagner knew full well that solemnity is enhanced by comic interruption,[93] and the antics in which he himself indulged (disapprovingly noted by Cosima) do more than hint that a sense of the absurd was by no means alien to him. Both idolatry *and* iconoclasm were rightly produced by such an eruption of genius, and a balanced assessment of the man and his art must exclude neither extreme.

Notes

1 Nietzsche, *Werke, ed. cit.*, I, p. 386: 'wie auch alles und jedes parodiert worden ist'.

2 Mark Twain: 'At the shrine of St Wagner', article in the *New York Sun*, 6 December 1891; reprinted in *What is Man? and Other Essays*, London, 1919, pp. 215–16. *A propos Parsifal* we should not forget that Wagner jokingly suggested to Mathilde Wesendonck that he would never touch such a theme: 'Und so etwas soll ich noch ausführen? und gar noch Musik dazu machen? – Bedanke mich schönstens! Das kann machen, wer Lust hat; *ich* werde mir's bestens vom Halse halten!' Such 'nonsense' was not for him – let Geibel write it and Liszt compose the music! Mark Twain comments on the inordinate length of the work; the most famous statement concerning Wagner's *longueurs* was made by Rossini: 'Monsieur Wagner a de beaux moments mais de mauvais quart d'heures' (said to Emile Naumann, April 1867. See the latter's *Italienische Tondichter*, 1883, IV, p. 541).

3 W. B. Yeats, *Autobiographies*, London, 1970, p. 208. Yeats did, however, include Wagner with such names as Gérard de Nerval, Maeterlinck, Villiers de l'Isle-Adam and Verlaine as a man who was contributing to the fund of mystical knowledge, but otherwise seems to have avoided the composer's influence.

4 Hartmut Zelinsky, *Richard Wagner: ein deutsches Thema*, Frankfurt, 1976, p. 276.

5 See H. Hakel (ed.) *Richard der Einzige: Satire, Parodie, Karikatur*, Vienna, 1963, pp. 210–23.

6 'Zukunftsposse mit vergangener Musik und gegenwärtigen Gruppierungen in drei Akten.' Heine's 'Jung-Katerverein für Poesiemusik', published in his *Romanzero* collection of 1851, may be an ironic reference to the new tendency in music, the 'höheren Ernst' which is expected in the howling of cats, and although Liszt is referred to at the end of the poem it is difficult *not* to think of that musician's illustrious son-in-law. The newly formed society is described as follows: 'Er will die Poesiemusik / Rouladen ohne Triller / Die Instrumental- und Vokalpoesie, / Die keine Musik ist, will er ... / Das tolle Konzert! ich glaube, es ward / Ein großes Tedeum gesungen, / Zur Feier des Siegs, den über Vernunft / Der freche Wahnsinn errungen.' In *Werke und Briefe* (Aufbau, 1961), II, pp. 236–7.

7 Johann Nestroy, *Gesamtausgabe*, Vienna, 1925; *Die Parodien*, II, pp. 388–9.

8 Nestroy, *op. cit.*, p. 204: I apologise for the dreadful paraphrase, but a translation eludes me. The German runs: 'So fand ich dich und ward dein treuer Schäfer, / O

Venus – du bist ein famoser Käfer.'

9 Nestroy, *op. cit.*, p. 226: 'Wollt ihr gleich mir das Glück mit Löffeln essen, / Wohlan, so geht und kneipt im Venusberg!'

10 Nestroy, *op. cit.*, p. 238: ('Setzt eine Nachtmütze auf und stirbt.')

11 Nestroy, *op. cit.*, p. 248: 'Kehr' wieder heim zum Zauberschlaf, / Sei fein geduldig, lieb und brav, / Wie ich fürwahr kein Schaf noch traf . . .'

12 Cosima Wagner, *Tagebücher*, I, p. 33: 'Zum Schluß erzählt R.: Hebbel habe ihm einst von Nestroy gesagt: "Es ist ein so gemeiner Mensch, daß, wenn er eine Rose beriecht, so muß dieselbe stinken.".' Wagner certainly admired that other great Viennese, Ferdinand Raimund, calling him 'eine der originellsten und liebenswürdigsten Erscheinungen auf dem Gebiet der öffentlichen Kunst' (*Gesammelte Schriften und Dichtungen*, VII, p. 295). It is also known that Wagner consulted Raimund's *Die gefesselte Phantasie* while working on *Die Meistersinger*: the Viennese 'Zauberspiel', the dramatic fairy tale with music and allegorical figures greatly interested him. The relationship between Wagner and Hebbel was never a friendly one, despite the attempts of the composer Peter Cornelius to bring them together. Hebbel described the Ride of the Valkyries in the following terms: 'Ich selbst wage nicht zu entscheiden, ob die Musik mehr die Seele oder das Rückenmark schüttelt', believing that it might make a splendid overture to a Viennese carnival (see the essay by Paul Bornstein in *Die Musik*, VIII, Berlin, 1908–9, p. 280). He did, however, admit in a letter to his wife (from Mainz, 1857) that he had to admit the merits of *Tannhäuser*, and in August 1858, after hearing *Lohengrin*, he wrote an enthusiastic letter to the Princess Wittgenstein. Hebbel never read Wagner's *Nibelungen* (only thirty copies were printed in 1853); Wagner later rejected Hebbel's trilogy in *Über Schauspieler und Sänger*, 1872.

13 Richard Wagner, *Das braune Buch*, *op. cit.*, pp. 189–91.

14 See *Kuriosa, Kitsch, Kostbarkeiten im Richard Wagner Museum* (ed. Eger), Bayreuth, n.d., p. 24: 'Dramatische Verslein mit Worten ohne Melodie, gegenwärtige Parodie von einer Zukunfstoper in drei Aufzügen, wo darüber viel losgezogen wird, und einem Vorspiel des Vorspiels von Richard Wagnermeister und Stückschreiber, sowie musikalischem Dramatiseur.'

15 *Kuriosa*, *op. cit.*, p. 24: 'Die Handlung spielt in der Vorzeit und ist in der Gegenwart zu Allem reif – teils zu Wasser, teils zu Land, weshalb auch der Text bald zu schlüpfrig und bald zu trocken ist. Textbücher werden keine ausgegeben, weil der Text hierdoch nicht so recht verstanden wird. Für dieses Stück sind nur drei Vorstellungen ausgesetzt: wenn es das Publikum aushaltet und die Schauspieler nicht umbringt, wird man doch sehen, was weiteres geschieht: vor der Hand wurden einmal die Preise erhöht, damit das Stück mehr an Wert gewinnt.'

16 See the article in *Die Gesellschaft*, 1891, 4, pp. 1363–4 (Kraus reprint): 'Bei der Premiere waren die Leute nach dem ersten Akte aus dem Theater gestürzt; einige

mit rotem zornglühendem Kopfe wegen der niederträchtigen ihren Ohren zugefügten Beleidigung; andere eilten mit gähnendem aufgesperrtem Rachen ins nächste Cafe; Bekannte, die sich trafen, platzten vor Lachen heraus; man sprach von Mozart – sich-im-Grab' – 'rumdrehen' ... Aber bald sollte es anders kommen. Bei gelegentlicher Wiederholung dieser oder jener ein bis zweihundert Takte der Oper auf dem Klavier oder im Konzertsaal zeigten sich nämlich bei einzelnen der Anwesenden, besonders bei Damen, feierlich gespannte Mienen, glänzende Augen, Starrheit der Glieder, allerlei Anzeichen der Geistes- abwesenheit; wie Frösche, die sich abends gegen das Licht kehren, saßen sie da, für alles abgestorben, bis auf die kleine Quelle, die sie fasciniert; erst nach Schluß des letzten Akkords wich der merkwürdige Zustand.' Panizza also delighted in absurd (and not so absurd) speculation concerning sexual perversion in Wagner; in 'Bayreuth und die Homosexualität' (*Die Gesellschaft*, 1895, 1, pp. 88–92) he quotes an advertisement found in a Bayreuth newspaper ('Young cyclist seeks male partner', etc.) and meditates upon the nature of the relationship, finding it appropriate that the advertisement appeared a few days before a *Parsifal* performance. The article describes the pederasty of the knights of the grail and ends: 'Zieht hin! Zieht in den Berg der *Venus masculinus* ein!' Thomas Mann was associated with *Die Gesellschaft* in his early Munich days and might well have read Panizza's article.

17 In *Punsch*, XVIII (1865), p. 169: '*Maxl*: "Du, für die Tristan und Isolden-Plag' bekommt jeder Hofmusikus fünfzig Gulden." *Sepperl*: 'So? Wonne – hehrstes Beben!" *Maxl*: "Aber sie haben's noch nicht." *Sepperl*: "Haben's noch nicht? Wahnlos holdbewußter Wunsch!" '

18 *Kuriosa, op. cit.*, p. 31.

10 Franz Grillparzer, *Sämtliche Werke* (Reclam ed.), I, p. 386: 'Ein neuer Salbader / Bezaubert euern König; / Werft ihn, ein zürnender Landsturm, / Nicht in die Isar, doch in den Schuldturm!' With commendable resignation Grillparzer saw that there was little point in combating the 'Music of the Future': the best thing to do was to let it blow itself out. 'Ein Thor, wer der Thornheit entgegenstrebt, / Man muß es der Zeit übergeben; / Habe die Hegel'sche Philosophie überlebt, / Werd' auch die Zukunftsmusik überleben' (*Sämtliche Werke*, Munich, 1969, I, p. 540). Wagner visited Grillparzer in 1848 to attempt to arouse the latter's interest in his operatic plans; Grillparzer was polite, but cool. The meeting is described in *Mein Leben*; Wagner notes that Grillparzer was the first dramatist he had ever seen wearing an official's uniform.

20 Paul Heyse, *Briefwechsel mit Theodor Storm* (ed. Plotke), Munich, 1917–18, p. 147.

21 Fontane, *Sämtliche Werke*, Munich, 1962, II, p. 33: '... ein Behexer wie es nur je einen gegeben hat. Und an diesem Tannhäuser und Venusberg-Mann setzt ihr ... euer Seelen Seligkeit und singt und spielt ihn morgens, mittags und abends. Oder dreimal täglich, wie auf euren Pillenschachteln steht.' Among the great nineteenth-

century German novelists it was Raabe who came out unequivocally in Wagner's defence. In a letter to Hans von Wolzogen (28 August 1883) he writes: 'Richard Wagner hat mich eigentlich nur als Mensch, Kämpfer und Charakter beschäftigt, aber in dieser Beziehung in herzerfreuendem Maße. Der Mann hat es auch erkannt, wie und was die Welt ist, und mit Frohlocken sah man wieder einmal einem nach, der "von Berge zu Bergen" hinüberschritt.'

22 F. Th. Vischer, *Aesthetik oder Wissenschaft des Schönen*, Stuttgart, 1857, III, pp. 1453–4: '... moderner Überreiz ... überladener, phantastischen Theaterpomp.' This is not the place for a discussion of Vischer; let it be noted, however, that Vischer, Keller and Wagner were associates in Zurich in the early 1850s, and that all three realised the importance of the *epic* (it might indeed be more appropriate to call Wagner's major works musical epics rather than music-dramas). Keller, of course, is the chief master here; like Wagner he had been greatly influenced by Feuerbach, but unlike Wagner and Vischer he had not passed through a Schopenhauerian crisis. (Wagner, incidentally greatly enjoyed Keller's *Spiegel, das Kätzchen* and delighted in reading it aloud.)

23 Vischer, *Auch Einer* (Volksausgabe), Stuttgart, 1904, p. 217. Again, my translation of this German Jabberwocky musts needs be unsatisfactory, and the original runs: 'Sende, o Neblige / Mondscheinschweblige! / Sende das kitzlige, / Prickelnde, bitzlige, / Kratzende, kritzlige / Uebel uns nur! / O Silinur! / Pfisala, Pfnisala, Pfeia!'

24 Newman, *Life*, *ed. cit.*, II, pp. 25–7.

25 Vischer, *op. cit.*, pp. 221–2: an approximation, only, to the following: 'Du aber, Grippo! / Grimmiger Greifer, / Grunzender Lindwurm, / Dräuender Drache! / Jegliche Dumpfheit, / Dickung und Dämmung, / Die das Gehirn drückt / Wenn sich der Pfnüssel / Sperret und pferchet, / Spare den Pfahlmann ... Feuer soll flammen, / Blutrote Zacken / Hoch aus der Beuge / Brennender Scheiter! / Griffolo, Griolo, Grio! / Gruffulu, Grugulu, Gruffu!'

26 Quoted in M. Gregor-Dellin, *Richard Wagner: die Revolution als Oper*, Munich, 1973, p. 16: 'Meine Herren, was halten Sie von Wagner?'

27 Quoted in Anna Jacobson, *Nachklänge Richard Wagners im Roman*, Heidelberg, 1932, p. 14: 'Hehrstes, wonniges Weib! ... Unglücklicher Wehwalt!'

28 See *Meister der deutschen Kritik*, II, (ed. Hering), Munich, 1963, p. 270: 'Weh, wie wenig Wonne ward mir wanderndem Wiener Spazierwalt durch Wagners *Walküre* ... Wir finden keine andere Deutung, als daß die Geschwister Musik und Drama hier eine blutschänderische Ehe geschlossen haben und der arme Hunding Verstand auf den verächtlichen Handwink Wotan-Wagners hin für immer zu schweigen hat. Die Wagnerianer waren ganz weg vor Entzücken, und ich war ganz entzückt, als ich weg war.'

29 Peter Altenberg, *Was der Tag mir zuträgt*, Berlin, 1919, pp. 137, 140 and 235. For a more scurrilous reduction of Wagnerian heroics see Georg Grosz, 'Gedenkblatt für Richard Wagner', in *Ecce Homo*, Berlin, 1923 (Zelinsky, p. 161).

30 Robert Musil, *Der Mann ohne Eigenschaften* (Frisé ed.), p. 49: 'Trotzdem spielte er Wagner; mit schlechtem Gewissen; wie ein Knabenlaster . . .'

31 Frank Wedekind, *Ausgewählte Werke*, Munich, 1924, II, p. 272: 'Ich muß morgen abend in Brüssel den *Tristan* singen!'

32 Carl Sternheim, *Die Hose*, in *Dramen* I, Neuwied, 1963, p. 94: 'Wagner! Das heiligste Gut der Menschheit!'

33 Heinrich Mann, *Der Untertan*, Leipzig, 1918, p. 371: ' "Des Reiches Ehr' zu wahren, ob Ost, ob West" Bravo! So oft er das Wort sang, reckte er die Hand hinauf, und die Musik bekräftigte es ihrerseits . . . Diederich wünschte sich, er hätte zu seiner Rede in der Kanalisationsdebatte eine solche Musik gehabt.'

34 Heinrich Mann, *op. cit.*, p. 372: 'Schilder und Schwerter, viel rasselndes Blech, kaisertreue Gesinnung, Ha und Heil und hochgehaltene Banner . . .'

35 Quoted in Hans Mayer, *Richard Wagner: Mitwelt und Nachwelt*, Stuttgart, 1978, p. 311: 'Für gewisse hypermoderne Moden ist Bayreuth nicht da, das widerspräche dem Stil der Werke, die ja nicht kubistisch-expressionistisch-dadaistisch gedichtet und komponiert sind.'

36 Hans Mayer, *op. cit.*, p. 25: 'Rettung Wagners durch surrealistische Kolportage.'

37 Carl von Ossietzky, *Schriften II*, pp. 128–34: '. . . die Bordell-Atmosphäre und das tingeltangelhafte Nuttenballett der Blumenmädchen – die Klingsor-Girls!'

38 Ossietzky, *op. cit.*, p. 133: '. . . diese Tristane und Lohengrine mit Doppelkinn und Bierbauch, und dazu die Sängerinnen mit flachsgelber Perücke, das Auge verzückt erhoben, Wogebusen und Wackelpopo durch ein rotumbortetes, urtümlich deutsches Nachthemd unterstrichen.'

39 Fest, *Hitler, op. cit.*, p. 37.

40 Arno Schmidt, *Zettel's Traum* (facsimile ed.), Frankfurt, 1977, pp. 539, 1029 and 1092.

41 James Joyce, *Finnegans Wake*, London, 1966, p. 565.

42 See William Blissett, 'Ernest Newman and English Wagnerism' in *Music and Letters*, vol. 40, October 1959, p. 314.

43 See E. T. Cook, *The Life of John Ruskin*, London, 1911, II, p. 457.

44 Mark Twain, 'At the Shrine of St Wagner', *op. cit.*, p. 216.

45 Quoted in Max Moser, *Richard Wagner in der englischen Literatur des XIX Jahrhunderts*, Berne, 1938, p. 103. For an amusing description of R. C. Trevelyan (elder brother of G. M. Trevelyan) see P. N. Furbank, *E. M. Forster. a Life*, Oxford, 1979. Trevelyan had written *The Birth of Parsifal* before *The New Parsifal*, an earnest and philosophical poem with Nietzschean overtones. Its sequel is a much more rewarding piece of work.

46 Benson, *The Rubicon, op. cit.*, p. 252.

47 Rupert Brooke, *The Complete Poems*, London, 1934, p. 13.

48 E. M. Forster, *A Room with a View*, London, 1962, pp. 159–60.

49 Ford Madox Ford, *No More Parades*, London, 1963, p. 191.

50 See Moser, *op. cit.*, p. 29

51 George Moore, *Parnell and his Island*, London, 1887, pp. 18–19.

52 George Moore, *Ave*, London, 1911, pp. 203–4.

53 George Moore, *Memoirs of my Dead Life*, London, 1906, p. 294.

54 On William Archer, see 'The World' (14 December 1892). Also quoted in the preface to the *Bodley Head Bernard Shaw*, I, 1970, p. 37.

55 See Hesketh Pearson, *Bernard Shaw: His Life and Personality*, London, 1961, p. 136.

56 Bernard Shaw, *The Perfect Wagnerite*, in *Major Critical Essays*, London, 1930, pp. 184 and 191.

57 William Blissett, 'Bernard Shaw, the Imperfect Wagnerite'. Reprint from the *University of Toronto Quarterly*, p. 198. Dzamba Sessa also makes a pertinent point when reminding us of G. K. Chesterton's remark on Shaw; she writes: 'It is just possible, as G. K. Chesterton said, that music, and especially Wagner's music, might "itself be considered in the first case as the imaginative safety valve of the rationalistic Irishman" ' (*Richard Wagner and the English*, p. 64).

58 *Bodley Head Bernard Shaw*, V, p. 14. Shaw could also not resist mentioning Wagner in a drawing-room boxing demonstration: a smart flick of the wrist, in *Cashel Byron's Profession*, knocks Lucien Webb into a chair, while Cashel is expostulating on 'Professor Wagner's' cunning.

59 *Bulletin of the John Rylands University of Manchester*, vol. 61, p. 479.

60 See *Selected Letters of James Joyce*, (ed. Ellmann), London, 1975, pp. 149–50.

61 DiGaetani, *op. cit.*, p. 132.

62 Joyce may have borrowed from George Moore here: in *Vale* a motif associated with Siegfried is used by Moore outside the door of Edward Hyde to gain admittance (p. 262) and later in the same book the sword-motif is printed on the page as a resounding clarion call for the Irish literary renaissance (see Chapter Three).

63 Joyce, *Ulysses* (Bodley Head ed.), 1955, p. 530.

64 See the introduction to the German translation by Georg Goyert, Zurich, 1956, pp. 826–7: 'Ich habe dieses Kapitel mit den technischen Mitteln der Musik geschrieben. Es ist eine Fuge mit allen musikalischen Zeichen: piano, forte, rallentando usw. Ein Quintett kommt auch darin vor, wie in den *Meistersingern*, der Oper Wagners, die ich bevorzuge ...' DiGaetani (p. 145) quotes Bowen's article on the 'Sirens' and quite plausibly asserts that Joyce was amused by the credulity of his readers and led them deliberately astray. Joyce had indeed sung in a performance of the quintet in his Zurich days, but can scarcely be said to have modelled the opening of the 'Sirens' on it.

65 Joyce, *Ulysses*, *op. cit.*, pp. 242–3.

66 Joyce, *op. cit.*, p. 246. In Wagner we read: 'Deinen stechenden Blick, deinen struppigen Bart, o säh ich ihn, faßt ich ihn stets! Deines stachligen Haares strammes Gelock, umflöss es Flosshilde ewig!' (*Das Rheingold*, scene 1).

67 I am indebted for these references to Adaline Glasheen's *Third Census of Finnegans*

Wake: An Index of Characters and their Roles Berkely, Calif., 1977. See also Zack Bowen's *Musical Allusions in the work of James Joyce*, New York, 1975.

68 Zelinsky, *Richard Wagner, op. cit.*, p. 182.

69 Newman, *Life*, IV, p. 277.

70 Jean Cocteau's comment might be recalled here: he complained that he found it impossible to rebuild a genuinely French theatre because of the all-pervasive Wagnerian influence (see F. Ferguson, *The Idea of a Theater*, New York, 1953, p. 112). A generation before, Strindberg had similarly remarked on the ubiquitous presence of the Master in Paris, and described the pseudo-medieval atmosphere prevailing in 1897 which was derived from Wagner's works: 'Young men dressed themselves in monk's cowls, cut their hair in a tonsure and dreamed of the monastic life; they wrote legends and performed miracle-plays; they painted madonnas and sculpted figures of Christ, gaining inspiration from the mysteries of the magician who has bewitched them with Tristan, Parsifal and the Grail' (*Legender*, in *Samlader Skrifter*, Stockholm, 1919–20, vol. 28, p. 347).

71 See K. E. Schmidt, 'Richard Wagner in der französischen Karikatur', in *Velhagen und Klasings Monatshefte*, Bielefeld, 1906, I, p. 125.

72 Wagner's music is, alas, frequently associated with war and destruction: it seems obligatory to play excerpts from Siegfried's funeral march whenever the ruins of Hitler's bunker are shown, and the fact that one of the basic themes of the *Ring* is the illusory nature of power is conveniently ignored. It is only appropriate to use military metaphors when dealing with Wagner's total *control* over the orchestra, and William Blissett's pertinent phrase 'Wagner was to total art what Schlieffen was to total war' (in 'Thomas Mann, the Last Wagnerite', *Germanic Review*, February 1960, p. 58) refers to Wagner's powers of organisation, the fusion of enthusiasm and order in his work, the constant vigilance, total employment of physical and spiritual resources, and contempt for mere security. The first German Kaiser had congratulated Wagner after hearing him conduct the Ninth Symphony with the words: 'Now you can see what a good general can do with his army' (quoted in Francis Hueffer, *Richard Wagner*, London, 1874, p. 294). See also Cosima Wagner *Tagebücher*, I, p. 870, for Wagner's own comparison between himself and Moltke.

73 Catulle Mendès, *Le Roi vierge*, Paris, 1882, p. 299; 'Frédérick tourna la tête et vit l'un des convives debout, serrang les poings, et dont les joues se crispaient en petites rides de colère – comme de l'eau remuée d'un vent – pendant que les débris d'une pile d'assiettes s'éparpillaient sur la table, ou roulaient sur le carreau jusqu'à la plinthe des murailles . . .'

74 Mendès, *op. cit.*, pp. 299–300: '. . . petit, maigre, étroitment enveloppé d'une longue redingote de drap marron: et tout ce corps grêle, quoique très robuste peut-être – l'air d'un paquet de ressorts – avait le tremblement presque convulsif d'une femme qui a ses nerfs; mais le visage, quand il n'était pas déformé par la grimace de colère, devait avoir une magnifique expression de hauteur et de sérénité . . .'

75 Mendès, *op. cit.*, p. 301: 'Et pourtant, la musique, c'est le vrai art allemand! L'Angleterre a Shakespeare, la France a Victor Hugo, L'Allemagne a Sébastian Bach, Beethoven et moi!'

76 Colette, *Claudine s'en va*, in *Oeuvres complètes*, Paris, 1948, II, p. 274: 'Claudine même, mal peignée, le canotier sur l'oreille, m'arracha à peine un sourire, quand, sur la place de la Gare, elle me brandit sous le nez une saucisse fumante qu'elle tenait à pleine main.'

77 Colette, *op. cit.*, p. 274: '. . . espèce de facteur des postes . . . il a des saucisses chaudes dans sa boîte en cuir bouilli, et il les pêche avec une fourche, comme des serpents.'

78 Colette, *op. cit.*, p. 276: '. . . le chapeau mal remis, des cheveux admirables noués en corde disgracieuse.'

79 Colette, *op. cit.*, p. 279: '. . . l'odeur de caoutchouc brûlé et de cave moisie.'

80 The grossness of the Germans was emphasised in 1906 not by a French chauvinist but by Georg Fuchs in his *Der Tanz*: 'The Germans' failure to recognise even today the beauty of the human body is revealed no more clearly than here, where its absurd distortions are unbearable to watch: Siegfrieds with tight corseted 'Bierhaus' bellies; Siegmunds with sausage-shaped legs crammed into tights; Valkyries who appear to spend their leisure time in Munich beer-halls over plates heaped with steaming offal and steins of foaming beer; Isoldes whose sole ambition is to play the part of fairground fat ladies and exercise their irresistible charms on the imagination of butcher's shop assistants.'

81 Paul Claudel, *Rêverie d'un poëte français* (critical ed. by Michel Malicet), Paris, 1970, pp. 60–1: 'Les confabulations du cordonnier avec Evchen ont failli me faire mourir. Nous pleurions de sommeil. Et quand est arrivée la Kermesse avec les bourgeois en justaucorps groseille et les femmes enceintes en jupes oranges . . . nous nous sommes enfuis! . . .'

82 Claudel, *op. cit.*, p. 61: 'Il est impossible de comprendre Wotan et les Walküres si on ne songe pas à ces grosses femmes aux "corsages opulents" (style de l'époque) et à ces puissants industriels à barbe blonde buvant du café au lait dans un jardin d'hiver.'

83 Claudel, *op. cit.*, p. 65: '. . . tout petit et maigre entre deux énormes femmes avec son béret de velours et sa figure de polichinelle.'

84 Claudel, *op. cit.*, p. 65: 'Il y avait dans Wagner du farfardet et du Nibelung, non seulement du magicien mais du nabot malfaisant.' Claudel was probably unaware of Wagner's sympathy with Alberich; see Cosima Wagner, *Tagebücher*, II, p. 52: 'R. erzählt mir, daß er einst völlige Sympathie mit Alberich gehabt . . .'

85 Claudel, *Le Poison Wagner*, in *Oeuvres complètes*, Paris, 1959, XVI, p. 326: '. . . cette histoire à la fois puérile et confuse', 'musique empoisonée, ruisselante de sauce (on sait ce que les restaurateurs appellent une sauce *riche*) qui laisse au palais un goût de rogomme et de vert-de-gris!'

86 Claudel, *op. cit.*, p. 330: 'Pardon! pardon! assez! assez! Je vous assure que j'ai compris! Ne me faites pas de mal! J'ai peur! Voilà le Walhall que s'écroule! Laissez-moi chercher mon parapluie!'

87 Nietzsche, *Werke, ed. cit.*, II, p. 919: 'Wagners Kunst drückt mit hundert Atmosphären.'

88 Nietzsche, *op. cit.*, p. 922: '(—letztere als unentbehrlich zur *reinen Torheit*) . . .'

89 Nietzsche, *op. cit.*, p. 923: 'Parsifal ist der Vater Lohengrins! Wie hat er das gemacht? . . .' By 'Parsiphallic' methods? (Then pun is James Huneker's; see Elliot Zuckerman, p. 163).

90 Nietzsche, *op. cit.*, p. 932: 'Ah, dieser alte Räuber! Er raubt uns die Jünglinge, er raubt selbst noch unsre Frauen und schleppt sie in seine Höhle . . . Ah, dieser alte Minotaurus!'

91 William Blissett, 'Wagner in *The Waste Land*', in Campbell and Doyle (eds.)., *The Practical Vision: Essays in Honour of Flora Roy*, Ontario, 1978, p. 85. For further references see R. M. Schafer, *Ezra Pound and Music*, London, 1977.

92 Thomas Mann, see letter to Julius Bab (14 September 1911): 'dieser schnupfende Gnom aus Sachsen mit dem Bombentalent und dem schäbigen Charakter'. Quoted in *Wagner und unsere Zeit, op. cit.*, p. 30.

93 See the article by William Mann on 'The humorous side of *The Ring*' (*The Times*, 13 October 1967). William Mann rightly points out that the creator of the slithering, sneezing Alberich, the Wagnerian 'zoo' and the grotesque serenade of Beckmesser was certainly not devoid of humour. Professor Erlin, in Somerset Maugham's *Of Human Bondage*, believed that Wagner was the greatest charlatan of the nineteenth century, a man who sat in his box laughing till his sides ached at the sight of all those who took his work seriously (chapter twenty-four).

'Et puis, quelle page écrite arrive à la hauteur des quelques notes qui sont le motif du *Graal?*'
   Valéry, 1891

'Sleepless one night in Venice, I stepped on to the balcony of my window overlooking the Grand Canal: like a deep dream the fairy city of lagoons lay stretched in shadow before me. From out of the breathless silence there rose the strident cry of a gondolier on his boat; again and again his voice went forth into the night, till from the remotest distance its fellow cry came answering down the midnight length of the canal ...' The crucial essay *Beethoven* contains this description, which continues: 'What could a Venice steeped in sunlight, gorgeous with colour, tell me that the sounding dream of night had not brought infinitely deeper, closer to my consciousness?'[1] Wagner then recalls the lofty solitude of an upland valley at Uri, the call of the cowherds across the 'monstrous silence', and that sense of wonder which overcame him, that 'dreamlike state in which the ear reveals to man the inmost essence of all that his eye had held suspended in the illusory show of manifold phenomena, and tells him that his inmost being is one with all, and that only in *this* manner can the essence of external things be truthfully known'.[2] It is the musician who is able to express the ultimate truth of things, Wagner writes; ignoring the specious glitter of transient objects the listener turns away from appearances and attains a state akin to trance. 'And in truth it is in this state alone that we immediately belong to the musician's world. From out of that world, which nothing else can picture, the musician casts a mesh, so to speak, of tones; or, if you like, he dews our brain with his wonder-drops of sound as if by magic, and robs it of the power of seeing anything save our own inner world.'[3] This is Wagner's clearest statement concerning the power of *music* to express an inner vision: with *Tristan und Isolde* particularly he had insisted (in '*Zukunftsmusik*') that 'Life and death, the whole import and existence of the outer world, here hang on nothing but the innermost movements of the soul'[4] – the purely extrinsic being relegated to a penumbrous existence. The 'absolute inwardness' of which Hegel had spoken is here celebrated, that principle which chapter one described as the true principle of Romantic art; the outer world can exercise no special claim over the human spirit, which flees into remoter and ever more lonely worlds.[5]

It is to be regretted that Wagner did not complete his *Die Bergwerke zu Falun*; its detailed sketch describes the descent of the young miner Elis into the depths of the mine, where he sees the Mountain Queen herself, surrounded by glittering crystals which assume the forms of flowers, trees, and maidens frozen in seductive attitudes. He is entranced by this subterranean world of jewels, caverns and bluish light against which his betrothed, the hapless Ulla, cannot fight.[6] G. H. von Schubert's anecdote in *Concerning the Darker Realms of the Natural Sciences* (Dresden, 1808) dealing with the preservation of the body of a young miner at Falun in Sweden begat some remarkable progeny, from Hoffmann via Wagner to Hofmannsthal, whose five-act verse play of 1899 deepened the psychological and mystical implications of the story; it exemplifies perfectly that mysterious path within ('nach innen) of which Novalis, inspector of salt mines and quintessental Romantic dreamer, had spoken. The metaphors of mine, mountain and golden treasure are apparent in Eduard von Hartmann's *Philosophy of the Subconscious* (1869), where the surface of this fruitful earth is rejected in favour of the chthonic realms; the cult of inwardness and mysticism associated with French symbolism elevated, as we have seen, the recondite symbol into a quasi-religious invocation and music to an ultimate revelation. The dissolution of the traditional structure of the work of art is at hand, and associative images, musical in organisation, become of paramount importance, the imitation of natural forms giving way to the free cultivation of private, self-sufficient universes.[7]

Baudelaire's 'forest of symbols', Mallarmé's abstract theatre, the cross-reference of symbol and image in many a novel characterised by a stream-of-consciousness technique we related to Wagner's art. 'It was like another art altogether. The sombre theme had to be given a sinister resonance, a tonality of its own, a continued vibration that, I hoped, would hang in the air and dwell on the ear after the last note had been struck'[8] – it is Conrad talking here about *The Heart of Darkness*, but the musical analogy can only be possible *after* Wagner. Literature as resonance, as tonality, as a seamless web of continuity, a narrative swelling to symphonic proportions – Wagner's method and imperious example revised the entire course not only of musical, but also of literary, development. The dissolution of all boundaries and the commemoration of the infinite unity of the world could not fail to enrich the traditional structure of prose, and those musical forms of poetry of which Schiller spoke, which give lasting shape to feeling without having recourse to any definitive state in the outer world, triumph over those plastic forms which create in accordance with the precepts of sense and the laws of reason.[9]

'But, of course, the real villain is Wagner. He has done more than any man in the nineteenth century towards the muddling of the arts . . . Every now and then in history there do come these terrible geniuses, like Wagner, who stir up all the wells of thought at once. For a moment it's splendid. Such a splash as never was. But afterwards – such a lot of mud; and the wells – as it were, they communicate with each other too easily now, and not one of them will run quite clean. That's what Wagner's done.'[10] Margaret Schlegel's reservations in *Howards End* concerning the great Mischief-maker, and her deploring her sister Helen's desire to 'translate tunes into the language of painting, and pictures into the language of music' impress the lowly Leonard Bast, but her strictures seem out of place if she is seen as being, as P. N. Furbank claims, Forster himself.[11] For Forster admitted, in the *Paris Review*, that he used a Wagnerian leitmotif system to help him keep so many themes going at the same time, and he also expressed the belief that 'in music fiction is likely to find its nearest parallel'.[12] Argue as she might with the warm and impulsive Helen, Margaret cannot bring herself to side with her brother, the limp and sterile Tibby, who 'treats music as music'; it is patently the *confusion* of the different art forms that Forster, through Margaret, condemns, a confusion that Wagner, as DiGaetani describes, never suggested.[13] The notion that the arts were somehow interchangeable, a purely mechanical interpretation of the *Gesamtkunstwerk*, was similarly rejected by Thomas Mann as 'bad nineteenth century':[14] this book has unequivocally stressed the hegemony of music both for Wagner and his for literary neophytes.[15] When a novel approximates to a musical score in the sense that there are leitmotifs associated with certain characters and situations which achieve a certain rhythm, then surely there is an enrichment of the narrative form rather than an impoverishment, despite the predictable strictures of a Lukács:[16] the famous simile with which this book began insists that the writer should admire and indeed embrace the musician's superior skill.

The musical structure and the total work of art: Wagner's presence dominates any discussion of these aspects of modernism, but it is his expression of the rich subliminal layer of psychic residua which makes his torrential creativity such a fascinating treasure house. Writing on *Ulysses* T. S. Eliot comments: 'In using the myth in manipulating a continuous parallel between contemporaneity and antiquity, Mr. Joyce is pursuing a method which others must pursue after him . . . Instead of narrative method, we may now use the mythical method.'[17] The return to myth in the modern novel was assessed in Chapter Three, and Wagner is the supreme mythophile, a Nordic Dionysus. His indebtedness to Greek mythology was commented on; both Nietzsche and Wagner, interpreting the ancient Greek world in remarkably startling ways, made European literature aware of potent archetypal situations. In section thirteen of *Human, All too Human* Nietzsche discussed the ability of dreams to transpose the dreamer back into the most distant origins of human culture, but it is Wagner who had taught him (*Meistersinger* III, ii) that the poet's task was to interpret these dreams, for within them was contained the very essence of human experience. The greatest European novelists have turned to myth and archetype in an attempt to portray the deepest preoccupations of the human psyche, but many critics have felt reservations concerning the obsession with ancient patterns. 'A yearning for ritualistic satisfactions can have a bad effect in literature as well as in politics, and it is a common enough complaint that the search in novels for mythical order reduces their existential complexity . . .'[18] 'Mythology . . . raises the whole question of belief. This could scarcely be so if it was only thought of as a breeding ground for images; in fact it is too often the anti-intellectualist substitute for science . . .';[19] 'Fictions can degenerate into myths whenever they are not consciously held to be fictive':[20] these comments by Frank Kermode betray a deep-seated unease at the blurring of distinctions between myth and belief and the substitution of simplistic and general solutions to individual crises. René Wellek goes further in his attack on 'the dangerously occult idea of the collective unconsciousness, or racial memory';[21] it is Jung who is the suspect here, but Wagner knew long before Jung of the unique power of his music to touch the deepest chords. Bryan Magee puts the point that 'Wagner's music expresses, as does no other art, repressed and highly charged contents of the psyche, and that is the reason for its uniquely disturbing effect . . . The feeling is of a wholeness yet unboundedness – hence, I suppose, its frequent comparison with mystical or religious experience.'[22] There can be no doubt that an obsession with primitive mythology can lead to cultural atavism rather than an inquisitive interest; Wagner's music can, as has been pointed out, lead to obfuscation and brutality. To quote Magee again: 'However beautiful it may be . . . it is never only an end in itself, always a carrier of something else; and it is how we react to the something else that is decisive. To some this music is like the poisoned flower of the Borgias; to others like requited love. There is no medium in which such differences can be settled, for the realm in which they lie is not merely deeper than words, it is deeper than music.'[23]

The first chapter of Lionel Trilling's book *Beyond Culture* (1966) considers a certain modernist tradition, a 'post-liberal' attitude informed by such works as Frazer's *The Golden Bough*, Nietzsche's *The Birth of Tragedy* and *The Genealogy of Morals*, Freud's *Civilisation and its Discontents*, Conrad's *Heart of Darkness*, Thomas Mann's *Death in Venice*, Dostoyevsky's *Notes from Underground* and Tolstoy's *The Death of Ivan Ilyich*.[24] It is not difficult to feel Wagner's *imprimatur* here, and, in fact, certain of these seminal works have already been mentioned in this book; the ethos they engender may indeed have little to do with liberalism, but a dark radiance is cast which seems to possess greater powers of illumination than the attitudes of enlightenment and humanism. An anti-mediterranean bias is here apparent (or, rather, anti-Latin, for the Greek gods, after Nietzsche, were reinstated in their barbaric splendour), and that pure Northernness which engulfed C. S. Lewis on seeing the words *Siegfried* and *The Twilight of the Gods*, that 'vision of huge, clear spaces hanging above the Atlantic in the endless twilight of Northern summer, remoteness, severity . . .'[25] is but one, simplistic, description of Wagner's mythical resonance. More central is the following comment on the poetry of T. S. Eliot: 'For all its professed classicism, the art of T. S. Eliot is unmediterranean because, like D. H. Lawrence and Thomas Mann, like James Joyce and Marcel Proust, like Jules Laforgue and Stéphane Mallarmé he owes no Roman obedience and remains liegeman to the great Despot from north of the Teutoberg forest.'[26] The final claim to be made is that Wagner deserves without question his place beside Marx, Nietzsche, Freud and Heidegger, those who have moulded European consciousness most palpably, and have 'invaded vast territories of the world's mind.'[27]

Notes

1 Richard Wagner, 'Beethoven', in *Gesammelte Schriften und Dichtungen, ed. cit.*, IX, p. 74: 'In schlafloser Nacht trat ich einst auf den Balkon meines Fensters am großen Kanal in Venedig: wie ein tiefer Traum lag die märchenhafte Lagunenstadt im Schatten vor mir ausgedehnt. Aus dem lautlosesten Schweigen erhob sich da der mächtige rauhe Klageruf eines soeben auf seiner Barke erwachten Gondolier's, mit welchem dieser in wiederholten Absätzen in die Nacht hineinrief, bis aus weitester Ferne der gleiche Ruf dem nächtlichen Kanal entlang antwortete . . . Was konnte mir das von der Sonne bestrahlte, bunt durchwimmelte Venedig des Tages von sich sagen, das jener tönende Nachttraum mir nicht unendlich tiefer unmittelbar zum Bewußtsein gebracht gehabt hätte?'

2 Richard Wagner, *op. cit.*, p. 74: '. . . jener traumartige Zustand . . . in welchem er durch das Gehör Das wahrnimmt, worüber ihn sein Sehen in der Täuschung der Zerstreutheit erhielt, nämlich daß sein innerstes Wesen mit dem innersten Wesen alles jenes Wahrgenommenen Eines ist, und daß nur in *dieser* Wahrnehmung auch das Wesen der Dinge außer ihm wirklich erkannt wird.'

3 Richard Wagner, *op. cit.*, p. 75: 'Und in Wahrheit ist es auch nur dieser Zustand, in welchem wir der Welt des Musikers unmittelbar angehörig werden. Von dieser, sonst mit nichts zu schildernden Welt aus, legt der Musiker durch die Fügung seiner Töne gewissermaßen das Netz nach uns aus, oder auch er besprengt mit den Wundertropfen seiner Klänge unser Wahrnehmungsvermögen in der Weise, daß er es für jede andere Wahrnehmung, als die unserer eigenen inneren Welt, wie durch Zauber, außer Kraft setzt.'

4 Richard Wagner, *ed. cit.*, VII, p. 123: 'Leben und Tod, die ganze Bedeutung und Existenz der äußeren Welt, hängt hier allein von der inneren Seelenbewegung ab.'

5 See Hegel's *Vorlesungen über die Aesthetik*, vol. 2, in *Sämtliche Werke* (ed. Glockner), XIII, pp. 130–3.

6 A full discussion of Wagner's sketch is given in the *Bayreuther Blätter* (1905), XXVIII, pp. 168–77. What Elis sees (in act two) is as follows: 'Die hintere Felswand beginnt allmählich sich zu lichten und zurückzuweichen. Eine immer zunehmende bläuliche Quelle verbreitet sich überall. Wunderbare Krystallbildungen zeigen sich immer klarer dem Blicke. Sie nehmen allmählich die Gestalten von Blumen und Bäumen an. Blitzende Edelsteine funkeln an ihnen; andere Krystallbildungen zeigen sich in der Gestalt von schönen Jungfrauen, wie im Tanze verschlungen. Endlich erblickt man im fernsten Hintergrunde den Thron einer Königin . . .' Wagner follows Hoffmann closely and tells us that Elis was once a sailor who returns home to find that his mother is dead.

7 See Lilian Furst, *Counterparts, op. cit.*, p. 102.

8 Quoted by M. Schorer: 'Technique as discovery' in *Forms of Modern Fiction*, ed. O'Connor, Minneapolis, Minn., 1948, pp. 9–29.

9 See August Wiedmann, *Romantic Roots in Modern Art*, London, 1979, p. 71.

10 E. M. Forster, *Howards End*, chapter five.

11 P. N. Furbank, *E. M. Forster: a Life*, Oxford, 1979, p. 173.

12 E. M. Forster, *Aspects of the Novel*, (ed. Stallybrass), London, 1974, p. 116.

13 J. DiGaetani, *Richard Wagner and the Modern British Novel*, pp. 101–2.

14 In *Leiden und Größe Richard Wagners*.

15 To those who persist in believing that Wagner held that all the arts were to be of equal value I can only refer to his essays *Beethoven* (1870) and *Über die Bestimmung der Oper* (1871), where the reverse is manifestly apparent. A perceptive essay is by Michael Turner, entitled 'The total work of art' in *The Wagner Companion* (ed. Burbidge and Sutton); a very good book is also Jack M. Stein's *Richard Wagner and the Synthesis of the Arts*, Detroit, Mich., 1960. The concept of the *Gesamtkunstwerk* which Wagner adumbrated in the early 1850s has been radically modified by the 1870s.

16 See *Essays über Realismus*, Berlin, 1945, p. 55, also 61: 'Mit vollem Rechte kann man . . . von den verschiedenen Richtungen der heutigen Bourgeoisie sagen, daß alle ihre verschiedenen Ausdrucksmittel – die mitunter mit nicht unbedeutender technischer Meisterschaft gehandhabt werden – nur dazu dienen, die oberflächlichen Erscheinungen des Alltagslebens der kapitalistischen Gesellschaft zu gestalten, und zwar noch alltäglicher, noch zufälliger, noch willkürlicher zu gestalten, als sie es in der Wirklichkeit sind.' Lukács also quoted with approval Ernst Bloch's rejection of the technique used by James Joyce.

17 Quoted in O'Connor, *Forms of Fiction, op. cit.*, p. 123.

18 Frank Kermode, 'This time that time' in *Continuities*, London, 1968, p. 40.

19 Frank Kermode, *Puzzles and Epiphanies: Essays and Reviews 1958–1961*, London, 1962, p. 38.

20 Frank Kermode, *The Sense of an Ending: Studies in the Theory of Fiction*, Oxford, 1966, p. 39.

21 René Wellek, *Concepts of Criticism*, New Haven, Conn., and London, 1963, p. 336.

22 Bryan Magee, *Aspects of Wagner*, op. cit., p. 59.

23 Bryan Magee, op. cit., p. 68.

24 Herbert Marcuse likewise comments that modern Western civilisation 'admires the convergence of death instinct and Eros in the highly sublimated . . . creations of the *Liebestod*'. See *Eros and Civilization*, Boston, 1955, p. 51.

25 C. S. Lewis, *Surprised by Joy*, op. cit., p. 74.

26 William Blissett, 'Wagner in *The Waste Lane*', op. cit., p. 85. Saxony is actually south of the Teutoburger Wald, as is Bayreuth; Blissett's geography is at fault here, but that is all.

27 Erich Heller in *Encounter*, April 1964, XXII, vol. 4, p. 59.

select bibliography

Writing on Wagner, Bryan Magee claims that 'The number of books and articles written about him, which had reached the ten thousand mark before his death, overtook those about any other human being except Jesus and Napoleon'. The biographer's task is not an enviable one with such a phenomenon: even when the topic under discussion is restricted to Wagner and literature the temptation to chase allusions and reverberations in the most unlikely places is difficult to resist. I have of necessity restricted my – very select – bibliography to those books and articles which I have felt to be most relevant; books dealing with more general literary topics are also included if they contain references to Wagner and his influence. I have not found it necessary to list all those primary texts referred to in this book, nor specific works dealing with these texts if Wagner does not loom large in them. For those interested in Wagner's own sources a useful bibliography is given in H. F. Garten's book (listed below); our prime concern, however, is not what Wagner took but what he gave.

Books

Adorno, Th. W., *Versuch über Wagner*, Frankfurt, 1952.

Beaufils, Marcel, *Wagner et le wagnérisme*, Paris, 1947.

Bertram, Johannes, *Mythos, Symbol, Idee in Richard Wagners Musikdramen*, Hamburg, 1956.

Block, Haskell M., *Mallarmé and the Symbolist Drama*, Detroit, Mich., 1963.

Bonilla y San Martin, A., *Los legendas de Wagner en la literatura española*, Madrid, 1913.

Bowen, Zack, *Musical Allusions in the Work of James Joyce*, New York, 1975.

Brown, E. K., *Rhythm in the Novel*, Toronto, 1950.

Braun, Edward (trans.), *Meyerhold on Theatre*, London, 1969.

Burbidge, P. and Sutton, R. (eds.), *The Wagner Companion*, London, 1979.

Coeuroy, André, *Wagner et l'esprit romantique*, Paris, 1965.

Cooke, Deryck, *I Saw the World End: a Study of Wagner's 'Ring'*, Oxford, 1979.

Cowley, Malcolm (ed.), *Writers at Work: the Paris Review Interviews*, New York, 1957.

Dahlhaus, Carl, *Richard Wagners Musikdramen*, Velbert, 1971.

DiGaetani, J., *Richard Wagner and the Modern British Novel*, Cranbury, N.J., 1978.

Donington, Robert, *Wagner's 'Ring' and its Symbols: the Music and the Myth*, London, 1963.

Dujard, Edouard, *Le Monologue intérieur: son apparition, ses origines, sa place dans l'oeuvre de James Joyce*, Paris, 1931.

Dzamba Sessa, Anne, *Richard Wagner and the English*, Cranbury, N.J., 1979.

Eger, Manfred (ed.), *Kuriosa, Kitsch, Kostbarkeiten im Richard Wagner Museum*, Bayreuth, no date.

Fischer-Dieskau, Dietrich, *Wagner und Nietzsche*, Stuttgart, 1974.

Forster, E. M., *Aspects of the Novel* (ed. Stallybrass), London, 1974.

Friedman, Melvin, *Stream of Consciousness: a Study in Literary Method*, New Haven, Conn., 1955.

Fries, Othmar, *Richard Wagner und die deutsche Romantik*, Zurich, 1952.

Furst, Lilian, *Counterparts*, London, 1977.

Garten, H. F., *Wagner the Dramatist*, London, 1977.

Gay, Peter, *Freud, Jews and other Germans*, Oxford, 1978.

Glasheen, Adaline, *A Third Census of Finnegans Wake: An Index of the Characters and their Roles*, Berkeley, Calif., 1977.

Grand-Carteret, John, *Wagner en caricatures*, Paris, 1892.

Gregor-Dellin, Martin, *Wagner und kein Ende: Richard Wagner im Spiegel von Thomas Manns Prosawerk*, Bayreuth, 1958.

Guichard, Léon, *La Musique et les lettres en France au temps du wagnérisme*, Paris, 1963.

Hakel, H., (ed.), *Richard der Einzige: Satire, Parodie, Karikatur*, Vienna, 1963.

Hanrieder, August, *Das Drama Richard Wagners im Urteil Friedrich Hebbels*, Munich, 1920 (dissertation).

Hellström, Victor, *Strindberg och musiken*, Stockholm, 1917.

Hildebrandt, Kurt, *Wagner und Nietzsche: ihr Kampf gegen das 19. Jahrhundert*, Breslau, 1924.

Ipser, K., *Richard Wagner in Italien*, Salzburg, 1951.

Jäkel, Kurt, *Richard Wagner in der französischen Literatur*, Breslau, 1931–2.

Jacobson, Anna, *Nachklänge Richard Wagners im Roman*, Heidelberg, 1932.

Jung, Carl-Gustav, *Symbols of Transformation*, New York, 1956.

Kaufnicht, Georg, *Richard Wagners Verhältnis zur romanischen Literatur*, Breslau, 1923 (dissertation).

Knust, Herbert, *Wagner, the King and 'The Waste Land'*, Pennsylvania, 1967 (dissertation).

Koppen, Erwin, *Dekadenter Wagnerismus*, Berlin, 1973.

Lehmann, Arthur G., *The Symbolist Aesthetics in France, 1885–1895*, Oxford, 1950.

Lessing, Th., *Schopenhauer, Wagner, Nietzsche: Einführung in moderne deutsche Philosophie*, Munich, 1906.

Loncke, Joycelynne, *Baudelaire et la musique*, Paris, 1975.

Loos, Paul Arthur, *Richard Wagner – Vollendung und Tragik der deutschen Romantik*, Berne, 1952.

Lyon, M. (ed.), *Books and Portraits: Some Further Selections from the Literary and Biographical Writings of Virginia Woolf*, London, 1977.

Magee, Bryan, *Aspects of Wagner*, London, 1968.

Mann, Erika (ed.), *Wagner und unsere Zeit: Aufsätze, Betrachtungen, Briefe*, Frankfurt,

1963.

Mayer, Erika, *Die Nibelungen bei Fouqué und Wagner*, Vienna, 1948 (dissertation).

Mayer, Hans, *Richard Wagner: Mitwelt und Nachwelt*, Stuttgart, 1978.

McGrath, William J., *Wagnerianism in Austria: the Regeneration of Culture through the Spirit of Music*, Berkeley, Calif., 1965.

Moser, Max, *Richard Wagner in der englischen Literatur des XIX. Jahrhunderts*, Berne, 1938.

Newman, Ernest, *The Life of Richard Wagner*, Cambridge, 1976.

Nordau, Max, *Entartung*, Berlin, 1892.

Park, Rosemary, *Das Bild von Richard Wagners 'Tristan und Isolde' in der deutschen Literatur*, Jena, no date.

Peckham, Morse, *Beyond the Tragic Vision*, New York, 1962.

Postic, Marcel, *Maeterlinck et le symbolisme*, Paris, 1970.

Reichelt, Kurt, *Richard Wagner und die englische Literatur*, Leipzig, 1911.

Richart, Franz, *Richard Wagners Verhältnis zu Johann Wolfgang von Goethe*, Vienna, 1949 (dissertation).

Schuppanzigh-Frankenbach, Alexandra, *William Morris: 'The Story of Sigurd the Volsung and the Fall of the Nibelungs' im Verhältnis zu Richard Wagners 'Der Ring des Nibelungen'*, Graz, 1943 (dissertation).

Shaw, G. B., *The Perfect Wagnerite*, London, 1898.

Sokel, Walter, *The Writer in Extremis*, Stanford, Calif., 1958.

Stein, Jack, *Richard Wagner and the Synthesis of the Arts*, Westport, Conn., 1960.

Steiner, George, *Language and Silence*, London, 1979.

Taylor, Ronald, *The Romantic Tradition in Germany*, London, 1970.

Vermeil, Edmond, *Das Problem der Dekandenz und der Regeneration, Nietzsche und Wagner*, Stuttgart, 1954.

Wagner, Cosima, *Die Tagebücher*, 2 vols. (ed. Gregor-Dellin and Mack), Munich, 1976.

Wagner, Wieland (ed.), *Richard Wagner und das neue Bayreuth*, Munich, 1962.

Wapnewski, Peter, *Der traurige Gott: Richard Wagner in seinen Helden*, Munich, 1978.

Wauters, K., *Wagner en Vlaanderen: 1876–1914*, Leuven, 1965.

Weininger, Otto, *Geschlecht und Charakter* (18th ed.), Leipzig and Vienna, 1919.

Weston, Jessie, *From Ritual to Romance*, New York, 1957.

Wiedmann, August, *Romantic Roots in Modern Art*, London, 1979.

Wilson, Edmund, *Axel's Castle: a Study of the Imaginative Literature of 1870–1930*, New York, 1931.

Woodley, Grange, *Richard Wagner et le symbolisme français*, New York, 1931.

Wunberg, G. (ed.), *Hermann Bahr: Theoretische Schriften 1887–1904*, Stuttgart, 1968.

Wysewska, Isabelle, *La Revue Wagnérienne: Essai sur l'interpretation esthétique de Wagner en France*, Paris, 1934.

Wyzewa, T. de, *Nos maîtres: études et portraits littéraires*, Paris, 1895.

Zelinsky, Hartmut, *Richard Wagner, 1876–1976: Ein deutsches Thema*, Frankfurt,

1976.

Zuckerman, Elliot, *The First Hundred Years of Wagner's 'Tristan'*, New York, 1964.

Articles

Auden, W. H., 'James Joyce and Wagner', in *Common Sense*, March 1941.

Barzun, Jacques, 'Nietzsche contra Wagner' in *Darwin, Marx, Wagner: Critique of a Heritage*, New York, 1958.

Bauer, Roger, 'Paul Claudel et Richard Wagner', in *Orbis Litterarum*, XI, 1956.

Benda, Julien, 'Mallarmé et Wagner', in *Domaine Français*, Geneva, 1943.

Blissett, William, 'Ernest Newman and English Wagnerism', in *Music and Letters*, 40, 1959.

—— 'Thomas Mann, the last Wagnerite', in *Germanic Review*, February 1960.

—— 'George Moore and literary Wagnerism', in *Comparative Literature*, 13, 1961.

—— 'Wagnerian fiction in English', in *Criticism*, 5, 1963.

—— 'From Wagner to Jung', review article in *Queen's Quarterly*, Toronto.

—— 'D'Annunzio, D. H. Lawrence, Wagner', in *Wisconsin Studies in Contemporary Literature*, 7, 1966.

—— 'Wagner in *The Waste Land*', in Campbell and Doyle (eds.), *The Practical Vision: Essays in Honour of Flora Roy*, Waterloo, Ont., 1978.

—— 'The liturgy of *Parsifal*', in *University of Toronto Quarterly*, 44, 1979–80.

Britten, Benjamin, 'Some notes on E. M. Forster', in *Aspects of E. M. Forster* (ed. Stallybrass), New York, 1969.

Bowen, Zack, 'The bronzegold sirensong: a musical analysis of the Sirens episode in Joyce's *Ulysses*', in *Literary Monographs* (ed. Rothstein and Dunseath), Madison, Wis., 1967.

Carcassone, E., 'Wagner et Mallarmé', in *Revue de la littérature comparée*, 16, 1936.

Donato-Petténi, G., 'Wagner e D'Annunzio, in *Rivista italia*, 2, 1921 (also published in book form, Florence, 1922).

Drougard, E., 'Richard Wagner et Villiers de l'Isle-Adam', in *Revue de littérature comparée*, 16, 1936.

Emrich, Wilhelm, 'Mythos des 19. Jahrhunderts: zu Thomas Manns *Leiden und Größe Richard Wagners*', In *Zeugnisse: Festschrift für Th. W. Adorno*, Frankfurt, 1963.

Ganz, Arthur, 'The playwright as perfect Wagnerite: motifs from the music dramas in the theatre of Bernard Shaw,' in *Comparative Drama*, 13, 3, 1979.

Hayman, David, '*Tristan und Isolde* in *Finnegans Wake*: a study of the sources and evolution of a theme', in *Comparative Literature Studies*, 1, 1964.

Heller, Peter, 'Some functions of the leitmotiv in Thomas Mann's Joseph Tetralogy', in *Germanic Review*, 22, 1947.

Hollinrake, Roger, 'Nietzsche, Wagner and Ernest Newman', in *Music and Letters*, 41, 1960.

Kloss, Erich, 'Richard Wagner und die Tanzkunst', in *Bühne und Welt*, 7, 1904–5.

Lucas, W. J., 'Wagner and Forster', in *Romantic Mythologies* (ed. Fletcher), London, 1967.

Mayer, Hans, 'Richard Wagners geistige Entwicklung', in *Sinn und Form*, 1953, Heft 3 and 4.

Moody, T. Campbell, 'Nietzsche's *Die Geburt der Tragödie* and Richard Wagner', in *Germanic Review*, 16, 1941.

Müller-Blattau, Joseph, 'Richard Wagner in unserer Zeit', in *Universitas*, 18, 1963.

Pierhal, Armand, 'Sur la composition wagnérienne de l'oeuvre de Proust', in *Bibliothèque universelle et Revue de Genève*, June 1929.

Prüfer, Arthur, 'Novalis's *Hymnen an die Nacht* in ihren Beziehungen zu Richard Wagners *Tristan und Isolde*,' in *Richard Wagner Jahrbuch*, I, (ed. Frankenstein), Leipzig, 1906.

Raphael, Robert, 'Strindberg and Wagner', in *Scandinavian Studies: Essays presented to H. G. Leach*, Seattle, Wash., 1965.

Scheltinga, Koopman E. Th., 'Die Funktion der Musik in Thomas Manns *Tristan* und *Zauberberg*', in *Duitsche Kroniek*, 17, 1965.

Schmidt, K. E., 'Richard Wagner in der französischen Karikatur', in *Velhagen und Klasings Monatshefte*, Bielefeld, 1906.

Stekel, Wilhelm, 'Nietzsche und Wagner: Eine sexual-psychologische Studie zur Psychogenese des Freundschaftsgefühles und des Freundschaftsverrates', in *Zeitschrift für Sexualwissenschaft*, 4, 1917.

Sypher, F. J., 'Swinburne and Wagner', in *Victorian Poetry*, spring 1971.

Vicentia, M., Sister, O.P., 'Wagnerism in Strindberg's *The Road to Damascus*', in *Modern Drama*, 5, 1962.

Vortriede, Werner, 'Richard Wagners Tod in Venedig', in *Euphorion*, 52, 1958.

The *Revue Wagnérienne* (1885–8, ed. Dujardin), reprinted by Slatkine, Geneva, 1968, contains articles on Wagner and French symbolism which are frequently illuminating, sometimes bizarre; the *Bayreuther Blätter* (1878–1938, founded by Hans von Wolzogen), apart from certain contributions by Theodor Fontane, Romain Rolland and Herman Bahr, and peripheral essays on Wagner and Winckelmann, Wagner and Grillparzer etc., can be largely ignored, although Wagner's own contributions are certainly worth reading. Gnomic utterances by Adolf Hitler, and attempts to identify the Russians with Fafner, the English with Mime, the French with Alberich and the Americans with the Gibichungs do not inspire confidence in either the integrity or the intelligence of the editor. The theosophical leanings of *The Meister* (1888–95, ed. W. Ashton Ellis) have already been noted; the contributions are of mixed quality, and are described in Anne Dzamba Sessa's book (pp. 40–4). Other defunct periodicals include *Parsifal: Halbmonatsschrift zum Zweck der Erreichung der Richard Wagner'schen Kunstideale*, Vienna, 1884, founded 'am ersten Jahrestag unseres erhabenen Meisters' (Zelinsky, p. 55) and the *Richard Wagner Jahrbücher* (1906–13, ed. Frankenstein, five volumes in all). Useful and stimulating articles are often to be found in the *Programmhefte der Bayreuther Festspiele* which have been published every year since 1953 and contain much that relates to Wagner and literature; the adulation and crankiness of earlier years seem to have gone for ever. Other current periodicals which appear irregularly include the *Tribschener Blätter: Zeitschrift der schweizerischen Richard Wagner Gesellschaft*, Lucerne (1956 onwards), the *Bulletin de Cercle National Richard Wagner*, Paris, the *Feuilles Wagnériennes: Bulletin d'Information de l'Association Wagnérienne de Belgique*, Brussels (1960 onwards) and *Monsalvat: Revista Wagneriana*, Barcelona (1973 onwards).

For those interested in Wagner and literature and unable to read German the following translations can be recommended:

The Brown Book, trans. George Bird, London, 1980.

Cosima Wagner Diaries, trans. Geoffrey Skelton, London, 1979–80.

Wagner Writes from Paris, ed. and trans. R. L. Jacobs and Geoffrey Skelton, London, 1973.

Stories and Essays, ed. and selected by Charles Osborne, London, 1973.

Wagner on Music and Drama, selected and introduced by Albert Goldman and Evert Sprinchorn, London, 1977. This is a selection from Wagner's prose works translated by W. Ashton Ellis: the translations are frequently weird, but the anthology might at least help the reader with no knowledge of German to find his way through Wagner's voluminous meditations.

index

Mengs, Ismael, 83
Meyer, Henri, 128
Meyerhold, Vsyevolod, 7, 13–14, 23
Mickiewicz, Adam, 68 note 69
Montesquiou, Robert de, 55–6, 67 notes 66–7
Moore, George, 41, 43–5, 49, 57–8, 59, 75, 80, 85, 110, 121–2, 137 note 62
Moravia, Alberto, 121
Morgan, Charles, 64 note 37
Morgenstern, Christian, 90
Morice, Charles, 8
Morris, William, 91–2
Musil, Robert, 107 note 97, 116, 136 note 30
Musset, Alfred de, 68 note 69

Nerval, Gérard de, 34, 132 note 3
Nestroy, Johann, 111–12, 132–3 notes 7–11
Nietzsche, Friedrich, 5, 23, 32, 41, 46, 47, 48, 57, 63 note 32, 67 note 69, 73–4, 75, 84, 92, 93, 110, 126, 131, 140 notes 87–90, 143–4, 145, 146
Noël, Michel, 127
Nordau, Max (i.e. Südfeld, Simon), 30 note 61, 32, 49, 59 note 2
Novalis (i.e. Hardenberg, Friedrich von), 40, 81, 143
Nunque, Degouve de, 82

Offenbach, Jacques, 127
O'Neill, Eugene, 15
Ossietzky, Carl von, 94, 106 note 86, 118, 136 notes 37–8

Panizza, Oskar, 113, 133–4 note 16
Pater, Walter, 2
Payne, John, 62 note 16
Péladan, Joséphin Sar, 35–6, 61 note 13, 90
Platen-Hallermünde, A. von, 47
Poe, Edgar Allan, 12, 14, 32
Pound, Ezra, 131
Powell, Anthony, 121
Powys, John Cowper, 103 note 61
Proust, Marcel, 7, 18–20, 23, 29 notes 40, 42, 45–9, 146
Przybyszewski, Stanislaus, 14

Qualtinger, Helmut, 111
Quiroga, Horacio, 41

Raabe, Wilhelm, 135 note 21
Raimund, Ferdinand, 133 note 12
Rathenau, Walther, 70, 93, 106 note 84
Reinhardt, Max, 88
Renoir, Pierre, Auguste, 32, 50
Richardson, Dorothy, 20
Rilke, Rainer Maria, 2, 82
Roche, Edmund, 127
Rodenbach, Albert, 99–100 note 24
Rossetti, Dante Gabriel, 91
Rossetti, William, 91
Rossini, Gioacchino, 5, 132 note 2
Rubinstein, Joseph, 95
Ruskin, John 119–20

Saint-Saëns, Camille, 33
Schelling, Friedrich Wilhelm, 6
Schiller, Friedrich von, 143
Schlaf, Johannes, 88
Schlegel, Friedrich, 72
Schmidt, Arno, 119